Pages 254–255
"How do Birds fly?"
Sara Stracey for SITE
Bombay, India
August (Monsoon season)
2004

Published in Australia in 2005 by
The Images Publishing Group Pty Ltd
ABN 89 059 734 431
6 Bastow Place, Mulgrave, Victoria, 3170, Australia
Telephone: +61 3 9561 5544 Facsimile: +61 3 9561 4860
Email: books@images.com.au
Website: www.imagespublishing.com

Copyright © The Images Publishing Group Pty Ltd 2005
The Images Publishing Group Reference Number: 494

National Library of Australia
Cataloguing-in-Publication entry:

ISBN: 1 92074 421 5

Edited by Steve Womersley

Concept design by Sara Stracey

Production by The Graphic Image Studio Pty Ltd, Mulgrave, Australia
Website: www.tgis.com.au

Film by Mission Productions Limited, Hong Kong
Printed by Everbest Printing Co. Ltd, in Hong Kong/China

IMAGES has included on its website a page for special notices in relation to this and our other publications.
Please visit this site: www.imagespublishing.com

CONTENTS

Art will no longer aspire to account for everything; it will have left forever the ambiguous sphere of transcendency for the scattered, humble, everyday universe of the relative.

PIERRE RESTANY, *POOR ART, POOR WORLD*

1

2

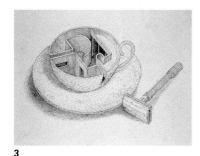

3

Teacup Transformation
This sequence of three teacup images is part of a lecture by James Wines used to illustrate the differences in conceptual thinking between architecture and art. It proposes that design is often limited to an exercise in form and space—or, in other words, a compromise of art in deference to the expedient—while art is about idea and attitude, without any concessions to practicality. The rather facetious diagram to the left compares (in sequential order) the following relationships:

1. The classic teacup as a useful artifact.
2. An inversion of meaning applied to this same object by Swiss Surrealist artist, Meret Oppenheim, who transformed its state of usefulness into a psychologically compelling sculpture, entitled *Fur-lined Teacup* in 1936.
3. The Oppenheim artwork, cleansed of its erotic implications by a hypothetical Modernist architect, who would probably misunderstand its conceptual intentions, shave off the hirsute effrontery, and subject the teacup to formalist re-design.

The imagery that a work of architecture generates as an extension of its own functions or formal relationships are never as interesting as the ideas it can absorb from the outside. A building should be like an environmental sponge, soaking up the most interesting fragments of information from its surroundings. In this way, architecture can be seen as a filtering zone for the communication of contextual feedback.

JAMES WINES
GREEN ARCHITECTURE, **TASCHEN VERLAG 2000**

SITE was founded in 1970 in New York City as a multi-disciplinary architecture and environmental art studio. From the beginning, the purpose was to integrate visual art, architecture and the surrounding context as part of a unified vision. The group's philosophical foundations grew out of a belief that buildings, artworks, and public spaces should not be conceived as objects sitting in the environment; instead they should be seen as a fusion of inside and outside elements interpreted as the environment.

The early development of SITE was motivated by a sympathy for many of the social, political and environmental causes of the early 1970s, as well as a resistance to the ubiquitous presence of Modernist, Cubist and Constructivist influences in architecture at that time. In the search for alternatives, the group proposed a narrative and contextually responsive interpretation of the building arts. This approach was based on the observation that wall surfaces, interiors, landscape and surrounding spaces can absorb and reflect certain cultural and psychological information; in other words, they can be used as sources for ideas that question many 20th century architectural traditions. Rather than follow the normal process of conceiving a building as a composition of form, space and structure, SITE shifted the emphasis to idea, attitude and context. By expanding on this objective, a number of the firm's projects today continue to serve as some form of critical commentary on design conventions.

The term "Identity in Density"—chosen as a title for this book—was originally used to describe a 1982 apartment building idea, called "High-rise of Homes." The concept offered city dwellers the freedom to establish their own personal identities within the typically homogenized environment of multi-story housing. It provided residents with an opportunity for individual façade treatments, exterior/interior amenities, and garden spaces. The intention was to shift aesthetic evaluation in architecture away from orthodox design continuity, by encouraging inhabitants to contribute the riskier (and far more intriguing) elements of indeterminacy, idiosyncrasy, cultural diversity, and their own spontaneous acts of choice, chance and change. Through this displacement of conventional design values, SITE proposed that a typical condominium tower could be seen as an example of what Marcel Duchamp once referred to as "canned chance."

While the High-rise of Homes represented a specific attitude toward personalized living in an urban environment, the uses of inversion and commentary have been emblematic of SITE's work from the beginning. In some cases, the notion of identity in density has been predicated on a dialogue in the mind. For example, many archetypes—office towers, shopping centers, civic edifices, suburban homes, etc—are accepted by people as ubiquitous artifacts and objects of reflex identification in their daily lives. By taking advantage of this subliminal level of recognition, SITE has frequently treated buildings as the subject matter of art, as opposed to an objective of the usual design process. Gradually, after the 1970s, this change of focus has become a way of questioning traditional definitions in architecture. It has also provided a means of using commonplace structures as the raw material (or as a foil) for critical interventions in a continuing search for altered meanings.

During the past decade, SITE has become increasingly involved with environmental issues in architecture—not only the challenge of energy conservation, sustainability, and the integration of landscape—but also with the psychological and aesthetic aspects of green design. The firm's most recent work has been based on a view that buildings and public spaces should move away from those influences associated with the 20th century Age of Industry and Technology, in order to respond more comprehensively to the present Age of Information and Ecology.

The architectural challenge of creating places of special identity, as an antidote to the impersonal legacy of the 20th century built environment, has always been a fundamental mission in SITE's work. Since this objective has become increasingly relevant in the context of a new millennium, it continues to motivate our work in research and design.

^ **Passages Diagrams—**
Architecture as a filtering zone
for information
1996

< **Strip Architecture**
Las Vegas, Nevada, USA
1970

< **Aboriginal Lean-To Habitat**
Northern Territory, Australia
1970s

< **PUNK Graffiti**
Paris, France
1970s

< **Subway**
New York City, USA
1970s

< **American Television**
Anywhere, USA
1970s

< **Object Plethora**
USA
1969

< **Urban Graphics**
Venezuela, South America
1970s

< **West Side Highway**
New York City, USA
1971

The crisis of communication in architecture is a crisis of sources. Architects have become incapable of filtering out, comprehending, and utilizing new sources in design of buildings, yet the orthodox Modernist imagery still being used is increasingly irrelevant in this disordered, pluralistic world.

JAMES WINES
DE-ARCHITECTURE, RIZZOLI 1987

> **Fantasy**
> Photographic Phenomena
> 1970s

> **Uluru ("Ayers Rock")**
> Northern Territory, Australia
> 1980s

> **Nathan's**
> Coney Island, Brooklyn, New York, USA
> 1970s

> **Freeway**
> Los Angeles, USA
> 1984

> **Cowboy/Western Film Genre**
> 1970s

> **Directive**
> Long Island, New York, USA
> 1970s

> **Destruction of the Traymore Hotel**
> **"Castle-By-The-Sea"**
> Atlantic City, New Jersey, USA
> ON SITE NOT SEEN
> 1972

> **Cadillac Ranch**
> **Ant Farm**
> Amarillo, Texas, USA
> 1974

> **Stop Missiles**
> 1970s

SITE: GERMAN MIESLES AND PLAZAMANIA MEET THE ROCKET RED LAUGH

TOM WOLFE

The architect James Wines won my Pritzker Prize for 1977 the moment he said, "I don't mind if they keep building those boring glass boxes, but why do they always deposit that little turd in the plaza when they leave?" Up to then, turds had not figured prominently in the canon of wit in the English language.

Everybody knew about "those boring glass boxes." During the Great Depression of the 1930s the socialist worker-housing theories of a pair of young German architects, Walter Gropius and Ludwig Mies van der Rohe ("Gropius and Mies"), raged through American architecture schools in an epidemic of German Miesles. Their Bauhaus or International Style purged architecture of all bourgeois rot, from pitched roofs to comfortable chairs, leaving only a ribs-showing anorexia of steel skeletons, concrete floors, flat roofs, glass walls (the "glass boxes"), and uncomfortable chairs. By the end of World War II the new generation of American architects was as obsessive and monomaniacal as any other anorexics and fired up with logorrhea and a skull-crushing rap known as theoryspeak. They brow-beat a bewildered new generation of American CEOs into pitching their spindly, fat-free, skin-and-bones socialist worker housing 40, 60, ultimately 100 stories into the air as the corporate office towers of the mightiest capitalists on earth. That was a laugh and a half, but Wines had put his finger on something still funnier: the plazas that went with them.

Plazamania began in 1958 with the Seagram Building, a 39-story glass box on the capitalists' street of dreams, New York's Park Avenue, by Mies himself. The plaza out front took up one third of a city block, and on it was... nothing. It was a bare flat plane of travertine and two anemic fountain pools set flush with the stone. In winter the wind howled across it as if on the Siberian steppes. In summer temperatures on the slab topped the three-minute sunstroke threshold. But that was what Mies, the original god of anorexic International Style worker housing, had decreed. Seagram's ruler, Samuel Bronfman, despised the whole idea, glass box, plaza and all, but his daughter Phyllis had contracted German Miesles while earning a fine arts degree at Vassar and battered him to jelly with worker-housing theoryspeak. In the end the old mogul gave up, bent over, and took it like a man.

From then on, as the glass boxes soared throughout America, the empty plazas spread with them. The poor CEOs whined and whined, but no architect would allow them anything other than a Miesly slab. Finally, the fiery puritans relented and allowed them to have a single piece of sculpture. But in the name of the workers it had to be bourgeois-proof, i.e. abstract, preferably by Isamu Noguchi or Henry Moore. The typical Moore looked like a sun-dried bolus with a hole in it. The typical Noguchi looked like a fresh bolus with severe descending colonic twists and squiggles. Later, when Noguchi was commissioned to do an entire plaza for SOM's new Beinecke Library at Yale, he did a piece of sculpture resembling the sort of rock-hard bolus, thick as it is long, that is egested in agony after a long bout of colonic hyper-retention.

Wines pronounced them "turds in the plaza" at considerable risk to his standing as an architect. The puritans seethed. It was not that Wines opposed the International Style. Far from it. In the late 1950s, in Italy on a Pulitzer Fellowship, he had chilled in Rome with the great god Gropius himself. As late as 1987 he was publishing a book called *De-architecture* that theory-rapped with the best of them. It was just that when the puritans' long faces reached a certain length, he couldn't restrain a certain red laugh.

^ **Seagram Building**

^ **Plop Art**

^ **BEST Forest Showroom**
BEST Products Company
SITE
Richmond, Virginia, USA
1980

^ **BEST Inside/Outside Building**
BEST Products Company
SITE
Milwaukee, Wisconsin, USA
1984

You really have to hear—and see—this laugh. Wines is a tall man with a raging mane of hair, mustache, and beard, halogen eyeballs, a long nose, and a mirthful smile that is... armed. When the eyes go to high beam, the lips part, the mouth opens, and the red laugh is launched, rising slowly at first, then rocketing faster than Mach 1 to the treacherous zone where atmosphere runs out and space has not yet begun and human humor is apt to go into a flat spin from which there is no recovery. Young artists gravitated to him just to hear it. His studio became a collective called SITE, in one of the great legends of bohemian life in New York, a tale Michael McDonough is about to tell us with intoxicating relish in the introduction that follows—including an account of the only great burst of comedy that ever lit up the sky of Modern architecture: SITE's storefronts for the BEST Products discount retail chain.

Those works, which cannot be contained in any of the known categories of art, are Rabelaisian enough when one looks at them in the photographs that await us in these pages; but nothing can take the place of having... been there. To go to the Forest Showroom in Richmond, Virginia, and walk through the front entrance of a BEST Products store—and find yourself in an already existing virgin forest—and then walk through 20 feet of soaring trees on God's own sod to the showroom floor—was to experience shopping as theater. To approach the Inside/Outside Building in Milwaukee and find jagged holes of catastrophic dimension in the walls amid crumbling brick, as if the place has just been attacked by fighter-bomber aircraft—was to know (in those innocent days) without the need of an essay that one had come upon the only touch of intentional humor and joie de vivre in the entire history of Modern architecture. BEST Products' owners, Frances and the late Sydney Lewis, commissioned SITE and gave them free rein. They are justly remembered as two of the greatest of all American patrons and collectors of Modern art, ranking with Albert C. Barnes, John D. Rockefeller, Jr., Solomon R. Guggenheim, and Joseph H. Hirshhorn. But to borrow a phrase from William Condren, owner of 1991's long-shot Kentucky Derby winner Strike the Gold, "they always knew where the rice bowl was." The Lewises' stores with SITE fronts inevitably achieved AMS—"anticipated market share"—at least twice as fast as others in the chain. As the saying went, "they stop to jaw-drop and plop to shop-shop."

TOM WOLFE

Wines was by far the most colorful of the International Style architects who in the 1980s and 1990s became known as the Post-Modernists, others being Robert Venturi, Robert Stern, Michael Graves, and Charles Moore. The old International Style fundamentalists regarded Post-Modernism as an "aberration," but they reserved their special resentment for Wines. He was more than aberrant; he was an apostate.

The fundamentalists suffered setbacks in the late 20th century but never lost their faith, which by now was reactionary in the literal sense. Even as I write (2004) they stand like South Pacific cargo cultists, torches in their hands, eyes searching the sky, waiting for the Advent, the second coming of the gods of the International Style who will return American architecture to the pure state of those happier days back in the 1950s. A member of the fundamentalists' ultra-conservative far right wing, Terence Riley, curator of architecture at the Museum of Modern Art, torch held overhead, eyes fixed upon the sky, says he has recently sighted them... up in the empyrean... and they are indeed coming... and they are young, just as Mies and Gropius were at the times of the first coming... and they are bringing with them an architecture so pure, so distilled to first principles, that it is, in Riley's words, "beyond style"... meaning the gods come bearing the very archetypes of architecture, hatched by virgin birth from Plato's "matrix of creation."

So goes the human comedy, and God bless them, one and all. When the time comes, we will still have James Wines to lead us in a chorus of rocket red laughs. And the turds—God bless them, too—are still there in the plazas. Meantime, Wines and SITE, whose E is for Environment, have their high-intensity eyes fixed upon the Green ground, figuring God is more likely to be found in the sod than in a to-the-rear march back into the miserly constipated bowels of the Bauhaus. SITE's latest design is for an apartment house in which every floor is a garden, literally, with an apartment abutting the single stout service column that supports the entire building like a tree trunk. Me, I'm waiting for the day when I can look up from an outrageously lush posh plaza in the heart of Manhattan, Jakarta, or Jersey City and see not sheer glass cliffs but 40, 60, 100 stories of trees, gardens, groves, arbors, orchards, and organic crops. You may have to hire a staff of soil-toilers in addition to the maids, the laundress, the nanny, the personal shopper, and the driver, but not even Wines and SITE can guarantee a sunny future without a price.

∧ **The Greening of Chicago**
SITE
Concept
1984

I first arrived at the cast iron columns of 60 Greene Street in SoHo, the abandoned factory building that housed the radical architecture collective SITE, on May 31, 1976 at 2:30 P.M. I remember the moment precisely because it changed my life. More than that, it reflected changes in the way people all over the world would live, work, and look at the world around them. To understand this, however, to understand that it was part of something much more than an old building and a group of artists toiling away at making a new type of architecture, you have to understand the setting for my story.

Downtown New York City in the late 1960s and early 1970s was an area of grassroots transition and artistic populist activism. What is now known internationally as SoHo, was then an historical building technology testing-ground and economic boom story gone bust. Born, essentially, in the 1870s post-Civil War boom period, the area served as an artisan quarter supporting the great late 19 century department stores and amusements of Lower Broadway. Hat makers, box makers, small purveyors, and tradesmen, manufacturers of every stripe toiled away, moving their goods eastward to Broadway where the monied classes consumed them. The buildings were far larger and grander than anything the city had ever seen, the direct result of newly made fortunes and newly minted constructional and structural systems, especially those employing cast iron and steel. Eventually the money moved Uptown and Downtown declined. By the mid-20th century bright-lights-big-city had become "Hell's Hundred Acres," and urban planner Robert Moses devised a sort of urban euthanasia: most of the district would be replaced by a cloverleaf of on and off-ramps, this part of a still more megalomaniacal scheme to run Fifth Avenue down to Canal Street, linking it to the Holland Tunnel and Manhattan Bridge via vast expressways blown right through the heart of what many saw as urban blight incarnate.

The whole shebang might have gone the way of Bruckner Boulevard and its attendant South Bronx spaghetti of roadways but for a glitch: artists. Artists, you see, had moved into the area, taking refuge in the high-ceilinged, day-lighted, and abandoned or dirt cheap buildings, and using them as studios. Sculptors, painters, poets, writers, dissident architects and engineers, free-thinkers of every stripe made it Bohemia on the Hudson. They soon saw what the urban planning and road-building powerbrokers had missed: this was the largest repository of historic cast iron façade structures in the world (these, a marriage of American technological innovation and the Florentine palazzo). It was surrounded by stable ethnic neighborhoods where life was lived at the pace of a European village, had a well-diversified wholesale and retail infrastructure, and was a transportation hub virtually unrivaled in the City. The artists were well educated and had powerful patrons as allies. They organized and fought in court and in the halls of government. The SoHo (its new name, from South of Houston Street) Cast Iron District grew into landmark status while coalescing as a community during the first glimmers of its economic rebirth. Art galleries sprung up, as did purveyors of fine foods, globally sourced furniture and other artifacts, world-class restaurants featuring an international range of cuisines, computer businesses, industrial and graphic designers, and fashion boutiques (these rivaling anything in Uptown, or in Paris or London for that matter). Loft living, then a necessity of artistic production and limited income, would become a new style of urban living, a minor economic engine, a work-live model, and a balm for urban decay now associated with the rebirth of cities all over the world.

In 1976, however, when I walked past the rag-picking business on the ground floor and up a set of rickety stairs to the second floor of that abandoned factory building, I stepped across a well-worn threshold into the incubator of something also a-birthing in SoHo: the world's most important artistic testing ground.

By the mid-1970s, Downtown New York City had become a sort of Mecca for artists. Art itself had not yet become the corporatized commodity it is today. While art sold, it sold without the market pressures for living artists that now are taken for granted. It was the "art world" and the "art scene," not the "art market." American abstract expressionism had become the dominant art movement internationally in the 1950s. Pop Art had

MICHAEL MCDONOUGH

established itself and was beginning to wane. Then along came the environmental art and conceptual art movements. The emphasis here was on scale, new materials, and especially on the idea behind the object, not the object itself. Many artists resisted the production of traditional objects altogether, preferring to make guerrilla art in the form of events, graffiti, manifestos, music, performances, plants, and Xerox-ed broadsides.

Architecture was in the midst of an extended private-sector building slump, and was suffering from the intellectual exhaustion of post-World War II Modernism. American cities were in crisis. "White flight" to the suburbs, inner-city poverty, decay, and violence were pervasive. Government support for attempts to mitigate these circumstances in the form of urban renewal (cynically and vulgarly called "Negro-removal"), highway construction, and other publicly financed building projects had been in place since after World War II, but with mixed results at best.

Crisis and creativity often made good handmaidens, and the architecture and planning professions had been encouraged to think beyond curatives in the 1950s and 1960s, to dream about what the nature of the modern city might be. Their idealistic solution to urban ills was generally the housing project and the office tower. Simply put, large-scale urban renewal projects of the post-War period—projects that affected millions of people and violently reshaped the American landscape—looked good as dreams, but failed terribly in practice. Fed by anti-urban, anti-neighborhood European Modernism ideals of the 1920s, this generation loathed cities as they had evolved, and revered clusters of sleek concrete towers in idyllic parks. What they built was under-class poverty barracks in desperate parking lots.

The most famous example of failure was the ill-fated Pruitt-Igoe Housing project in East Saint Louis, Missouri. It won accolades and a medal from the American Institute of Architects when it was built in the 1950s. Completely unlivable, dangerous, impossible to maintain, and otherwise inappropriate as housing, it had to be demolished in 1972. How could things have gone so wrong? Reaction and resistance to bulldozer aesthetics and its implicit paternalistic social engineering began to solidify. Younger professionals, often allied with artists, were more sophisticated, less cynical, and more egalitarian in their outlook than the previous generation. Having grown up in newly minted, soulless suburbs, they liked and longed for cities. Less class-conscious, more open-minded and tolerant, suspicious of authority and its unrestrained excesses (the big lesson of Vietnam), non-xenophobic, they wrote, observed, and absorbed the potentialities of urban life with glee.

SITE was born of this era. A crew of dissident intellectuals and artists in 1969, they advocated the presence of sculpture in the environment (hence the SITE acronym). By 1975 the paradigmatic Indeterminate Façade building in Houston, Texas (BEST Products Company) was completed and SITE burst onto the international architecture scene. Hailed as architecture married to social criticism, as ironic humor, as a marriage of art and architecture, and as a serious challenge to Modernist aesthetics, its deftly composed crumbing façade rocked the international architecture world.

SITE got their energy and intellectual direction from the environmental art movement. The work was consistent with the post-Vietnam War-era art theories that held art should exist outside the museum walls, be readily available to the public, and challenge existing aesthetics. Allies and co-travelers during this period included Gordon Matta-Clark, whose "House-Cutting" piece featured a perfectly iconic little American house sliced up the middle with a chain saw until one half of it fell off its foundations a bit. Voila. Anti-architecture was born. Robert Smithson, whose "Spiral Jetty" in Great Salt Lake had expanded the boundaries of environmental sculpture to include industrial waste and lakes, had known the members of SITE. Smithson's idea was that the large-scale jetty would disappear over time and that its progressive decay and absence was the work. Entropy became a sort of fashion.

∧ **Spiral Jetty**
Robert Smithson
Great Salt Lake, Utah, USA
1970

∧ **Low Building with Dirt Roof**
Alice Aycock
New Kingston,
Pennsylvania, USA
1973

∧ **Splitting**
Gordon Matta-Clark
Englewood, New Jersey,
USA
1974

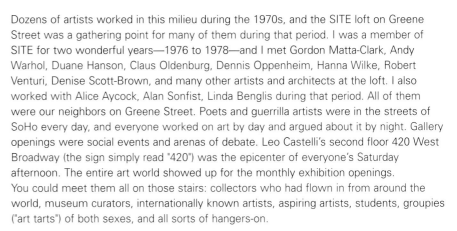

Dozens of artists worked in this milieu during the 1970s, and the SITE loft on Greene Street was a gathering point for many of them during that period. I was a member of SITE for two wonderful years—1976 to 1978—and I met Gordon Matta-Clark, Andy Warhol, Duane Hanson, Claus Oldenburg, Dennis Oppenheim, Hanna Wilke, Robert Venturi, Denise Scott-Brown, and many other artists and architects at the loft. I also worked with Alice Aycock, Alan Sonfist, Linda Benglis during that period. All of them were our neighbors on Greene Street. Poets and guerrilla artists were in the streets of SoHo every day, and everyone worked on art by day and argued about it by night. Gallery openings were social events and arenas of debate. Leo Castelli's second floor 420 West Broadway (the sign simply read "420") was the epicenter of everyone's Saturday afternoon. The entire art world showed up for the monthly exhibition openings. You could meet them all on those stairs: collectors who had flown in from around the world, museum curators, internationally known artists, aspiring artists, students, groupies ("art tarts") of both sexes, and all sorts of hangers-on.

We were all very young, mostly broke, serious-minded, and determined to change the world. The world, curiously, mostly noticed. I remember when Dino DeLaurentis filmed his campy remake of King Kong in 1976. Most of Downtown turned out as unpaid extras in the plaza of the World Trade Center, all of us celluloid witnesses to the great ape's denouement. SITE celebrated the event with a King Kong Christmas Tree party that year, the centerpiece a cardboard confection of the Empire State building topped by the angel Kong himself. The then still oh-so-dowdy *New York Times* reported on the event, complete with a group portrait. It was like Paris in the 1920s, our Greene Street Mafia, but the style was grunge before there was grunge. Tee shirts and jeans were the anti-style style of the day. Disco sucked and art rocked. I remember seeing Mick Jagger and John Lennon walking through the streets together one afternoon. At that point in time, they were as living gods to most young, culturally aware people on the planet. No one in SoHo bothered them or spoke to them. We had our work; we were Mick Jagger and John Lennon and they were visiting us.

The Italian cultural connection—especially through the worlds of painting, sculpture, and industrial design, and the *arte povera* (poor art) art movement—was also important in New York at that time. The *arte povera* idea was that you could make art from concrete blocks, from earth, from any "degraded" material, and SITE's low cost stripmall retail structures fit this mold perfectly. Sydney and Frances Lewis ("The Lewises"), who owned BEST Products, basically allotted an amount equal to the National Endowment for the Arts' "one percent for art" criterion to their buildings. That is, they told us at SITE, you have one percent of the construction budget to transform the BEST Products buildings into art. Do as you will. And those buildings were constructed at a cost of around $17 a square foot. So SITE had 17 cents per square foot to change the world, and it did.

The relaxed urbanism and hybridized art and architecture, art, and landscape, typical of Italy from the Renaissance forward were also important models during the mid-1970s. This artistic integration at the scale of a nation held tremendous sway over a generation of designers, and in many ways still continues to shape the contemporary notion of what a building, a suburb, a city should be. City as festival, as open-air museum, as walk-able cultural and culinary celebration were all nascent ideas during this period. They eventually matured into the historic preservation movement and other positive notions of city and urban landscape, lending the energy and insight that saved the historic cores of many American cities.

Conceptual and unbuilt projects were thought of as very serious architecture in this context. (SITE published its *Unbuilt America* book in 1976—a sort of virtual snapshot of the period.) Drawing and making models was a way to communicate ideas about architecture without the need for the power politics and big money required to make

ᵛ **King Kong Cookie**
Susan Wines (Age 10)
1976

MICHAEL MCDONOUGH

^ Trowel 1
Claus Oldenburg
Kröller-Müller Museum,
Otterlo, Netherlands
1976

buildings. And big private money for building was rare during this period of economic stagnation and high inflation. People had the room and predilection to experiment. The intellectual playing field became larger and more inclusive. The range of design had expanded. (I examined this confluence of art, architecture, and urbanism as an independent artist in my 1978 project Grid House and in my 1983 essay *Architecture's Unnoticed Avant-Garde: Taking a Second Look at Art in the Environment* among others.)

SITE's Indeterminate Façade was followed by a building with an entry corner that sheared off and moved into the parking lot (Notch Building); a building with a vertically displaced but otherwise intact façade (Tilt Building); and a building where the roof was a lifted rolling extension of the asphalt parking lot itself (Parking Lot Building). The Europeans, the Japanese, intellectuals, and avant-garde-ists around the world seemed to revel in these deceptively simple, violated concrete box projects. The great hue and cry of the conservative, mainstream architecture world in New York, however, was: "That's not Architecture." Where we saw Dada-ist aesthetics and the legacy of Duchamp, they saw one-liners. While we reveled in the anonymous but pervasive American warehouse building, a symbol as powerful as the Coca-Cola bottle and the Campbell's Soup Can, a found-object and suitable for intellectual speculation, they saw triviality.

If you leap forward to where we are today, the ideas embodied in those buildings have become part of architecture's institutionalized avant-garde. The idea that architecture should be dematerialized, or ephemeral, that it should be psychological or phenomenological—as if its creator had conceptually inserted or subtracted an object into or through the building as part of its composition—has become part of the canon of architecture. Academic architects and theoreticians in the very institutions that decried SITE as trivial and invalid now routinely draw on these very ideas in creating, justifying, and codifying their own work. SITE was interested in the idea of frozen phenomena some 30 years ago, way ahead of their time. SITE considered the academic and mainstream American rejection of their work as "not-architecture" as a badge of honor. Bear in mind that SITE was truly a collective. We made very little money and what we made we shared. Like many SoHo artists of the period, we had little interest in selling anything related to traditional art and little chance of selling it anyway. And yet we all persisted, determined to change the way the modern world sees and builds, lives and works.

^ Campbell's Soup Can
Andy Warhol
Acrylic, Silkscreen on
Canvas
1964

"Whither, Greene Street, best beloved of friends,

O whither hast thou gone, and left me here

Alone amid the many toils of earth

wither hast thou gone now?"

Everywhere.

(Apologies to St. Gregory of Nazianzus, Elegy
for his tutor Carterius, circa 4th century A.D.)

^ Grid House
Michael McDonough
Boston, Massachusetts, USA
1978

PLOP ART AND TURD IN THE PLAZA: The descriptions of outdoor sculpture as "plop art" or "turd in the plaza" were originated by James Wines, for various lectures on the advent of a new environmental sensibility during the early 1970s. The purpose in using these critical terms was to separate the contextually inclusive ideas of an emerging environmental art movement from the kind of "object thinking" that characterized institutionalized interpretations of public art during that same period. In Wines' view, public art since the late 19th century had seldom functioned as anything more than cosmetic decor—meaning, a form of aesthetic tokenism, where art was treated as a minor accessory and architecture was seen as the big event. His derogatory terms were directed against works that had been conceived from a "private art" point of view. This referred to sculptures that already existed in plan or fact (independent of any environmental considerations) and were supposed to enhance the public domain by the mere act of installation. From Wines' perspective, whatever aesthetic value emerged from this awkward confrontation was based on subjective compositional preferences and the self-conscious decision to install art in the first place. The result was simply an object that pedestrians leaned against while waiting for a taxi—lacking both content and context.

This project by early SITE member Cynthia Eardley proposes an under-lake environment constructed in glass and intended to span a 300-foot distance across Fallen Leaf Lake, Nevada. The purpose is to enable visitors to experience the various levels of a clear mountain lake. As people enter, they have the sensation of walking on water. After crossing the surface level, participants can descend under water and experience a completely submerged contemplation chamber. Totally enveloped by water, they can experience a calm and meditative atmosphere.

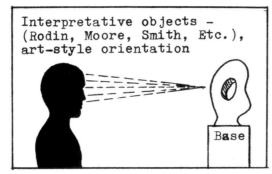

Spectator view - into and at the
object, enclosed directives for
viewing

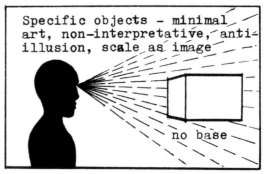

Spectator view - at and around
the object, scale and adjacent
peripheral environment affect
visual reception

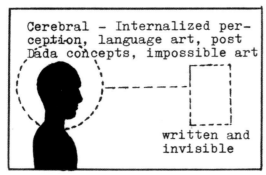

Spectator view - Inward, thought
process, conceptualized

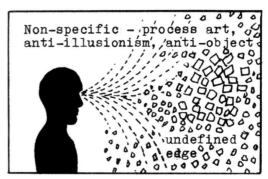

Spectator view - Fragmented and
dispersed, material oriented,
visual reception without the security of focal direction

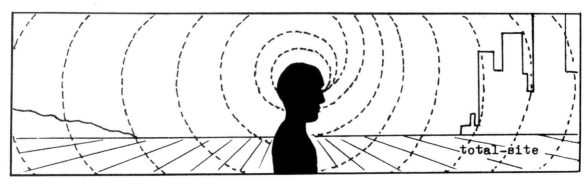

Spectator view - Expansive, inclusive of the far periphery, non-focal,
responsive to influences within the environment which determine the
concept of site-oriented art

^ **Ways of Seeing, Perceptual Habits in Viewing Art**
ON SITE N° 1 "ON SITE ON SITE ON SITE ON SITE,"
1972

> **Roadside House**
Barcelona, Spain
1970

This non-focal project by early SITE member Dana Draper works with an environment defined by the building, the plaza, and the adjacent spaces—all of which become a "base" for a sculptural event. The conflict of "scale to building" and "scale to man" is simultaneously resolved. The sculpture utilizes the stronger design elements and, at the same time, helps to detract from the side wings of the skyscraper, which are drastically out of scale relative to the 600-foot tower. From a distance one perceives the bright red enamel stripe, a shot of color, a statement of activity, in a city pervaded by dense neutrality. From a proximate view the spectator experiences the perceptual illusion of a two-dimensional stripe disappearing into the sky, as well as the real volume articulating the plaza area.

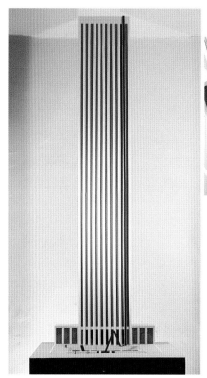

In the future perhaps remote (we shall see) the end of art as a thing separated from our surrounding environment, which is the actual plastic reality. But this end is at the same time a new beginning.
PIET MONDRIAN

METROPOLITAN OPERA HOUSE PLAZA   NEW YORK CITY, NEW YORK, USA   **1969**

This early environmental art project by James Wines proposes a large reflective wall of polished stainless steel that mirrors a plaza-hugging, partly incised in the paving, series of related structures. The intention is to transform a rather bleak urban site, by involving all of the existing architectural elements. This space is intended to engage human activity by means of a cinema screen-like reflection wall. The building façade and pavement surface become intrinsic parts of the sculptural environment.

< **Metropolitan Opera House Plaza**
1969

An early environmental art concept by James Wines for architect I.M. Pei's Everson Museum in Syracuse, New York, this concept proposes a randomly poured "distribution piece" in lead. The purpose is to visually activate a rigidly formal plaza space, adjacent to an institutional building. Although still identifiable as a work of sculpture in an architectural context, the conceptual approach introduces certain ideas of indeterminacy and undefined edges as part of SITE's emerging artistic vocabulary. This project was designed one year before the official charter of the group in 1970.

> **Plaza by Dan Kiley at Lincoln Center for the Performing Arts**
New York City, USA
1990

> **I.M. Pei's Everson Museum**
Syracuse, New York, USA
1969

< **Duck in Plaza**
New York City, USA
1969

Illustration for an essay in *Architectural Forum* (April, 1972) and subsequent lecture at the Southwest A.I.A. Convention in Yosemite Park, California (October, 1972) entitled "The Case for the Big Duck"—a response to Robert Venturi's 1971 negative critique of the Long Island poultry store as a means of supporting his theory in favor of the "decorated shed."

^ **The Big Duck**
Long Island, New York, USA
1970s

This public space concept proposes a gently undulating environment composed of 10-foot-square modules. The configuration suggests a massive chessboard that serves as a stage for human activity. Extending this analogy, the plaza is equipped with a series of fixed and variable units, incorporating natural and phenomenological elements, which offer users an infinite potential for change, movement, and creative interaction. Among the kinetic elements, there are contextually responsive uses of light, sound, laser beams, and cloud-like emissions of illuminated steam at night.

← 10 feet →

∧ **10-foot-square grey and white modules**

∧ **Plastic arc of colored light**

People who use the space should be there at the inception of the planning. This way the environment becomes a place where they belong.

CYNTHIA EARDLEY, *TIMES UNION*, 1971

^ Steam Square

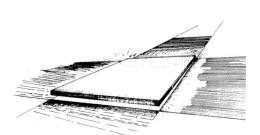

^ Raised Square Lighted from Beneath

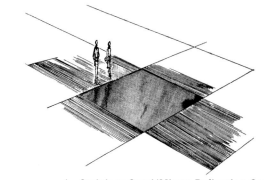

^ Stainless Steel/Mirror Reflection Square

^ Earth Square

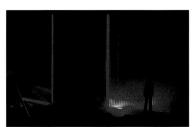

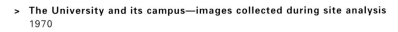

^ Variable modules of phenomenological events

> The University and its campus—images collected during site analysis
1970

The Binghamton project grows out of the special character of its environs (a riverfront community in upstate New York) and the need for visual relief from the relentlessly flat monotony of the township's Main Street and its unimaginative urban renewal. The site includes an abandoned space between buildings, a connective alleyway, and an adjoining shopping mall—in all, a total of six blocks of aligned real estate parcels. The program calls for the unification of these disparate spaces and architectural styles.

The final proposal evolved from the ideas generated during SITE discussions. The initial pooled proposals included: Wooden Waves, a dissipating undulation from the site's apex to alleyway; a Multi-tiered walk, weaving together the layers of levels; and a secondary Floating Boardwalk, skimming the water's surface. All are made entirely of locally produced and available wood beams. These materials are part of a stockpile, left in storage from years of pier removal after the waterfront shipping industry declined during the early 20th century.

The final proposal eliminates the alleyway and suggests an undulating dock-like structure. The project is intended to integrate both land surface and adjacent building walls, as components of an environmental art piece that can be seen to equal advantage from a walking position, or a moving automobile.

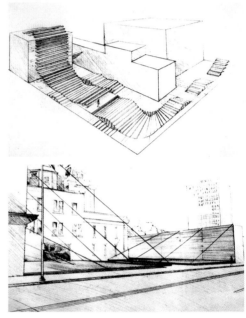

> **Floating Boardwalk and Wooden Waves**
Sketches, Cynthia Eardley
Model, James Wines

I have forced myself to contradict myself in order to avoid conforming to my own taste.

MARCEL DUCHAMP

< **Contextual information collected during site analysis**
Binghamton, New York, USA
1972

PEEKSKILL MELT   PEEKSKILL, NEW YORK, USA   **1972**

This public space project was developed for a middle-income housing complex in upstate New York. The community is distinguished by mountains, a rolling landscape, and densely forested areas. SITE was asked by the local development agency to provide a place of special identity, adjacent to one of the largest and most oppressive of these brick units. The solution proposes "melting" the base of the apartment block at each corner. This is achieved by allowing a flow of undulating brick to emerge from the rectangular volume of the building and spill over the surrounding landscape. The visual effect is intended to seem like a release of tension in the static walls—as though the internal cohesion of the architecture has responded to the forces of nature and the burden of its own existence. The project also challenges the categorical distinction between land surface as "left-over" space, next to a building, versus the conventional completeness of architecture as an object independent from context. By blurring these separations, the Peekskill Melt creates an ambiguous transition between structure and the environment.

COURTYARD PROJECT   INTERMEDIATE SCHOOL 25, NEW YORK CITY, NEW YORK, USA   **1973**

This work of environmental art for a schoolyard plaza proposes the de-materialization of an existing stair tower. The volume of the imposing concrete structure is physically reduced by gradually enlarging the size of the aggregate mix used to construct the face of the tower, until the outward flow of its adhesive mass disintegrates into a casual distribution of stones and boulders at the far end of the courtyard. The intention of this inversion is to question the sanctity of formalist architecture as an inviolable object. For example, it suggests that a building can be treated as the raw material, or subject matter, for an art statement. This conceptual approach became the premise for many of SITE's subsequent projects.

Public art since the late-19th century has seldom functioned as anything more than cosmetic decor. The inevitable results are a form of aesthetic tokenism, where art is assigned to the role of a minor accessory and architecture is seen as the big event.

JAMES WINES

ROBERT SMITHSON: O.K. we'll begin with entropy. That's a subject that's preoccupied me for some time. On the whole I would say entropy contradicts the usual notion of the mechanistic world view. In other words it's a condition that's irreversible, it's a condition that's moving towards gradual equilibrium and it's suggested in many ways. Perhaps a nice succinct definition of entropy would be Humpty Dumpty. Like Humpty Dumpty sat on a wall, Humpty Dumpty has a great fall, all the king's horses and all the king's men couldn't put Humpty Dumpty back together again. There is a tendency to treat closed systems in such a way. One might even say that the current Watergate situation is an example of entropy. You have a closed system which eventually deteriorates and starts to break apart and there's no way that you can really piece it back together again.

Another example might be the shattering of Marcel Duchamp Glass, and his attempt to put all the pieces back together again attempting to overcome entropy. Buckminster Fuller also has a notion of entropy as a kind of devil that he must fight against and recycle. Norbert Weiner in *The Human Use of Human Beings* also postulates that entropy is the devil with a very simple mortality of good and bad, the etropic devil is more Manichean in that you really can't tell the good from the bad, there's no clear cut distinction. And I think at one point Norbert Weiner also refers to modern art as one Niagara of entropy.

In information theory you have another kind of entropy. The more information you have the higher degree of entropy, so that one piece of information tends to cancel out the other. The economist Nicholas Georgescu-Roegen has gone so far as to say that the second law of thermodynamics is not only a physical law but linked to economics. He says Sadi Carnot could be called a econometrican. Pure science, like pure art, tends to view abstraction as independent of nature, there's no accounting for change or temporality of the mundane world. Abstraction rules in a void, pretending to be free of time. One might even say that the whole energy crisis is a form of entropy. The earth being the closed system, there's only a certain amount of resources, and of course there's an attempt to reverse entropy through the recycling of garbage. People going around collecting bottles and tin cans and whatnot and placing them in certain compounds like the one over on Greenwich Avenue across from St. Vincent's Hospital. Well this seems to be a rather problematic situation.

Actually right now I would like to quote from Georgescu-Roegen, The Entropy Law and the Economic Process, about what he calls entropic bootlegging. It's an interesting conception I think. This is what he says about recycling waste materials. "This is what the promoters of entropy bootlegging fail to understand. To be sure, one can cite numberless scrap campaigns aimed at saving low entropy (low entropy in his definition is raw materials before they're processed into refined materials. In other words raw ore would be low entropy and high entropy would be the refined material such as steel)… by sorting waste. They have been successful only because in given circumstances the sorting of, say, scrap copper required a smaller consumption of low entropy than the alternative way of obtaining the same amount of metal. It is equally true that the advance of technological knowledge may change the balance sheet of any scrap campaign, although history shows that past progress has benefited ordinary production rather than scrap saving. However, to sort out the scrap molecules scattered all over the land and at the bottom of the sea, would require such a long time that the entire low entropy of our environment would not suffice to keep alive the numberless generations of Maxwell's demons needed for the completed project." In other words he's giving us the indication that recycling is like looking for needles in haystacks.

Now, I would like to get into the area of, let's say the problem of waste. It seems that when one is talking about preserving the environment or conserving energy or recycling one inevitably gets to the question of waste and I would postulate actually that waste and enjoyment are in a sense couples. There's a certain kind of pleasure principle that comes out of a preoccupation with waste. Like if we want a bigger, better car we are going to have a bigger and better waste production. So there's a kind of equation between the enjoyment of life and waste. Probably the opposite of waste is luxury. Both waste and luxury tend to be useless. Then there's a kind of middle-class notion of luxury which often is called "quality." And quality is sort of based on taste and sensibility. Sartre says Genet produces neither spit or diamonds. I guess that's what I am talking about.

ALISON SKY: Isn't entropy actually metamorphosis, or a continual process in which elements are undergoing change, but in an evolutionary sense?

SMITHSON: Yes and no. In other words, if we consider the earth in terms of geologic time we end

^ **Stacking**
Indeterminate Façade Reference
SITE Archives

< **Cover of ON SITE N° 4—"NOT SEEN AND/OR LESS SEEN OF…"**
1973

up with what we call fluvial entropy. Geology has its entropy too, where everything is gradually wearing down. Now there may be a point where the earth's surface will collapse and break apart, so that the irreversible process will be in a sense metamorphosized, it is evolutionary, but it's not evolutionary in terms of idealism. There is still the heat death of the sun. It may be that human beings are just different than dinosaurs rather than better. In other words there just might be a different situation. There's this need to try to transcend one's condition. I'm not a transcendentalist, so I just see things going toward a... well it's very hard to predict anything; anyway all predictions tend to be wrong. I mean even planning. I mean planning and chance seem to be the same thing.

SKY: I wish the architectural profession would recognize that. In their grand master plan schemes for the world, architects seem to find the "final solution" to all possible solutions.

SMITHSON: They don't take those things into account. Architects tend to be idealists, and not dialecticians. I propose a dialectics of entropic change. There is an ongoing aspect of things that fascinates me like my recent involvement with Central Park (see "Frederick Law Olmsted and the Dialectical Landscape," *Art Forum*, February 1973). You see that photograph there showing a pit in Central Park. Now you might say that's a kind of architecture, a kind of entropic architecture or a de-architecturization. In other words it's not really manifesting itself the way let's say Skidmore Owings and Merrill might manifest itself. It's almost the reverse of that, so that you can observe these kinds of entropic building situations which develop around construction. That pit will eventually be covered, but it's there right now with all of its scaffolding, and people have been confused by the pit, they think it has something to do with the Met (Metropolitan Museum of New York). There's a lot of graffiti on it attacking the Met, but it's a really big city.

SKY: It's ironic that we've been able to perpetuate this attitude of set design solutions throughout the world. Travelling through Europe you can go for miles and it all looks exactly alike everywhere else. Mimic Lefrak City architecture is covering the earth. How did this manage to take over as opposed to the opposite view exemplified by places like Rome where there are no two buildings, angles, textures, etc the same. Ruins melt and merge into new structures, and you get this marvelous and energetic juxtaposition occurring—with accident a large part of the whole process.

SMITHSON: Well, Rome is like a big scrap heap of antiquities. America doesn't have that kind of historical background of debris. But I'd like to mention another mistake which is essentially an engineering mistake and that's the Salton Sea in southern California, which happens to be California's largest lake. It happened back during Teddy Roosevelt's administration. There was a desperate attempt to try to reroute the Colorado River. The Colorado River was always flooding and destroying the area. There was an attempt to keep the Colorado River from flooding by building a canal, in Mexico, and this was illegally done. This canal was started in the delta of the Colorado and then it was rerouted back toward Mexicali, but what happened was that the river flooded into this canal and the canal overflowed, and fed back into the Imperial Valley which is below sea level. So that this 30-mile lake was created by this engineering mistake, and whole cities were inundated, the railroad also was submerged, and there were great attempts to fight back this deluge, but to no avail. Since then, people have come to live with this lake, and recently I was out there. I spent some time in Salton City which is a city of about 400 people. And another example of blind planning is this maze of wide boulevards that snake through the desert. Now it was the idea that they would turn into a huge retirement village or whatever, maybe a new Palm Springs, but the bottom fell out of that so that if you go there now you just see all these boulevards going all through the desert, very wide concrete boulevards and just sign posts naming the different roads and maybe a few trailer encampments near this city. It's impossible to swim in the Salton Sea because barnacles have grown all over the rocks. There is some water skiing and fishing. There's also a plan to try to desalinate the whole Salton Sea. And there's all kinds of strange schemes for doing that. One was to bring down slag from Kaiser Steel Company, and build a dike system. So that here we have an example of a kind of domino effect where one mistake begets another mistake, yet these mistakes are all curiously exciting me on a certain kind of level—I don't find them depressing.

^ **Buried Woodshed**
Robert Smithson
Kent State University, Ohio, USA
1970

^ **Asphalt Rundown**
Robert Smithson
Rome, Italy
1969

> **Dissolving Clouds**
Peter Hutchenson
Aspen, 1970
ON SITE N° 4
1973

SKY: There's an inherent energy level present in an accident or mistake occurrence. I was listening to a discussion of I.M. Pei buildings near Washington Square Village, and apparently in two towers owned by New York University an attempt was made at "total control." Even the curtains were specified so as not to disturb the "aesthetic resolution" of the building façade. The third tower was not owned by N.Y.U. and houses the people replaced by the construction. These people were free to choose their own curtains and you get an incredible diversity of styles and colors which I find much more dynamic. Ironically the white curtains so carefully controlled have since faded to different tones of white so that the process is occurring anyway.

SMITHSON: Right. It's like the Anchorage earthquake that was responsible for creating a park. After the earthquake they set aside a portion of the earthquake damage and turned that into a park, which strikes me as an interesting way of dealing with the unexpected, and incorporating that into a community. That area's fascinated me quite a bit. Also, the recent eruptions outside of Iceland. At Vestmann Islands an entire community was submerged in black ashes. It created a kind of buried house system. It was quite interesting for a while. You might say that it provided a temporary kind of buried architecture which reminds me of my own Partially Buried Woodshed out in Kent State, Ohio where I took 20 cartloads of earth and piled them on this woodshed until the central beam cracked. There was a problem from one of the local papers. They didn't really see that as a very positive gesture, and there was a rather disparaging article that went under the heading "It's a Mud, Mud, Mud World."

But basically I think that those preoccupations do escape architects and I'm thinking of another problem that also exists, that of mining reclamation they wanted to put back in the mines the way they were before they mined them. Now that's a real Humpty Dumpty way of doing things. You can imagine the result when they tried to deal with the Bingham pit in Utah which is a pit one-mile deep and three miles across. Now the idea of the law being so general and not really dealing with the specific site like that, they were supposed to fill that pit in; now of course one would wonder where they were going to get the material to fill the pit in.

SKY: Did you ask them?

SMITHSON: Yes, I mean to have said it would take something like 30 years and they'd have to get the dirt from another mountain. It seems that the reclamation laws really don't deal with specific sites, they deal with a general dream or an ideal world long gone. It's an attempt to recover a frontier or a wilderness that no longer exists. Here we have to accept the entropic situation and more or less learn how to reincorporate these things that seem ugly. Actually there's the conflict of interests. On one side you have the idealistic ecologist and on the other side you have the profit desiring miner and you get all kinds of strange twists of landscape consciousness from such people. In fact there's a book that the Sierra Club put out called *Stripping*. Strip mining actually does sort of suggest lewd sex acts and everything, so it seems immortal from that standpoint. It's like a kind of sexual assault on mother earth which brings in the aspect of incest projections as well as illicit behavior and I would say that psychologically there's a problem there. There's a discussion of aesthetics on this book Stripping from the point of view of the miner and from the point of view of the ecologist. The ecologist says flatly that strip mines are just ugly and the miner says that beauty is in the eye of the beholder. So you have this stalemate and I would say that's part of the clashing aspects of the entropic tendency, in other words two irreconcilable situations hopelessly going over the same waterfall. It seems that one would have to recognize this entropic condition rather than try to reverse it. And there's no stopping it; consider the image that Norbert Weiner gives us— Niagara Falls.

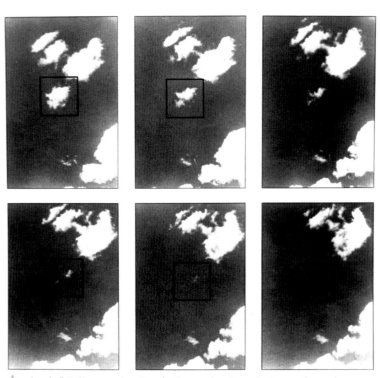

DISSOLVING CLOUDS

According to Hatha Yoga principles, if you breathe properly and concentrate your Pranic (electrical-mental) energy, you can dissolve a cloud. I tried it and photographed the result. This is what happened — see cloud outlined — Time elapsed was 3 minutes.

Peter Hutchinson, Aspen, August 1970

In fact they even shored up Niagara, speaking of Niagara. They stopped Niagara for a while because it was wearing away. And then they put these steel rods into the rock so that it would maintain its natural appearance.

SKY: Have they been able to stop it?

SMITHSON: They did stop it.

SKY: From wearing away?

SMITHSON: Well, it's still there. It didn't fall apart yet. Niagara looks like a giant open pit quarry. In other words it has high walls which offend people greatly in the strip mining regions. There are defects called "high walls" that exist in the strip mining areas and there's a desire on the part of ecologists to slope these down. The cliffs all around Niagara suggest excavation and mining, but it's just the work of nature. Is man not a part of nature? So this causes problems.

SKY: There is definitely some sort of perverse fascination attached to the process of inevitable and impending destruction that will occur either in your own environment or be observed vicariously because people persist in living at the bases of volcanoes, on earthquake zones such as the fault line which is supposed to destroy all of California, on top of sinking landscapes such as Venice which is a city built entirely on rotting wooden pilings and will eventually fall into the sea.

SMITHSON: Well, that may be something that's human... that's a human need. It seems that there's almost a hope for disaster you might say. There's that desire for spectacle. I know when I was a kid I used to love to watch the hurricanes come and blow the trees down and rip up the sidewalks. I mean it fascinated me. There's a kind of pleasure one receives on that level. Yet there is this desire for something more tranquil—like babbling brooks, and pastorals, and wooded glens. But I suppose I'm more attracted toward mining regions and volcanic conditions—wastelands rather than the usual notion of scenery or quietude, tranquility... though they somehow interact.

SKY: I think man turns on the wooded glens in the last moments for the most part. He probably wouldn't like to admit it but I don't think it's of prime importance to him—from a fascination viewpoint. I mean he really hasn't done much to protect these pockets of tranquility. At the last moment, after it's almost all destroyed he starts screaming "put up the trees" but only in a token gesture sense. That's always the answer, especially in public spaces in a city like New York—stick up a few isolated trees.

SMITHSON: Well, it seems that in a city like New York where everything is concrete there's this craving to stick up a tree somewhere. Also in regard to the origin of parks in this county it's interesting to note that they really started as graveyards. There's something in the mid-19th century that's called the "rural graveyard movement" where there was an attempt to get away from the dreary little churchyard graveyards. They introduced a kind of silvan setting so that nature would intermingle with the graveyards, and they developed a whole funerary school of art you might say. I know for a fact over near Fort Lee there are all these vaults... little pyramids, you know, for the dead.

There is an association with architecture and economics, and it seems that architects build in an isolated, self-contained, a-historical way. They never seem to allow for any kind of relationships outside their grand plan. And this seems to be true in economics too. Economics seem to be isolated and self-contained and conceived of as cycles, so as to exclude the whole entropic process. There's very little consideration of natural resources in terms of what the landscape looks like after the mining operations or farming operations are completed. So that a kind of blindness ensues. I guess it's what we call blind profit making. And then suddenly they find themselves within a range of desolation and wonder how they got there. So it's a rather static way of looking at things. I don't think things go in cycles. I think things just change from one situation to the next, there's really no return.

AMERICAN BICENTENNIAL COMMEMORATIVE
MONUMENT AT FOUR CORNERS NEW MEXICO, USA **1974**

The American Bicentennial Project developed to commemorate the Navajo Indian Nation and Jefferson Grid at the Four Corners area in New Mexico. This site is where the four states— Utah, New Mexico, Arizona, and Colorado intersect. It is a place symbolic to the Indian culture and representative of Thomas Jefferson's ideal land division plan for the United States. At the time of SITE's involvement, the location was marked only by a flat concrete slab.

The SITE concept is based on various symbolic images drawn from Navajo myths, as well as the rising and setting sun orientation in the Four Corners environment. This monument was intended to be built from a series of earth mounds with a massive horizontal directional. An underground section provided a Four Corners and Indian History Museum.

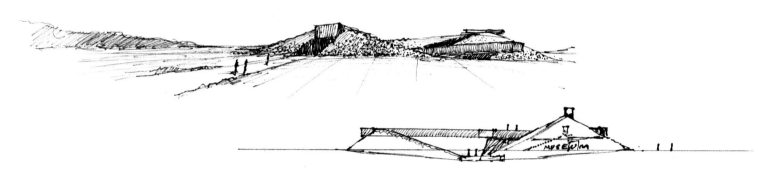

^ Landscape of the Four Corners region

The earth's surface
           and the figments of the mind
have a way
of

disintegrating
into discrete regions of art.
Various agents, both
              fictional and real,

somehow trade places with each other—one cannot avoid
muddy thinking when it comes to earth projects,
or what I will call "abstract geology."
One's mind and the earth are in a constant state of erosion,
mental rivers wear away abstract banks, brain waves undermine cliffs of thought, ideas decompose
into stones of unknowing,
and conceptual crystallizations break apart into deposits of gritty reason. Vast moving facilities occur in this
geological miasma, and they move in the most physical way.
This movement seems motionless, yet it crushes the landscape of logic under glacial reveries. This slow flowage
makes one conscious of the turbidy of thinking. Slump, debris slides, avalanches all take place within the cracking
limits of the brain. The entire body is pulled from the cerebral sediment, where particles and fragments make
themselves known as solid consciousness. A bleached and fractured world surrounds the artist. To organize this mess
of corrosion into patterns, grids, and subdivisions is an esthetic process that has scarcely been touched.
ROBERT SMITHSON, "SEDIMENTATION OF THE MIND: EARTH PROJECTS"
ART FORUM, 1968

Developed as part of a Bicentennial Project and sponsored by the State of Nebraska, this proposal by SITE incorporates the actual roadway as part of an environmental art concept to be seen from moving automobiles. The stenciled words REST STOP begin to appear, as though gradually emerging from the highway divider lines, approximately one mile before the actual rest area location. Approximately one-quarter mile from the site, the words become completely formed and then appear as three-dimensional units in the triangular gore space—starting with the letter "R" and continuing into the grass plot, until the words are repeated in both two and three-dimensional form. At the center of the gore area, these three-dimensional letters begin to dissolve and then gradually disappear at the end of the island. At this point, the stenciled letters reverse and slowly return into the pavement, where they again dissolve into the dotted road dividers. The reversed letters can then be seen by motorists in their rear-view mirrors, indicating that the rest area has been passed.

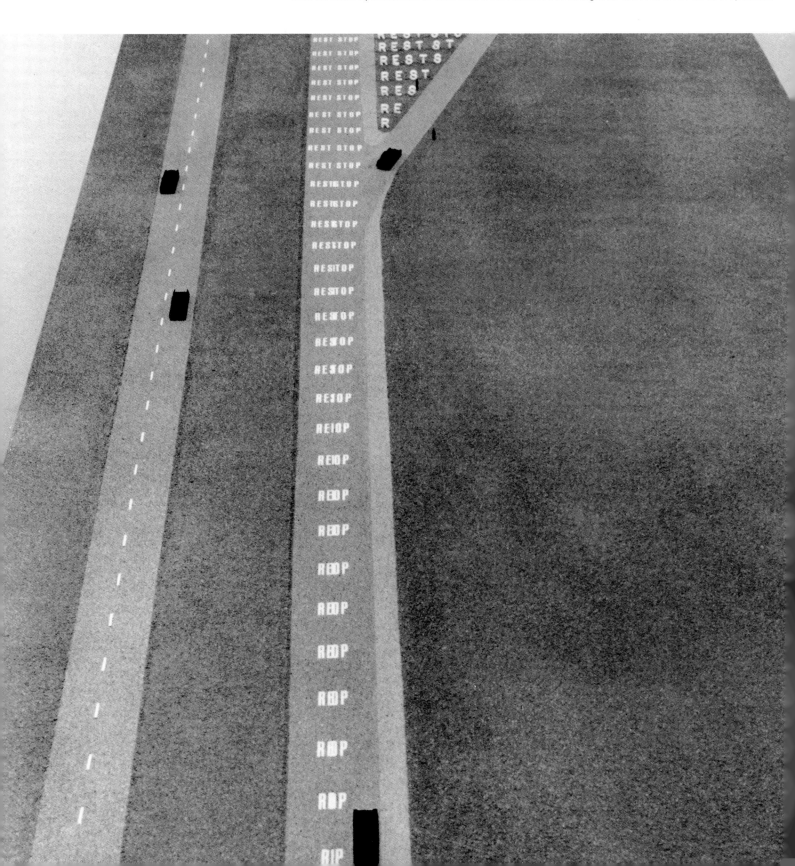

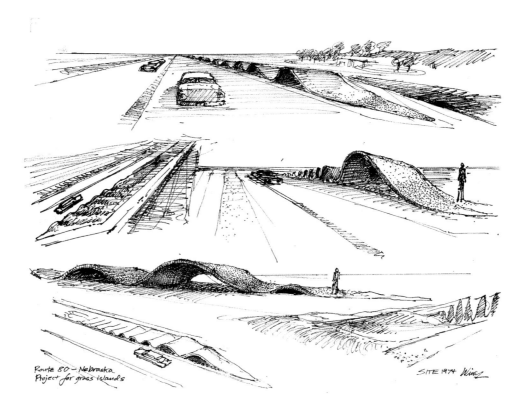

This second project is also part of the American Bicentennial and sponsored by the State of Nebraska. The proposal incorporates the gore sections adjacent to Interstate 80 as part of an environmental artwork, to be viewed by the drivers of moving automobiles. The strip separating the roadway shoulder from the rest stop area is elevated into a series of gradually diminishing, grass-covered, corrugations (achieved by an internal construction of pre-cast concrete units). The visual effect of these undulating mounds is intended to suggest an ambiguous ritual environment, located in an endlessly flat and uneventful landscape.

^ **Aerial view of prototype rest stop along Interstate 80**
Nebraska, USA
1973

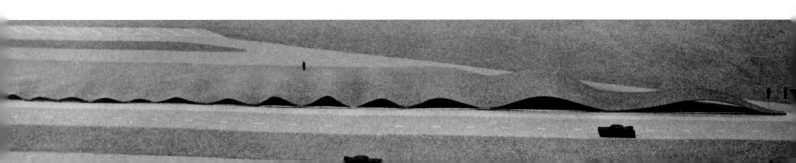

^ BEST Prototype
The Box/Found-Object

^ Strip Architecture
Los Angeles, California, USA
1970s

In 1972 SITE was retained by BEST Products, Inc., one of the nation's largest mail order corporations, to develop a series of projects for their merchandise showrooms in various parts of the country. The showroom prototype is a rectangular brick shoebox on an asphalt parking lot, variable only in size, and a more recent pedestrian canopy. They are usually situated on a peripheral strip area near a major city and always adjacent to a principal highway. In its analysis of the BEST buildings, SITE concluded that the standard brick model was important to retain and that any art ideas should grow out of its generic identity. The first of these projects completed in Richmond, Virginia was a "peeling building" where the actual brick façade inclines precariously away from the central structure. Located on Midlothian Turnpike, the structure captures public attention as an unusual interpretation of roadway art and as an inversion of conventional expectations for the proper behavior of brick walls.

SHOPPING CENTER ART, 1972   NANCY GOLDRING

PART ONE
What kind of art might be employed to affect qualitative change in the experience of the shopping center?

The Shopping Center—Prevailing Assumptions and Attitudes

1. Shopping centers are coherent environments with recognizable formats. They serve as easily identifiable landmarks on the contemporary landscape.

2. Such commercial buildings may be constructed according to economic dictates. "Aesthetics," in this sense, becomes irrelevant to Every Day.

3. Decorative elements added after the fact provide an expedient method for the embellishment or improvement of the shopping center.

4. Society's ultimate authority on decoration is the artist, whose sensibility is largely confined to the production of his own personal works.

The Art

1. *Select a "high quality" art product:*
the time-tested variety: a classical architectural sculpture or a contemporary success: a Henry Moore (blown up to large scale).

Situate the work within a shopping center complex:
BEST Products, Richmond, Virginia.

Resulting Conclusions:
The ludicrous juxtaposition of elements (a quasi-"assisted readymade") illustrates the inability of high culture artifacts to transform and redefine BEST Products, either as a work of art or a cultural product.

Art-as-Beautification within this context becomes self-defeating if not to say impossible.
The attempt to whitewash proves ineffectual, a BEST Products continues to insist upon the predominance of its identity as shopping center. The works of art themselves, out of a timeless and rarified atmosphere (i.e. the gallery or museum), either disappear amidst the general traffic, or begin to assume the quality of their new, commercial surroundings.

2. *Select an expression appropriate to the site:*
A billboard or kitsch art form.

Situate the "art" within the same shopping center.

Resulting Conclusions:
The stylistic consistency of the billboard and the site itself serve to reiterate the meaning of the shopping center. In no way has the place been transformed.

PART TWO
Why would the shopping center intrigue the artist?

The Pop Artist and the Shopping Center

As the archetypal shopping center, BEST Products could become a natural readymade, when situated within the gallery. It could become the easy object of its own facetious statement, thriving upon which it condemns.

If left in place (hypothetically the subject of Christo's wit), BEST Products provides a comment upon the consumer society which propagates shopping centers. In this form the "work of art" becomes the monumental product or the packaged package.

BEST Products looks like the cardboard container that it is.

Minimalist and the Shopping Center

"Art-as-Art" rejects "Shopping Center-as-Art" on any level.

The purist approach, particularly during the last several decades, has attempted to reduce the scope of the art making process to its essentials; and the advocates of this tendency would, therefore, struggle to keep the artist free from the complexity (banalities) of everyday life.

BEST Products does, in fact, resemble the simple forms used by Minimalists. Furthermore, the building calls attention to itself as "shopping center" just as Minimal works insist upon their own "presence." The similarity between the two (BEST Products and Minimal structures), however, fails to relate the shopping center to any pure art form. The shopping center exists as pure use, not pure form.

The Conceptual Artist (Process) and the Shopping Center

The conceptual artist need only make his presence felt within the mall in order to qualify BEST Products as "work of art."

By exposing the rituals of the market, he has focused his artistic intentions upon the particular process. The articulation of his propositions concerning the shopping center becomes the "art object" which entices the audience. The public, anxiously awaiting the artist's return to the gallery with his photographs and notes, can then amuse itself with the artist's perceptions (judgements) of his everyday activities.

The shopping center remains essentially intact, having been subjected only to speculation. Untouched by the hand of the artist, BEST Products continues to assert its meaning as use rather than art.

Classical

Time-Tested

Blow Up

Kitsch

Minimalist

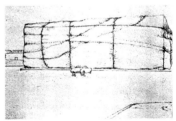

Pop

Conceptual

1

2

3

4

5

6

7

8

9

10

11

14

15

16

17

68'-4 1/2"   78'-6"   78'-6"

398'

12

13

1 Floating Roof Showroom, Concept 1970
2 Colonnade of Color, Concept 1970
3 Mirror Project, Concept 1970
4 BEST Reflection, Concept 1970
5 Peeling Project, Richmond, Virginia, USA, Built 1971
6 Word Project, Concept 1974
7 Indeterminate Façade Building, Houston, Texas, USA, Built 1975
8 BEST Notch Showroom, Sacramento, California, USA, Built 1977
9 BEST Tilt Showroom, Towson, Maryland, USA, Built 1978
10 BEST Reversible, Concept 1978
11 BEST Anti-Sign, Ashland, Virginia, USA, Built 1978–79
12 Twist Showroom, Concept 1979
13 Scale Reference Showroom, Concept 1979
14 Cutler Ridge BEST, Miami, Florida, USA, Built 1979
15 BEST Products Hialeah Showroom—(Rainforest Building), Hialeah, Florida, USA, Built 1979
16 BEST Forest Building, Richmond, Virginia, USA, Built 1980
17 BEST Inside/Outside Building, Milwaukee, Wisconsin, USA, Built 1984

^ **Sydney and Frances Lewis**
Clients for the BEST Products

^ **Indeterminate Façade**
SITE Archives
1975

The assumption that art should be viewed on exclusively proximate terms must be expanded to include, for instance, the spectator seated in a passing automobile or departing airplane.

SITE, *NOTES ON PUBLIC ART*, 1975

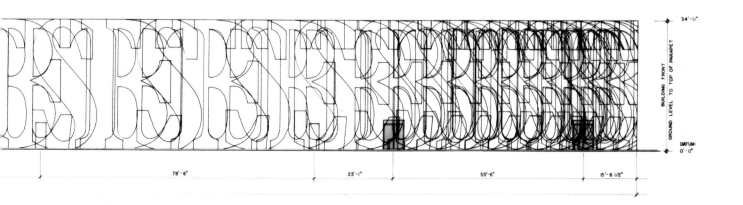

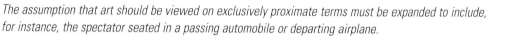

The Peeling Project by Cynthia Eardley was the first of nine commercial buildings designed (between 1971 and 1984) for the BEST Products Company of Richmond, Virginia, a retail merchandiser of hard goods in the United States. Each of these concepts treats BEST's standard prototype as the subject matter or raw material for an art statement. As a result, the building itself becomes a means of commentary on the social, psychological, and aesthetic aspects of architecture. It is also a way of changing public response to the significance of commercial structures in the suburban environment. Portions of the façade's brick veneer are peeled away precariously into space (achieved by the use of Sarabond mortar) to reveal the masonry wall underneath. This sculptural innovation produces the effect of architecture in a state of tentativeness and instability. By engaging a context of normalcy, the result becomes a juxtaposition of routine utility with visual ambiguity. Since the project is not about formalist design, it opens up the possibility of considering alternative relationships between art and buildings.

PEELING PROJECT – ALTERATION TO RETAIL CENTER

BEST PRODUCTS CO., INC.   RICHMOND, VIRGINIA   SITE, INC.   NEW YORK, NEW YORK

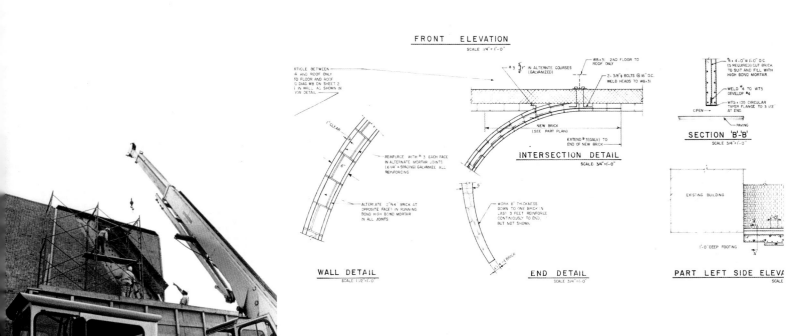

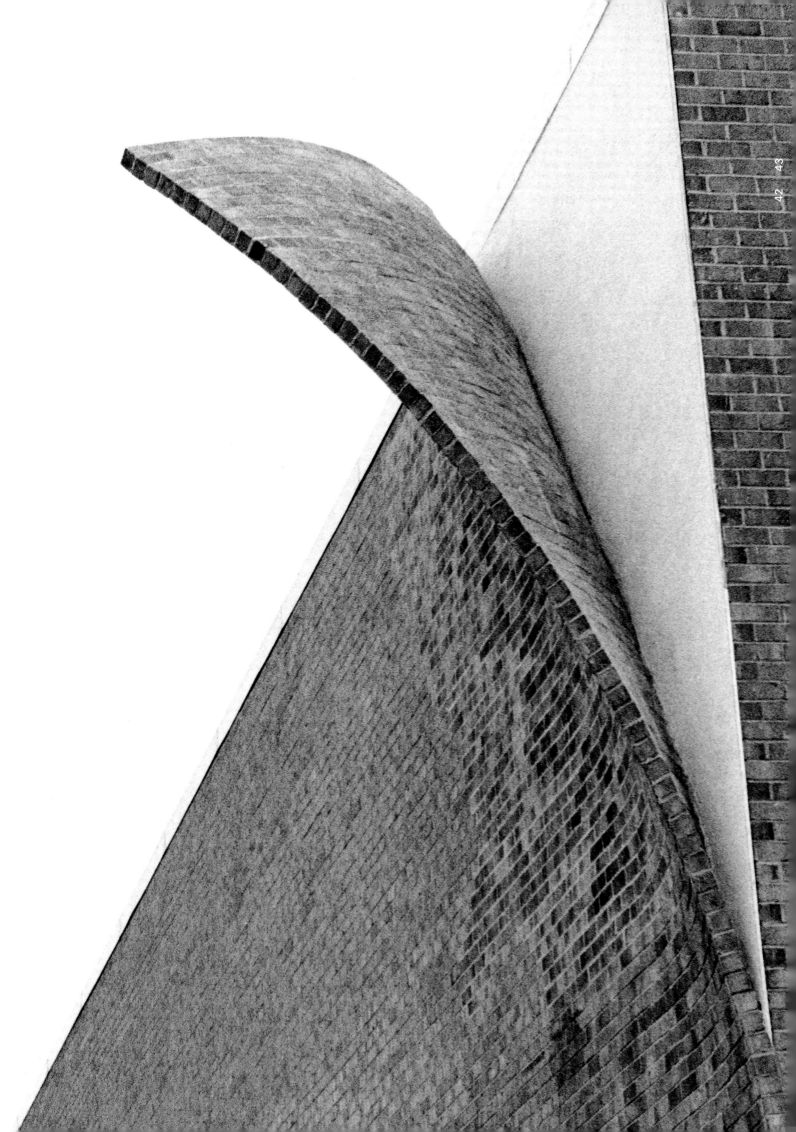

This is the second structure in the BEST Products Company series of retail merchandising showrooms. The dematerializing walls are intended as a critical commentary on American consumer culture, the standard shopping center box, the tradition of false-front façades, and the signage conventions found in typical commercial strips. The message is communicated by extending the brick veneer of the façade as a ragged profile beyond the logical edge of the roofline, resulting in the appearance of architecture arrested somewhere between construction and demolition. To intensify this feeling of indeterminacy, a section of the central façade breaks away into a cascade of waste bricks, spilling over the top of a pedestrian canopy. The Houston building became one of SITE's most famous early projects and set a highly visible precedent for using a ubiquitous building style as the foil for an art idea.

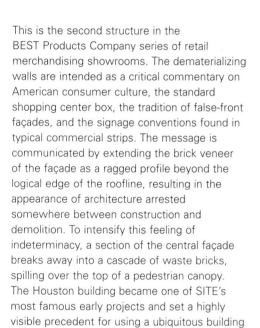

SITE
Projects and theories
1969-1978
Dedalo libri

Typical response to the showroom has been to interpret it as a symbol of apocalypse and/or destruction—or, as proposed by the French critic Pierre Schneider, "The new American pessimism". These metaphors are implied, but the intended dialogue is primarily concerned with missing parts, with the gap between the know and the void, with equivocation versus expectation as a source for urban imagery.

In a paradoxical sense this reduction by construction is a reversal of Mies van der Rohe's famous maxim "Less is more." The inclusion of more (material) in the Houston showroom gives the impression that there is less (physical substance) and suggests that the intention of "less" can be as intriguing as the aspiration to "more". Or, as Marxist philosopher Georgi Plekhanov has suggested "Negative thinking is simply positive thinking in the other direction."

SITE, *PROJECTS AND THEORIES 1969–1978*, EDITED BY BRUNO ZEVI

The Parking Lot Building proposes rolling a central section of asphalt paving over the roof of the store, as an inversion of the traditional relationship between retail architecture and its ubiquitous parking environment. The showroom is intended to appear as though it has been consumed by an undulating blanket of pavement—with its car culture imagery further emphasized by the continuation of parking lines over the top of the building. Consistent with SITE's other projects for BEST, this concept utilizes inherent materials and a generic building type associated with the commercial strip. In this case, two universal elements—the parking lot and the retail warehouse—are fused together as part of a surreal experience. In a sense, this notion of buildings invaded by their own contexts implies the elimination of architecture as an independent sculptural object—replacing the "shape-making" conventions of formalist design with an exploration of alternative possibilities for the integration of buildings and their surroundings.

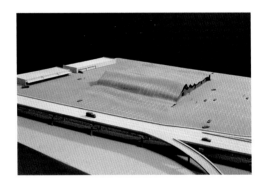

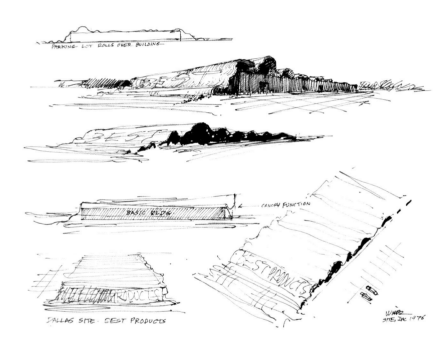

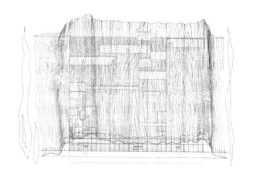

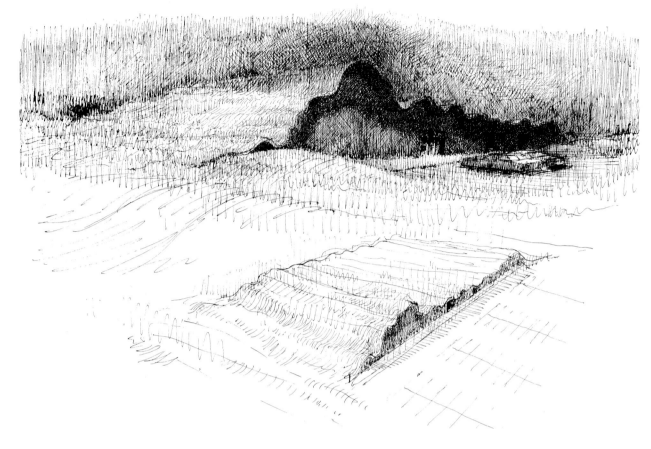

^ **60 Greene Street Studio**
New York City, USA
1976

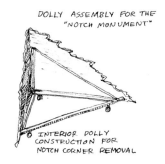

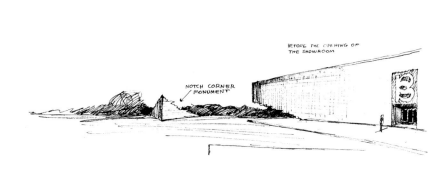

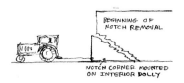

The Notch Showroom represents a further exploration of SITE's interest in an iconography of fragmentation and subtraction. Whereas the crumbling sections of the Indeterminate Façade in Texas suggest a process of dematerialization, the segmented corner of the Notch building is more like a jigsaw puzzle. It is intended as a stage for interaction—involving shoppers in a kind of theatrical event—as well as a form of commentary on positive and negative elements in architecture. A 14-foot-high, raw edged notch penetrates the masonry block building, functioning as a main entranceway. The 45-ton wedge, extracted from this gap, is mounted on a rail system incised into the paving and mechanized to move a distance of 40 feet to open and close the showroom. This concept takes advantage of the routine habits of shopping center visitors—accustomed to their own movements, while buildings remain stationary. In this case, the building is in motion, while the people stand still. The project is also a critique of the tradition of "integrating the arts." By becoming both monument and building, the Notch Showroom questions the entire process of integration. Its visual imagery is based on interaction and displacement, which establishes an entirely new relationship between art and architecture.

^ **Notch under construction showing cantilevered negative section with partially completed masonry work and view of the "wandering wall" steel work**

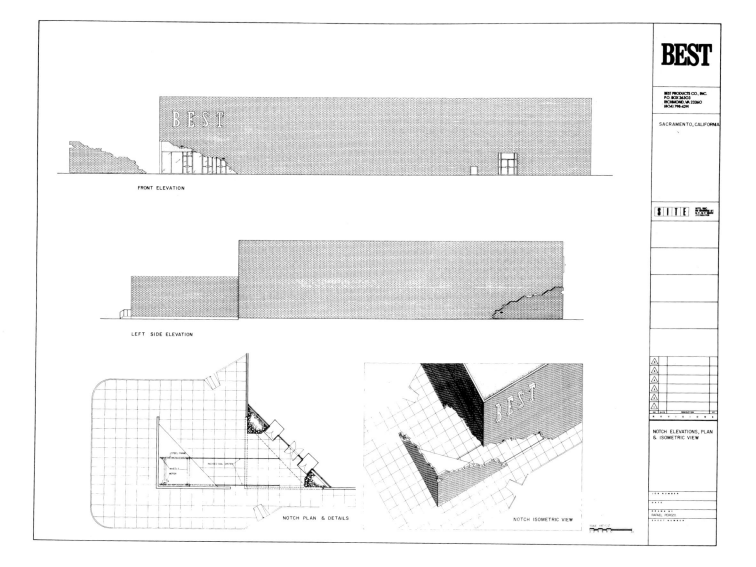

FRONT ELEVATION

LEFT SIDE ELEVATION

NOTCH PLAN & DETAILS

NOTCH ISOMETRIC VIEW

BEST

BEST PRODUCTS CO., INC.
P.O. BOX 26303
RICHMOND, VA 23260
(804) 798-4211

SACRAMENTO, CALIFORNIA

SITE

REVISIONS

NOTCH ELEVATIONS, PLAN
& ISOMETRIC VIEW

JOB NUMBER
DATE
DRAWN BY
RAFAEL PEROZO
SHEET NUMBER

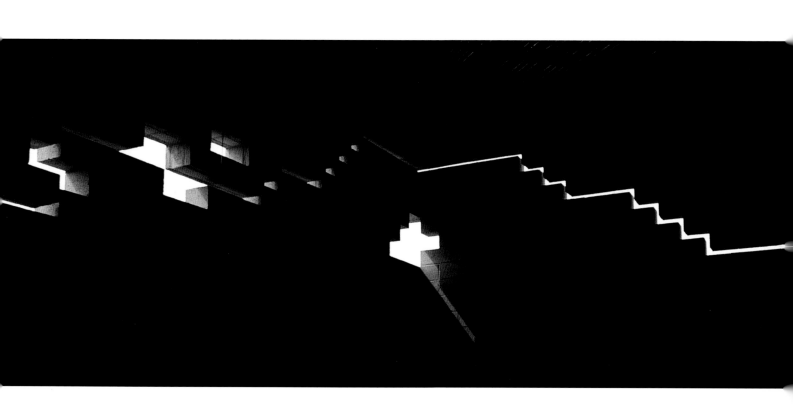

The Tilt Showroom in Eudowood Mall questions people's routine expectations for a standard retail structure and the architectural traditions of formal design and equilibrium. The façade of the Eudowood Mall showroom is dislodged from its normal position,—transformed into a massive, casually tilted, plane of masonry block—which takes advantage of people's predisposition toward the physical and psychological components of the American shopping center. Since the Towson site is a U-shaped retail center composed of rigidly vertical and horizontal elements, this displacement opens up a visual dialogue between normal utility and a sense of precariousness. The building is also a commentary on modern architecture's obsession with form as an expression of function. In this case, the function is not "expressed," but simply "revealed" by lifting up one corner of the usual impediment between outside and inside.

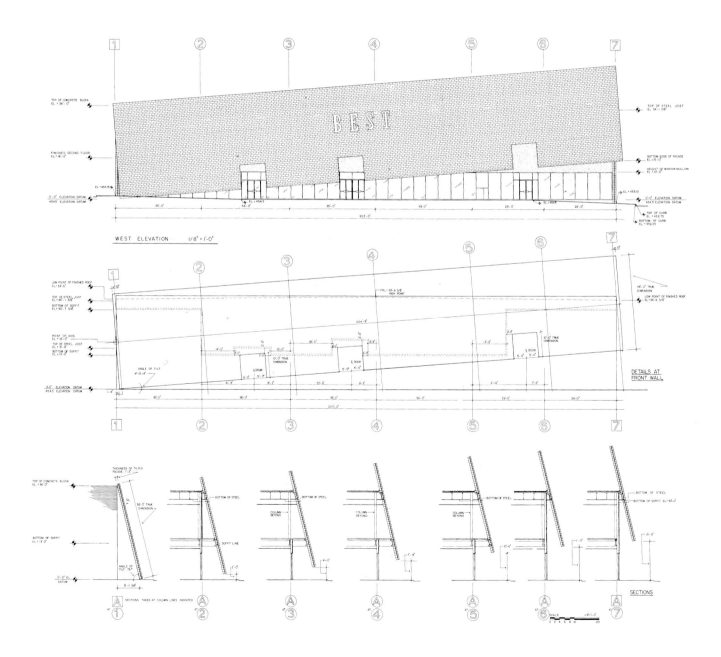

∧ **Metamorphosis Project—Terrarium Showroom Alternate**

∧ **Urban Baroque Apartment Building**
Sicily, Italy
1970s

The BEST Terrarium Showroom is designed for a highly visible plateau, near a major highway and surrounded by mountainous landscape in South San Francisco. The concept proposes using the volume of earth, excavated during foundation preparations, as an intrinsic part of the architecture—transforming the geology of the region into a visual iconography for the finished building. The supporting walls are made of cement block and the roof is radically inclined to receive a series of terraced landscapes. A transparent skin of glass surrounds this basic structure, allowing an eight-inch gap between glass and masonry. The negative space left between the walls is filled with soil and rock, approximating the geological strata of the area, while the entire roof supports a mixture of earth and regional vegetation. The Terrarium Showroom serves as a biographical microcosm of South San Francisco topography, geology, and landscape features. In time, as subterranean plant life takes root in the walls, this horticultural phenomenon will result in an evolutionary and ever-changing imagery; as a result, inviting the community to watch the building grow.

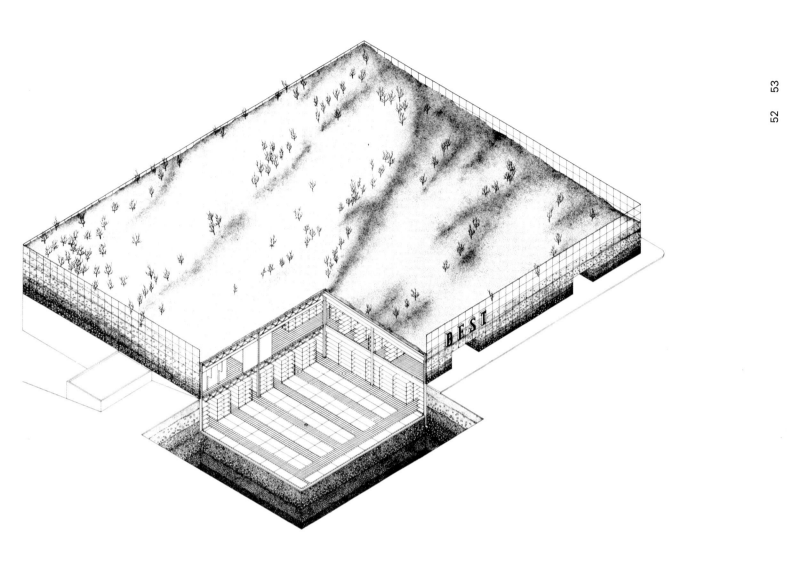

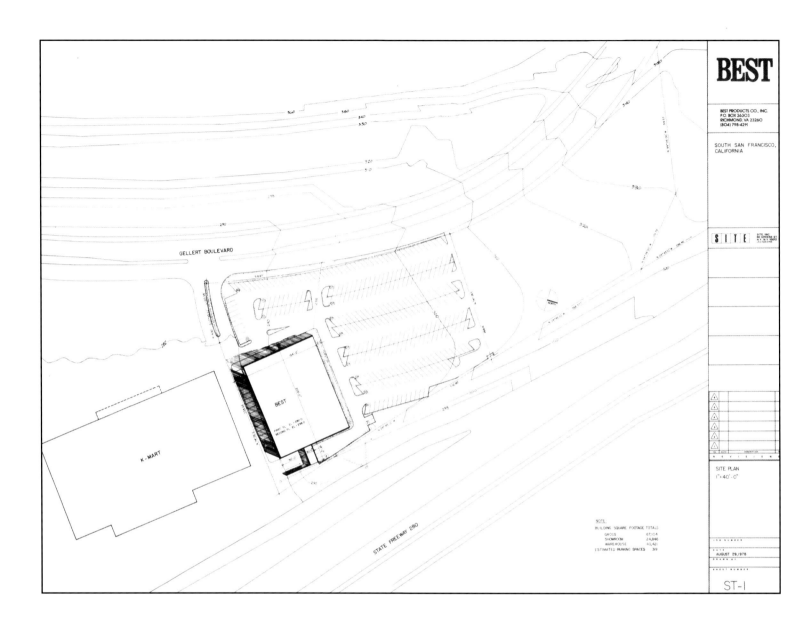

GELLERT BOULEVARD

K-MART

BEST

STATE FREEWAY 280

NOTE:
BUILDING SQUARE FOOTAGE TOTALS
GROSS   67,104
SHOWROOM   24,846
WAREHOUSE   40,421
ESTIMATED PARKING SPACES   319

^ Site Plan—Terrarium Showroom and Metamorphosis Project
Pen and ink on mylar 24″ x 30″

Continuing the BEST Products Company showroom series, the Hialeah, Florida structure is one of the first buildings to incorporate the natural environment as an intrinsic part of architecture. The emphasis, in this case, is on the relation of the shopping center to a nearby roadway and the tropical vegetation of Florida. The entire façade is constructed as a microcosm of the surrounding landscape—including a terrarium of water, trees, plants, earth, and rock. This "living iconography" is achieved by enclosing the natural elements behind a wall of glass, which supports a continuous waterfall from the roof level. Contrary to the traditional use of immobile sculptures, signage, or decorative graphics to enhance a commercial building, in this case the entire building becomes an example of mutable and evolutionary architecture. From a visual perspective, the blurred impressions of the BEST logo and plant life, as seen through the refraction of water, emphasize the kinetic experiences associated with the ever-changing processes in nature and Florida landscape, when viewed from a moving vehicle. The building also represents an early use of vegetation and water as cooling elements in architecture, which led to SITE's increasing commitment to green design.

The showrooms were invaded by the environment in such a way they seemed to be consumed in a portentous role reversal—or, "nature's revenge." This sense of intrusion by plants and trees was achieved in the Virginia structure through a massive incision, splitting apart the walls and in Florida, by means of a glass waterwall that locks in fragments of the tropical landscape. In each case, nature appeared liberated, hyperbolized and surreal; instead of its conventional function in architecture as suppressed, contained and rational.

JAMES WINES

^ Existing conditions collected during site analysis

This retail-merchandising store for BEST Products Company in Richmond, Virginia is intended to both preserve and celebrate the location's natural environment and create an inside/outside architectural experience. The Forest building is constructed in a densely wooded suburban area and carefully planned to save the maximum number of trees, bushes, and other forms of vegetation. To accomplish this goal, the surrounding forest is allowed to penetrate and envelop the showroom. The outer perimeter is enclosed by glass terrarium walls, which reveal the underground geology of the area. The explosion of nature is further emphasized by contrast to an asphalt parking lot and adjacent roadway. This invasion of forest elements creates the appearance of a typical American commercial structure consumed by its own surroundings—or, described another way, architecture as a victim of nature's revenge. There is a 35-foot gap, separating the façade and the actual front of store, with an irregular cleft at each end of the building to accommodate a cluster of massive oak trees. Store customers are able to participate in these inside/outside relationships on foot, by walking through the glass wall of the outer façade and crossing a pedestrian bridge that spans the densely forested interior—thereby entering the store as part of a "nature walk" experience.

^ Alternate approach

The BEST showroom in Milwaukee is the eighth in a series of special buildings for the Virginia based catalogue merchandiser. It is the purpose of these buildings to use architecture as a means of generating psychological reactions and as a way of changing public response to the role of commercial structures in the suburban landscape. The exterior masonry walls of this inside/outside showroom are invaded by gaping incisions that reveal the (usually hidden from view) heating and cooling ducts, structural support systems, and commercial products sold by the store. Whereas the communicative imagery of architecture is traditionally interpreted as surface decoration—for example, the façades of Gothic and Renaissance buildings—in this case the iconography is achieved by cutting through the successive layers of exterior walls. To emphasize this intervention, the total building is painted a monochrome gray. Many merchandise items, which would normally be contained inside the showroom, have been installed as part of a transitional connection between interior and exterior. For thermal sealing purposes, there is a recessed glass wall separating these products into real and surreal components of the same objects. This effect is accomplished by using the glass as a point of dissection; as a result, every object in the interior remains in natural color, while its extension on the outside appears in monochrome—suggesting interplay between the actual and the metaphysical.

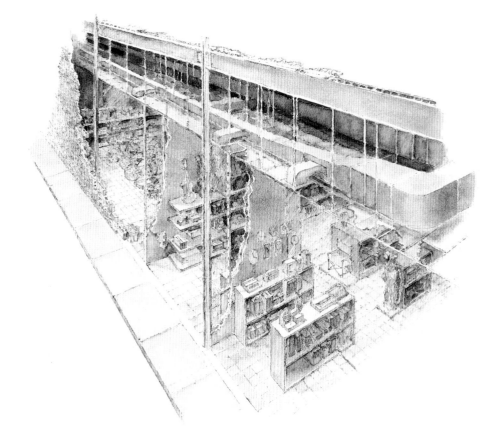

The Ghost Parking Lot incorporates two ubiquitous elements of the suburban shopping center—automobiles sitting on an asphalt parking lot surface—and then inverts their relationship to each other. Twenty historical cars are partially buried in Hamden Plaza and covered by a thin skin of asphalt paving. Each vehicle is embedded, on graduated levels, from full exposure of the body contours to complete interment. This work of environmental art deals with a number of factors connected to the American automotive experience; for example, the blurred vision associated with motion, the fetishism of car culture, and the questions evoked by the contrasts between inertia and mobility. The Ghost Parking Lot is consistent with SITE's view of public art, by engaging both physical and psychological elements. Contrary to the prevalent tendency to install "object art" as a decorative accessory in public spaces, this project is neither "placed" nor "integrated" in the usual formal sense. Instead, the project becomes part of its environment by the inclusion of certain subliminal relationships between the rituals of merchandising and the mythology of the automobile. Also, unlike conventional public art (which is often conceived from a "private art" sensibility), this project cannot be isolated or exhibited apart from its context without a total loss of meaning.

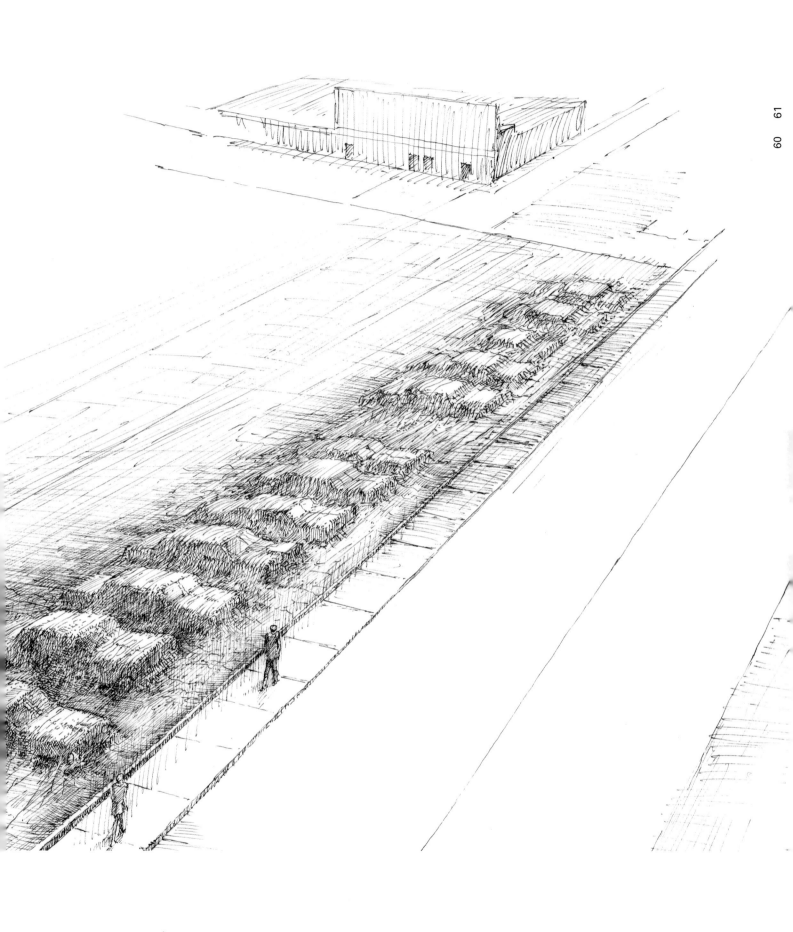

Art made for the museum or gallery has the luxury of being showcased under conditions of reflex identification, relaxed contemplation and protective isolation. Art in the street confronts a relentless competition of chaos and disorder. For public art to be successful, it has to rise above these distractions—or to include them as part of its source material—then assert itself as a situational (not objectified) presence. Otherwise, public art fails to address one of the most interesting challenges of a true community-oriented statement—that is, serving as a commentary on the urban environment.

JAMES WINES, *DE-ARCHITECTURE*, 1989

< Documentation of Construction process—
surveying the site, locating and reinforcing
cars, spraying flexible sealant and
submerging with asphalt

^ Local children interpreted the Ghost Parking
Lot project as the "ultimate prank"

The only true role of anti-art is in the streets and marketplace.

HERBERT MARCUSE

Ghost Parking Lot – Hamden, Conn.

^ **Elevage de Poussiere from the Green Box**
Marcel Duchamp, photographed by Man Ray
1934

The High-rise of Homes is the architectural equivalent of what Marcel Duchamp once referred to as "canned chance."
In this respect, the project becomes a stage for the infinite variety of unpredictable performances.

SITE

The 1923 "Dust Breeding" experiment by Marcel Duchamp (photographed by Man Ray) was the result of watching several months of dust accumulate on the surface of his "Large Glass," during a time when this renowned work of art was being stored horizontally in his New York Studio. Duchamp was fascinated by the aesthetic implications of an uncontrolled natural process, taking place within the context of one of his own creations—an auxiliary category of art experience, which he referred to as "canned chance."

As an architectural equivalent for Duchamp's faith in the merits of chance, SITE's High-rise of Homes proposes that the role of the architect should be confined to the design of a functional matrix— only structure and services—allowing the final aesthetic qualities of the building to be determined by an arbitrary collage of the inhabitants' choices of dwellings and gardens, plugged into allotted spaces on each floor. This converts the evaluation of artistic value in a building away from traditional formalist design and opens up the indeterminate territory of risk.

> **Kowloon Walled City**
> Hong Kong, China
> 1990s

> **Christmas Lights**
> Anywhere, USA
> 2002

> **Trailer Park**
> Anywhere, USA
> 1995

> **Housing Indifference**
> Tribeca, New York, USA
> 2003

> **Cruising Suburbia**
> Pennsylvania, USA
> 2003

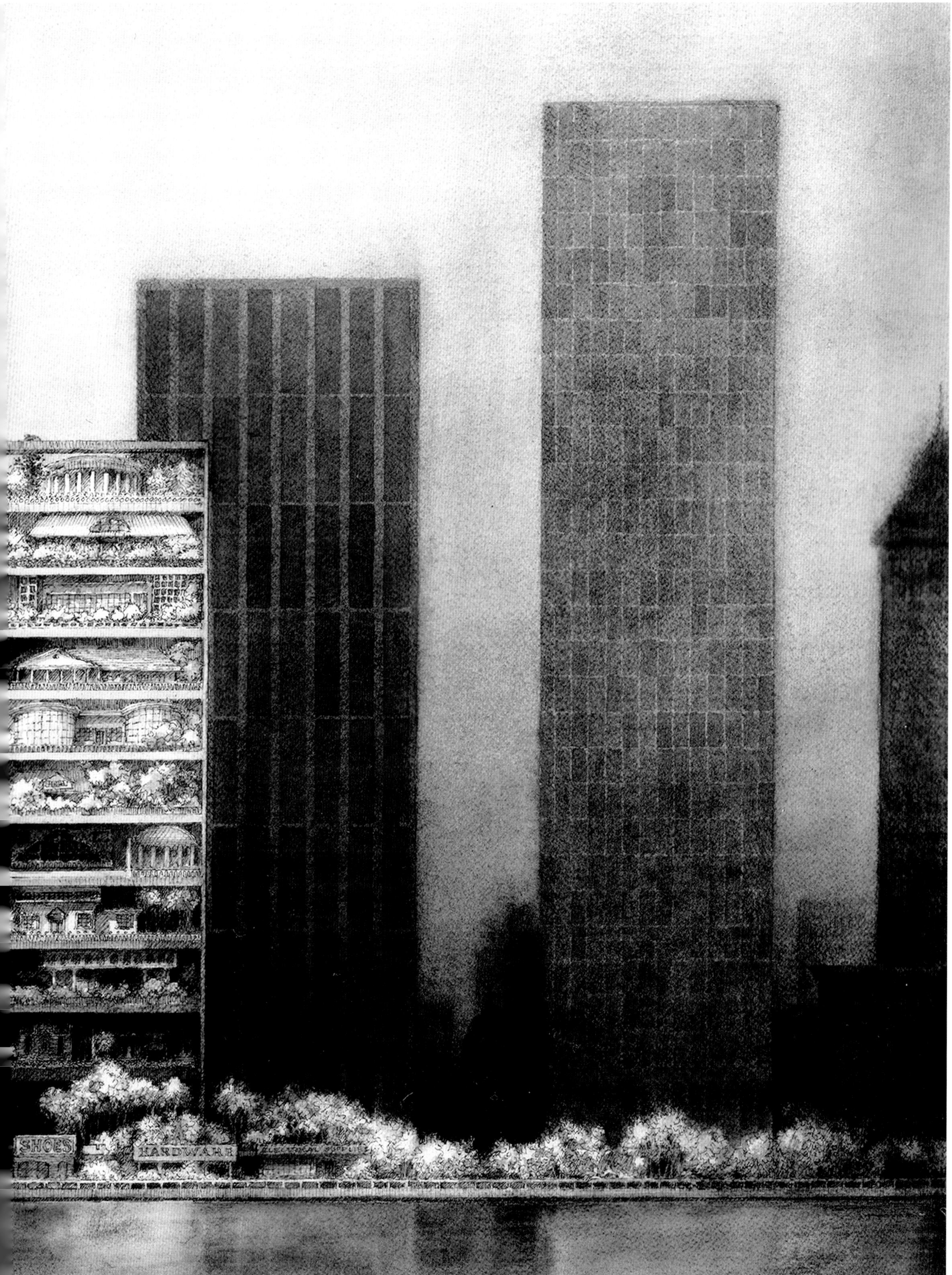
SHOES

SITE

Highrise of Homes

This experimental high-rise housing proposal is composed of 15 to 20 stories to be located in a densely populated urban center. It is intended for mixed-income residents and includes shopping, parking, and residential facilities. The configuration of the structure is a steel and concrete matrix that supports a vertical community of private houses, clustered into distinct village-like communities on each floor. Every level is a flexible platform that can be purchased as separate real estate parcels. A central elevator and mechanical core provide services to the individual houses, gardens, and interior streets. The philosophical motivation behind this concept is a critique of the 20th century tradition of homogenized and faceless multi-story buildings, which eliminate the possibility for urban dwellers to demonstrate any evidence of their presence in the cityscape. As an alternative, the High-rise of Homes offers residents a unique opportunity to achieve an individual statement of identity. The purpose is to shift the premises for aesthetic evaluation in high-rise buildings away from orthodox design continuity in favor of the artistic merits of collage architecture, based on indeterminacy, idiosyncrasy, and cultural diversity.

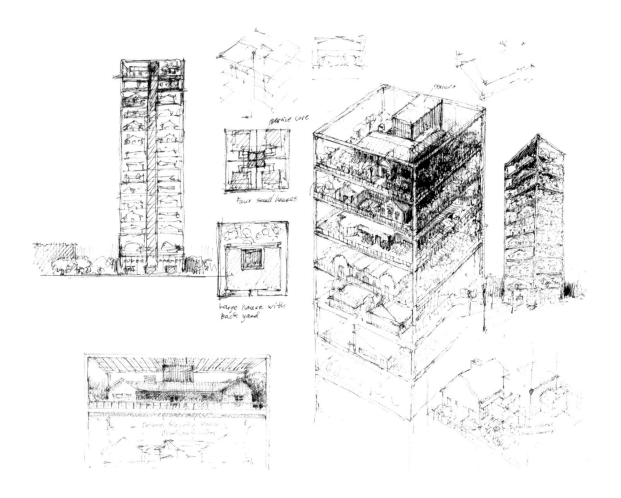

The house as an architectural form and symbol is the one artifice where private worlds and public domains converge. Like all architecture, the house is expressive of a larger cultural realm, yet there is a persistent and changing dialogue between the personal preferences and tastes of the different inhabitants and architectural convention.

SITE, *HIGH-RISE OF HOMES*

^ **Generic home, apartment complex and suburban neighborhood**
SITE Archives
1981

^ **Photomontage**
SITE Archives

^ **Vernacular Extensions**
Valetta, Malta

> **Axonometric of Low-Cost Prototype**
Ink on Mylar

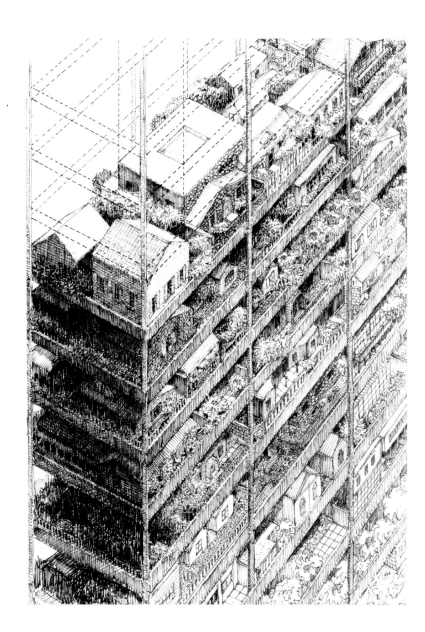

^ **Proposal for Algiers Viaduct Block**
Le Corbusier
1934

Le Corbusier's Viaduct Housing project for Algiers in 1934 is another precedent for the High-rise of Homes. The purpose of his project was to combine the urban transportation advantages of a high-speed roadway along the seafront, with the need for a radical expansion of regional housing. Since the Algerian culture resisted the loss of individuality—exemplified by European apartment blocks—the architect proposed that the structural support under the viaduct should be built as descending platforms, in order to accommodate a linear city of Arabic style houses.

In those parts of the world where man still builds his own house and makes with his own hand the objects that go into it, the house has always been a fairly accurate indicator of his needs and the accumulated experience of his race, not so with us. It is a long time since we lost the ability to find out what is good for us. We have little more to go by than what we are told. Most of our demands are "created" and built into goods we consume...

BERNARD RUDOLFSKY

Modernism and the objectives of industrial capital fostered a mass faith in technology and system. It seems evident that an expedient solution to habitat wa[s] foisted on the public and, by the time people had taken stock of its effect on their visual and living environment, it was too late for reversal. Like the factor[y] workers indentured by both contract and a compulsion to own the artifacts produced, the urban dweller was seduced by the idea of economical shelter an[d] then entrapped by its rampant proliferation. In protecting the business interests of developers and the egos of architects, city inhabitants were led to believ[e] that they neither needed, nor wanted, interventions of their own—everything would be taken care of. The repressive implications of this process are obviou[s] when applied to politics or social systems, so why should architecture be an exception?

JAMES WINES, "HIGH-RISE OF HOMES", NEW YORK, RIZZOLI INTERNATIONAL PUBLICATIONS 198[3]

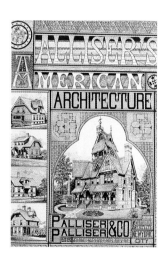

^ Doors, Windows and Sidings

^ Alliser's American Architecture—
Guide to Homes Cover

> Axonometric of Catalogue
Components

The theory of de-architecture holds that throughout history the successful edifices, at their most intense level of communication, have been the product of psychological, social, cosmic, and metaphysical influences.

JAMES WINES, *DE-ARCHITECTURE*, 1987

GEHRY

SITE

TIGERMAN

TROIS PORTRAITS

DE L'ARTISTE

EN ARCHITECTE

olivier boissière

ÉDITIONS DU
MONITEUR

JAMES WINES

^ **Floating McDonald's**
SITE Construction Image
1983

< **Gehry SITE Tigerman**
Oliver Bossiére
1981

< **De-Architecture**
James Wines
Rizzoli
1987

> **65 Bleeker Street Studio**
Bayard-Conduit Building
1984

DE-ARCHITECTURE
DE-ARCHITECTURE
DE-ARCHITECTURE

ISBN 0-8478-0862-9

MOLINO STUCKY BIENNALE DI VENEZIA, VENICE, ITALY **1978**

The Venice Biennale Committee of 1978 and regional government asked several international architects to design concepts for the 19th century Stucky Mills, located on the Island of Giudecca. The city's purpose in focusing attention on these abandoned industrial buildings was to revitalize a neglected area and convert the unused complex into a place for student housing, recreation, and academic activities. The SITE proposal reverses the familiar relationship between the front of the building and its reflection in the canal. In this case, the façade becomes the canal and the canal becomes the façade. This inversion is achieved by extending the front promenade as a horizontal replica of the actual façade and then installing a vertical glass wall to bridge the gap between the two adjacent wings of the factory. A hydraulic sprinkler system, suspended on a steel space frame, allows a continuous cascade of water to flow over the glass. The shimmering, transparent water wall stands out in marked contrast to the monumentality and ornate decoration of traditional façades of Venice.

GHOST HOUSES VARIOUS TRACT HOUSE COMMUNITIES IN NEW JERSEY, USA **1980**

Most of SITE's early projects were based on an inversion of meaning, using various building archetypes, with the purpose of altering public reaction to commonplace situations. Within this row of planned houses for New Jersey, each homeowner is required to purchase in an identical dwelling, where only the façade materials are variable. In SITE's conceptual approach, the development company prototype has been retained, but the materials are changed to create a kind of "illusion versus reality" commentary on suburban lifestyle. For example, shingle-style façades are constructed in cement, wood houses are covered in asphalt, stone houses are constructed in latex rubber, brick houses are transformed by modules of stainless steel and so forth. As a result, each structure seems to be built of one material, but actually produced in another. In the event of a future increase of these stylistically indistinguishable houses, it will become increasingly difficult to discern what actually exists, as opposed to what seems to exist. As the members of the community become familiar with this game of inversion, they may ultimately become active participants, by initiating their own conversions of household artifacts into alternative materials. This phenomenon could lead to an entirely new interpretation of shelter and furniture, where the notion of function itself may be revolutionized by the proliferation of such architectural and domestic artifacts as asphalt windowpanes and rubber screwdrivers.

Located between two condominium towers in an overdeveloped environment, Independence Place Plaza is designed as an explosion of paving and regional vegetation.

This special McDonald's restaurant was commissioned for its commemorative significance, among all of the company's thousands of buildings. Located near the hometown of founder Ray Kroc, it is also in the vicinity of the first McDonald's roadway stand built in the United States. While developing the concept, SITE observed that every freestanding restaurant in the chain is composed of standard ingredients—mansard roof, Colonial-style windows, brick-faced exterior, and the familiar "Golden Arches" logo—symbols that have become ubiquitous and instantly recognizable to a global audience. For the Berwyn facility, each of these architectural elements is dislodged from its customary position and then suspended above ground level to produce the effect of a floating building. The interior utilizes this flotation engineering system as a means of providing an under-the-building garden and clerestory illumination for the customer seating areas.

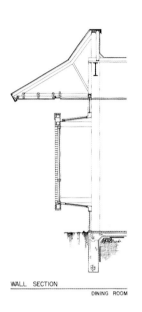

WALL SECTION

DINING ROOM

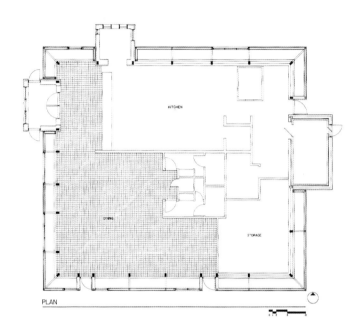

PLAN

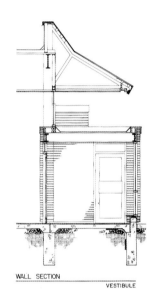

WALL SECTION

VESTIBULE

WEST ELEVATION

NORTH ELEVATION

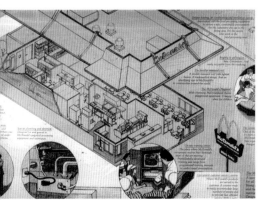

∧ **McDonald's Prototype Floorplan**
SITE Archives
1983

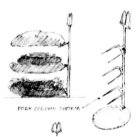

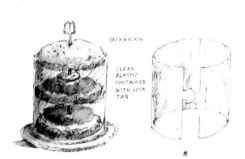

^ **Big Mac**
SITE Archives
1980s

The competition program for this museum of contemporary art described the sponsor's preference for a "factory-like" building, which would be ideal for the exhibition of conventional painting and sculpture, but flexible enough to accommodate environmental works, performance art, technology-based installations, and unpredictable interventions in the future. Based on an orchestration of "inside/outside" relationships, this project also responds to a triangular site, occupied by several partially destroyed buildings remaining from World War II. In order to accommodate these existing features and respect the precise north/south–east/west orientation of all public buildings in Frankfurt, the architectural solution places a rectangular structure on a triangular intersection. This conflict of formal strategies requires cutting away a major portion of one façade and allowing the upper floor planes to break off as fragmented tiers in space. In addition to the visual drama of these raw-edged platforms, they offer a unique opportunity for the display of outdoor sculpture. The inside/outside relationships continue on the ground level as interior paving materials that extend into the street. In order to provide a thermal barrier for the exhibition spaces, as well as provide an enclosure for the outdoor sculpture garden and museum cafe, a three-sided, 18-meter-high wall of glass penetrates the masonry building and defines the triangular shape of the entire site.

^ **Bomb-damaged Berlinerstraße**
Frankfurt, Germany

^ **View east of Braubachstraße**
Frankfurt, Germany

When architecture becomes organic to the degree that the other plastic arts have, then probably the blurring of boundaries in those will extend to include it.

ALLAN KAPROW

The "effect on civilization" is what a world exposition is all about.

JAMES WINES, 1982

REVENGE OF THE RIVER
WATERCOLOR POSTER DESIGN FOR THE 1984 LOUISIANA WORLD EXPO
DAWN DEDEAUX PRODUCTIONS   NEW ORLEANS, LOUISIANA, USA   **1984**

This watercolor by James Wines was part of a series of limited edition posters by invited architects and artists for the Expo 84 in New Orleans. Since most architecture of the exposition was designed as a pervasive decorative version of the historicist Post Modernism, the image in this painting is intended as a critique of the stylistic commitment. As a humorous commentary on the entire event, his poster places recognizable Expo buildings, a Disney-like central processional, and a variety of theme exhibitions at the bottom of the Mississippi River.

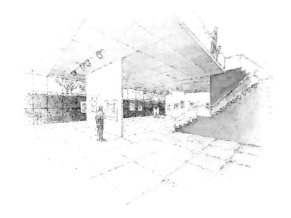

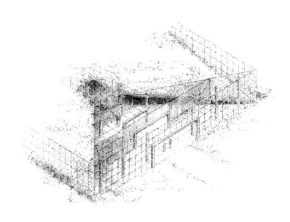

^ Camera Mechanics
SITE Archives

The Ansel Adams Center is the winning entry in a competition sponsored by the Friends of Photography for a building in Carmel, California. Located on a coastline hilltop, the museum is intended to function as a place for the study, exhibition, and production of creative photography. It is also a permanent tribute to the achievements of Ansel Adams, the great American nature photographer. This earth-sheltered building is covered by a section of its own meadow site—displaced, elevated, and re-planted to contain all of the identical vegetation that occupied the land surface before excavation. Instead of designing the center as an object sitting in its location, this project treats the context itself as the building. In order to allow sufficient natural light to penetrate the gallery and office spaces, a trapezoidal section of the roof plane is cut out and inclined upward for illumination. A second titled plane forms the covering for an entry plaza and creates a camera-like configuration for the total structure. The "X"-shaped interaction of volumes suggests a diagram of the kind of optical inversion and focal perspective associated with a photographic lens. Extending Adams' lifelong interest in American Indian civilization, the center of the building is designed as an above ground/below ground terrarium garden that houses the bookstore and reflects a Pueblo Indian belief that the human soul emerges from the earth and exits through the center of a dwelling.

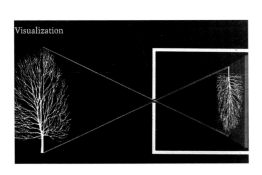

Visualization

< Pinhole Effect
SITE Archives

From their origin in the 15th century, these "landscapes of the mind" were infused with the spiritual and intellectual values that produced the timeless power of communication. They extended the Buddhist belief in the garden as a microcosm of a larger universe and as an embodiment of inside/outside. This is also the condition of Japanese architecture embracing these gardens. Here, duality is expressed by the flow of space from the interior to exterior and by the use of tissue-like membrane walls separating the two. It was this impressive Japanese achievement that profoundly influenced Frank Lloyd Wright and became the foundation for his philosophy of organic architecture.

JAMES WINES, *INSIDE/OUTSIDE—THE AESTHETIC IMPLICATIONS OF GREEN DESIGN*, 1991

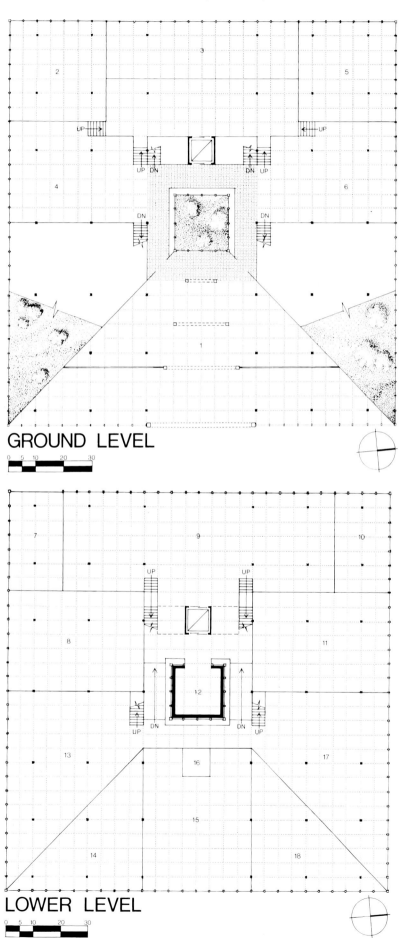

GROUND LEVEL

0 5 10   20   30

1· ENTRANCE PLAZA

CENTER FOR THE ADVANCED STUDY OF PHOTOGRAPHY
2· LIBRARY
3· SEMINAR ROOMS
4· OFFICES

THE FRIENDS OF PHOTOGRAPHY
5· DIRECTOR
ADMINISTRATIVE STAFF
6· RECEPTION
OFFICES

LOWER LEVEL

0 5 10   20   30

7· LOADING DOCK
SHIPPING & RECEIVING
MECHANICAL
8· PUBLICATION STORAGE
ARCHIVE STORAGE

MUSEUM AREA
9· GALLERIES
10· TRUSTEE LOUNGE
DOCENTS ROOM
11· EXHIBITION PREPARATION & STORAGE
KITCHEN & LUNCHROOM
12· BOOKSTORE

CENTER FOR THE ADVANCED STUDY OF PHOTOGRAPHY
13· PHOTOGRAPHER WORKROOM
14· DEMONSTRATION DARKROOM
15· LECTURE HALL
16· PROJECTION BOOTH

· THE FRIENDS OF PHOTOGRAPHY
17· OFFICES
CLERICAL
18· WORKROOM
DARKROOM
SUPPLY ROOM
COMPUTER & COPY CENTER
MAIL CENTER

**^ Garden at the Royal
Palace of Katsura**
Kabori, Ershu, Kyoto,
Japan

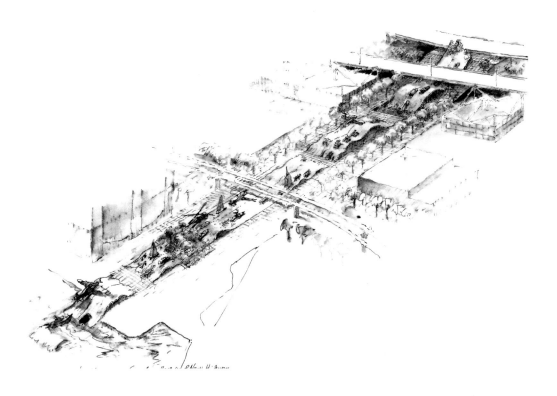

^ **Archaeological Dig**
SITE Archives

^ **Archaeology Pavilion**
Model, Alternate Pavilion Design

Highway 86 is a winning competition entry for the centerpiece public space at Expo 86, celebrating the history of 20th century air, land, and sea transportation technology. The structure is conceived as a 700-foot-long undulating ribbon of concrete and steel—integrating all means of transportation as part of a participatory sculptural event. The total project includes an area underneath two automotive viaducts, adjacent spaces for various national and corporate exhibits, plus a shoreline segment overlooking the Vancouver harbor. The processional rises out of the sea, crosses an expanse of land surface and, as it passes under the highway, the paving soars upward between the two viaducts. At this point, the structure comes to a fragmented conclusion, soaring into space above the viaducts. Highway 86 has been conceived as a commentary on people's ambivalent relationship with industrial technology during the 20th century. In view of the ominous warnings of environmental destruction, the transportation theme can be seen as leading to either apocalypse or utopia (depending on the level of earth-friendly responsibility by government and commerce in the future). Also, since the roadway emerges from the sea like some primordial creature, it can be interpreted as a commentary on Darwin's Theory of Evolution. The surface of the processional is encrusted with several hundred examples of transportation technology—everything from cars and boats to motorcycles, bicycles, wheelchairs, farm tractors, jogging shoes, wind surfers, airplanes, helicopters, space capsules, and lunar rovers. A water-resistant coating of monochrome gray protects each of these objects from the weather. One major innovation, from the perspective of Expo pavilion design, is the creation of an exterior exhibition, as opposed to the traditional enclosed building. As a result, Highway 86 can readily accommodate over 200,000 visitors per day, without forcing people to endure the usual interminable waiting queue at an entryway.

SITE based its concept for Vancouver's Expo on the belief that the highest level of communication is human interaction. The first call for entries in the competition specified an enclosed pavilion. SITE's view was that most of the exhibits at the Expo would be closed off, resulting in long lines of impatient visitors, and that the sensible alternative was to create a public space and a participatory event that would generate crowd but would be accessible without waiting.

SITE

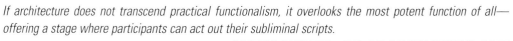

If architecture does not transcend practical functionalism, it overlooks the most potent function of all—offering a stage where participants can act out their subliminal scripts.

JAMES WINES, *DE-ARCHITECTURE*, 1987

One difficulty SITE faced in working within this particular context was that Expos are generally regarded as transient and exploitative events, where architecture built in deference to these expectations has to be superficial and conceptually meaningless. Since SITE had worked on commercial buildings in the most banal of circumstances, the attitude toward the Expo was that its motivations could be treated with humor as the raw material of art, without any particular compromise of aesthetic intentions.

SITE

^ **Expositione Universelle**
Paris, France
1889

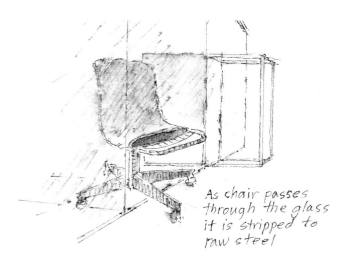

As chair passes through the glass it is stripped to raw steel

The ALLSTEEL furniture showroom is located in a converted warehouse structure, at the International Design Center in New York. The concept is developed as a visual and psychological extension of the company's high quality products and office systems. The communicative purpose is intended to capture the feeling of a factory environment and take advantage of people's associations with steel, as a material of strength and integrity. Taking into account the limited floor area for product display, SITE decided to utilize the ceiling and upper air space of the interior as an additional opportunity for exhibition. The entire ceiling is a skeletal reflection of the finished products and office stations in the showroom below. Every ALLSTEEL product attached to the ceiling has been stripped down to its raw steel state (excluding all other materials) to reveal its essential means of manufacture. In this way the ceiling becomes an inverted biographical counterpart of the floor display. As an extension of this "finished/unfinished" dialogue, certain ALLSTEEL furniture has been displayed against the glass walls facing a public access hallway, using the transparent partitions as invisible bi-sectors. On one side of the glass, the company's products appear in their finished state while, on the opposite side of the intersection, they are reduced to their raw steel skeletons.

ALLSTEEL ARCHAEOLOGY NEW YORK CITY, NEW YORK, USA **1986**

^ Prototype Office
SITE Archives

^ Steel Fabrication
SITE Archives

^ Archaeology Installation
ALLSTEEL Headquarters,
Aurora, Illinois, USA

The ALLSTEEL furniture manufacturers celebrated the company's 75th anniversary with special tableaux at the International Design Center in Long Island City. SITE was asked to create a special exhibition for this event. The concept is a humorous interpretation of the terrarium displays that often appear in archaeological museums as a way of simulating historical excavations. In this case, the archeological elements are seven decades of past ALLSTEEL furniture, half buried in a mix of sand, earth, rocks, and vegetation—all enclosed by a large glass container. In order to showcase the entire legacy of ALLSTEEL and also celebrate the present, a selection of recently produced furniture is placed on top of the earth-encrusted artifacts.

In modern cities throughout the world our sense of orientation, knowing where and who we are, is damagingly compromised. Offices, apartments and stores are piled together in ways which owe more to filing-cabinet systems or the price of land than to a concern for human existence or experience.

CHARLES JENCKS

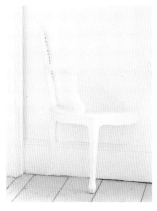

^ **Louis XV chair emerging from the living room wall. Bygone windows, doors, arches, fireplaces, and walls**

The Laurie Mallet residence was designed for the president of a prominent fashion company and her family in the Greenwich Village section of New York City. The project called for the renovation and expansion of an 1820s, three-story Greek revival house, protected by New York City landmarks preservation laws. The structure was originally built in the 19th century tradition of speculative housing. As the result of a lack of maintenance and the building's early construction methods, it required major restoration. Also, in order to expand the interior space for children's bedrooms, an area under the backyard has been excavated and the entire garden and patio is elevated to form the roof of this addition. The interior is based on a layering of narrative ideas, drawn from the history of the building, artifacts found inside, the legacy of the neighborhood, and the personal biography of the owner. In order to integrate this information and add a metaphysical dimension to the living spaces, a series of architectural features are partially buried in the walls. As these objects emerge from the vertical surfaces, at various levels of exposure, they create the impression of ghosted memories that have been left behind by generations of inhabitants. The scale, purpose, and psychological associations identified by the owner, as well as the physical restraints of the existing structure, have determined the choice and positioning of the surreal artifacts.

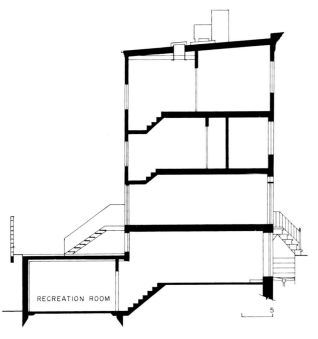

RECREATION ROOM

5

^ Façade of the 1820s
Greenwich Village home

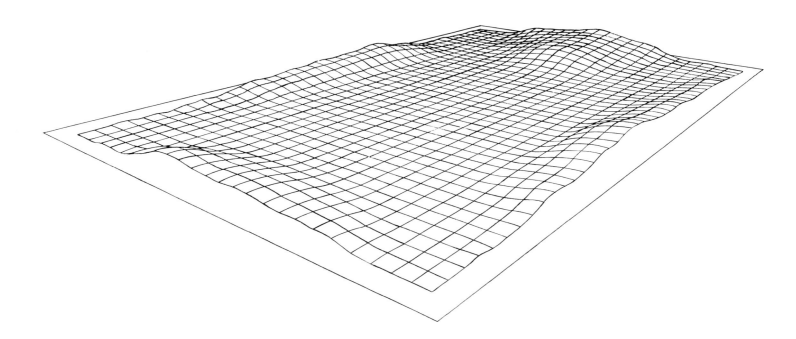

^ **Aerial view—Existing Condition
Pershing Square**

The City of Los Angeles, when viewed from the air, appears to be a vast carpet-like grid that has been carelessly installed, leaving rumpled corners where the hills and mountains surround the central plain. During the night hours, housing and roadway lights intensify the visual impact of this undulating matrix. The Pershing Square Concept represents a visual and participatory microcosm of the city's horizontal geometry. The idea is to compress virtually all of Los Angeles and its suburbs into a public space that is both narrative and abstract. The gridline articulated plaza is basically flat in the central portion, while all of the peripheral edges of the space are raised in a series of

undulating, mountain-like waves of concrete. These various elevations serve as a source of visual drama from the adjacent streets, a means of access for dramatic overviews, and as shelter for restaurants, bus stops, parking entryways, and service facilities. To provide a wide variety of botanical and participatory events, the modular grid is used to generate a series of mini-environments—each representing the regional characteristics of Los Angeles. These include its downtown ethnic diversity, Hollywood fantasies, pastoral life in the hills, oceanfront recreations, suburban sprawl, and automobile culture.

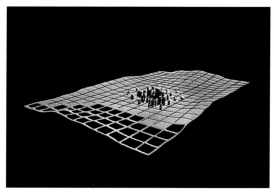

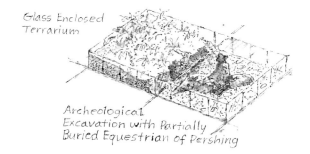

Glass Enclosed
Terrarium

Archeological
Excavation with Partially
Buried Equestrian of Pershing

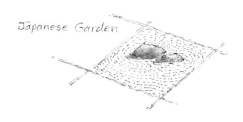

Japanese Garden

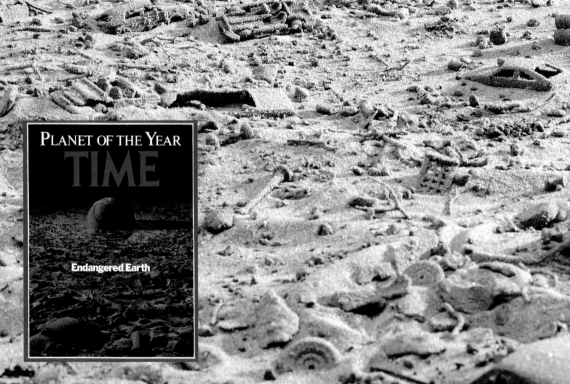

PLANET OF THE YEAR

TIME

Endangered Earth

A special exhibition of gardens by well-known architects was proposed for the Pompidou Center in 1989—financed by a prominent Japanese corporation with large investments in France. At the last minute, the sponsor withdrew support and the project was never realized. SITE's concept of a "ghost garden," utilizes a triangular corner of the public space facing the museum. This granite-covered wedge slopes downward toward the façade of the building, creating an incision in the plaza surface and two levels of graduating height. The idea, designed specifically to fit the triangle, proposes a memory garden that recalls a world of primordial vegetation, long before the city of Paris existed. The two-tiered structure offers an above grade plane (representing the land surface) and a below grade chasm to signify the underground. On top of the triangle, the area is covered with actual trees, plants, and ground cover which have been chemically treated to achieve a state of preservation—like embalming—which is then sprayed with a monochrome gray. On the underside of the platform, the exposed tree roots are suspended in space—creating the surreal impression of a forest without earth.

^ **Root System**
SITE Archives

^ **Centre Georges Pompidou**
Paris, France
1989

< **Cover Submission**
1988

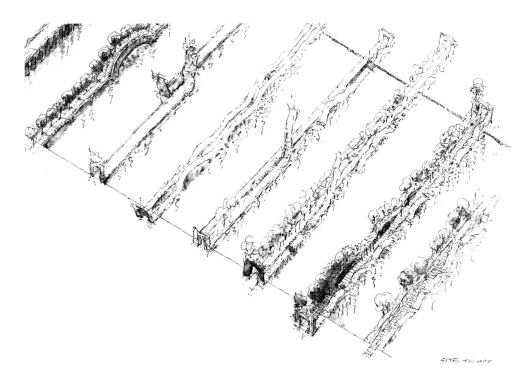

This commemorative bridge in Hiroshima celebrates the links between people and the natural environment. The form and gesture of SITE's design is based on the classical tradition of arched Japanese bridges and their connections to landscape. Rather than simply repeat these conventions, this concept integrates new technology with contemporary interpretations of the garden. The surface of the bridge is divided by a glass wall, punctured by three pedestrian crossways and terminated at both ends by lateral glass arches. On one side of the glass wall—spanning the entire length of the walkway—four landscape terrariums contain typical vegetation from the principal geological and climatic quadrants of the earth. On the opposite side of this transparent divider, pedestrians are able to see the layers of earth (with simulations of regional geology) in the form of terrarium gardens. The glass wall also supports a continuous flow of water that clings to the surface and feeds a series of river-like basins. The overflow becomes a waterfall, cascading into the lake below.

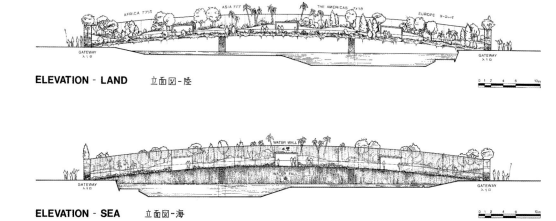

ELEVATION - LAND   立面図-陸

ELEVATION - SEA   立面図-海

^ **Japanese Historical Bridge**
SITE Archives

^ **Construction of Terrarium wall**
Hiroshima, Japan

In 1989 the combined patronage of the Isuzu Motors Company and Japan Railway sponsored a children's plaza for Yokohama. This public space was commissioned to celebrate the links between people, ground transportation, and space exploration. The design for this large public space, in front of the Sakuragicho Railway Station, also includes an exhibition inside the main pedestrian concourse. The entire exterior plaza is interpreted as a void in the universe. Since venturing into the cosmos is closely associated with the absence of gravity and the frequently publicized flotation of astronauts, the plaza plane supports an inverted world of people and (Isuzu) vehicles. To achieve this effect, the lower bodies and legs of a number of Yokohama residents have been cast (from life) into fiberglass and then installed in an upside down position. The intention is to create the impression of an invisible walking surface, suspended above the actual plaza level. In order to enhance the surreal dimension of this space, all of the human figures, automobiles, bicycles, street furniture, and tree roots are monochrome gray to match the color of the paving.

^ **Zero Gravity Effect**
SITE Archives

^ **Preparation of Castings**
Yokohama-SITE Studio
Japan

^ **Installation**
Yokohama, Japan

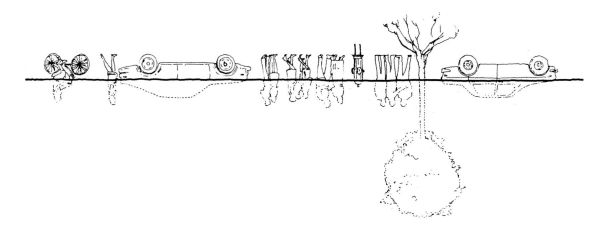

The imagery that a building generates as an extension of its own functions or formal relationships are never as interesting as the ideas it can absorb from the outside. An edifice should be like an environmental sponge, soaking up the most interesting fragments of information from its context. In this way, architecture can be seen as a "filtering zone" for information within its surroundings and, in this way, transforms the entire definition of public art.

JAMES WINES, *NOTES ON PUBLIC ART*

When first presented to the Mayor's Office in Vienna for approval, the plan to cut a new bookstore entranceway into the exterior wall of MAK was rejected on the grounds that this incision would violate an important historic institution. In an effort to compensate for this restriction, a solution was proposed by SITE to conscientiously preserve the extracted section of the museum as part of a public plaza in front of the bookstore. This solution was approved as a responsible act of historic preservation, so the permit was granted and the project was built. The fragment of window and wall removed to allow access to the bookstore is installed a few meters from the new entryway. This structure is mounted as an independent work of public art; but, at the same time, reveals its biographical origins as part of the original wall. The extracted section retains all of the chisel marks, sawed bricks, cracked plaster, iron radiator, and water pipes that declare its authenticity.

De-architecture's basic premise is that art, not design, is the supreme mission of a building, and that the creative process must be revised to reflect this objective.

JAMES WINES

This new display feature is designed for Frito Lay potato chips, as an installation in supermarkets throughout the United States. The purpose, during the research phase, was to identify an essential feature that visually connects the entire line of Frito Lay snacks and beverages. It was decided that the unifying characteristic is the function of the human hand in every aspect of manufacturing, distribution, and product consumption. The resulting "Hands of the World" display is a series of cast-from-life human arms and hands (representing all nationalities, professions, and walks of life) produced in approximately 20 different gestures for holding bags and eating Frito Lay products. These prosthetic units are monochrome gray, to achieve a certain abstract symbolic quality and to hyperbolize the colorful variety of packaging and food products.

The following selection of product designs by SITE shows a range of objects that reflect some aspects of the studio's approach to buildings and public spaces. The ideas in SITE's architectural works are usually drawn from sources of information that already exist within the surrounding environment. This aesthetic intention can take the form of visual commentary on a specific situation, or it can refer to the absorption, reflection, and inversion of elements within a larger context. In a similar way, each of these product designs has a narrative dimension that takes advantage of the people's reflex identification with certain functional artifacts and then uses these expectations as a premise for changing or expanding the meaning of the objects themselves. SITE's product designs perform the service requirements of standard products, while exploring the relationship between the conventions of function—or, in other words, "the use of use"—as a subject matter for art.

BLACK LIGHT PROTOTYPE   FOSCARINI ITALIA   MURANO, ITALY   **1991**

The Black Light is one of a group of "light bulbs as lamps," designed for a special exhibition of new Venetian glass at Italy's annual furniture fair in Milan. Produced by Foscarini Italia (a major manufacturer of glass products in Murano), the series is an alternative to conventional high-design lighting fixtures. As an inversion of the typical light bulb with socket, this project substitutes Venetian glass units that melt, bend, crack, split, and otherwise alter traditional configurations—a process which changes the context of a banal object by interpreting it in a precious material. The Black Light centerpiece of the ensemble plays with people's expectations concerning the function of a standard bulb as a source of light. In this case, the socket and electrical cord are illuminated, while the bulb remains dark. While on exhibit at the furniture fair, all of the light bulb variations were displayed in a black box room with a dark gray table and chair. This environment gave a surreal dimension to the project and emphasized the unique qualities of illuminated Murano glass.

Black Light
(white glass & frosted)

Melting Light
(white glass & frosted)

Broken Light
(Blue glass)

MELTING CANDLESTICK   SWID/POWELL USA AND BALERI ASSOCIATI ITALIA
NEW YORK, USA AND MILAN, ITALY   **1985**

The Melting Candlestick in silver is intended to compensate for the fact that today's "drip less" candles fail to provide the attraction of melting surfaces. Since cascades of wax are considered by most people to be romantic and evocative, this product design restores the tradition as part of the candelabrum itself, while still taking advantage of scientific advances in contemporary candle making. In keeping with the nature of SITE's design commentary in architecture, the selection of a Corinthian column is the object's source of reflex identification and the target of a humorous commentary on the tradition of classically themed candlesticks.

Split bulb.   Ghost bulb.

SITE was commissioned to redesign the plastic bottle for Vittel, a French producer of mineral water, in order to celebrate the company's product with a totally new kind of container. The concept for the "Iceberg" Bottle is inspired by the characteristics of both frozen water and melted plastic. The configuration of the new container is the result of hand-crushing a standard Vittel water bottle, which then becomes an evocative and indeterminate object. The distorted shape has the additional advantage of producing a surface condition of refraction and reflection that looks remarkably like a piece of melting ice. This effect, in turn, makes the water inside the bottle appear more refreshing and inviting.

BINARY WATCH   JACK MARKUSE PRODUCTIONS
WOBURN, MAINE, USA   **1998**

Markuse Productions commissioned SITE to design several watches as part of a special series of timepieces by internationally known architects; including Richard Meier, Charles Gwathmey, Eric Owen Moss, Stanley Tigerman, Michael Graves, and others. The SITE concept is based on binary systems. Since computers are operated on a logic gate of 2—as a way of simplifying the open (0) and closed (1) state of switching—this reference seemed appropriate for an Age of Information timepiece.

^ Bottled Water
SITE Archives

IDENTITY PEN, WATCH, CARD CASE, AND TIE
ACME STUDIO   MAUI, HAWAII   **2003**

The "Fingerprint" series of products for ACME Studio is a humorous commentary on the desire of people everywhere to retain evidence of their uniqueness in a world where escalating technology is destroying most opportunities to retain one's personal identity. In a world of digital connections, mass media, faceless apartment towers and mega-malls, the fingerprint is becoming the last available symbol of individuality (albeit, mostly associated with police work). The ACME pen, watch, card case, and tie use the fingerprint image as a white on black graphic, which suggests that even this traditional source of identification is receding into a negative dimension. It is assumed, however, that merely by possessing, using and/or wearing these products, the user will stand out in the crowd.

TERRA TAVOLA   SAPORITI ITALIA   MILAN, ITALY   **1999**

In 1998 Saporiti Italia commissioned SITE to design a series of earth-friendly products under the general title of ECOLOUNGE. This wood table is built as a waffle-like grid that contains earth, rocks, and plants. These pockets can also be filled with sand or pebbles and used for the display of collectibles. A glass top covers the entire table, providing a window into these microcosmic environments. The intention is to evoke the feeling of memory landscapes or transplanted archaeological excavations.

MONUMENTAL DESK   WILLIWEAR CORPORATION   NEW YORK CITY, NEW YORK, USA   **1985**

The SITE interiors for WilliWear, a prominent fashion house in the 1980s, were built out of rough construction materials and various artifacts found in the streets of New York. In order to maintain the industrial ambiance of the showrooms and workspaces, this monumental desk for the chief financial officer of WilliWear is designed as a composition of perforated metal and angle irons, with a glass panel as the tabletop. The desk is intended to evoke the feeling of industrial architecture—constructed as though it had evolved like a building—laying one element on top of another in a post-and-lintel fashion. The unit also includes surrounding shelving, file drawings, and storage cabinets in the same materials.

CARRARA TABLE   CASIGLIANI ITALIA   CARRARA, ITALY **1989**

This coffee table is one of a series designed for the Casigliani Marble Company. The idea is based on maintaining a sense of the origins of stone in the quarry as part of the design of each table. For this reason, the marble blocks are severed into two or more sections and the small pieces, left over from the cutting process, are gathered together as an intrinsic part of each table. The large blocks are mounted under the glass, with a raw-edged chasm in the middle, allowing the marble fragments to cascade into a mound on the floor.

Ancient cultures understood that humanity's final destiny lay in the balance between the structure of the universe and the resources of the earth and that the only role for art was to pay homage to these decisive forces.
JAMES WINES, *DE-ARCHITECTURE*, 1987

Nature is a mutable cloud which is always and never the same.
RALPH WALDO EMERSON

From an environmental perspective, mainstream architecture and landscape design for the past two decades have sent out confusing messages. The images communicated to urban dwellers by these two professions often seem to endorse a discard attitude toward the natural environment and a view that the earth is some remote location where commuters drive on weekends—but then, upon return to the city, can regard it as a distant memory, which is rarely associated with buildings, urban spaces, and the serious enterprises of daily life.

As a result of most designers' obsessive commitment to the early 20th century industrial/technological dream, the relationships between buildings and landscape are still dominated by the formalist traditions of Modernist design. It is a situation where the edifice is seen as the star attraction and vegetation is regarded as peripheral decor. At the core of the problem, there seems to be a paranoid fear among architects that foliage might upstage the building. In visual terms, this phobia usually results in a rigorous compositional hierarchy, where architecture is enthroned as a sculptural centerpiece and landscaping is reduced to a girdle of lollypop trees. This attitude has taken a negative toll on urban aesthetic; but, more irrationally, it has been bad for business and even worse for community well being. From a rather crass bottom line assessment, it is simply a fact that abundant garden spaces attract people to linger in city centers, spend more money, and thus have a positive impact on the local economy. From a health standpoint, one tree absorbs 26 pounds of carbon dioxide and this means four people can breathe. In large part, a city's quality of life can be determined by the equation between its population statistics and a proportional quantity of trees.

During the past few years, it has become increasingly apparent that architecture is desperately in need of a reunion with the natural environment and a total re-evaluation of its conceptual, philosophical, and aesthetic priorities. This does not simply mean more urban greening and conservation efforts—although these are obviously urgent issues—but it also indicates the necessity for a radically increased awareness of the "integrated systems" found in nature and the capacity to interpret them from an artistic perspective. Translated into environmental design, it means that the building arts today have an opportunity to physically and symbolically connect to a new green consciousness. Just as designers of the 1920s were inspired by the materials of industrial technology and the reforms of socialist politics, the equivalent sources of design ideas today are a combination of ecological awareness and the information revolution. These radical changes in priorities—social, psychological, cultural, topographical, geological, botanical, cosmological, and technological—should motivate new creative agendas and an expanded definition of "environmental thinking" over the next decade.

∧ **Avenue Number Five**
SITE
Seville, Spain
1992

It seems inevitable that architecture must exchange its roots in Modernist and Constructivist design, abstract art, and Industrial Age imagery for a more open ended visual language, consistent with the emerging Age of Information and Ecology. For example, people's reflex reactions to contemporary life have been shaped by a pervasive "ambient sensibility"—a world created by television, cinema, computer science, and a sense of foreboding concerning the consequences of environmental destruction. This awareness is a natural generator of subliminal references that have little in common with the industrial and technological sources that shaped the past century. It seems logical that buildings and their adjoining spaces should no longer be conceived strictly from the standpoint of form, space, and structure; but, instead, the emphasis should be shifted to idea, attitude, and context. Through narrative and environmental associations, architecture can now deal more directly with revised sources of content and earth-related issues. This shift of focus from physical/hermetic to mental/environmental seems consistent with both the informational and ecological revolutions. It also opens up the building arts and landscape design to a range of options that have been closed off for most of the last century.

Currently, a great deal of post-structuralist philosophy in architecture is turning away from references to deconstruction and chaos theory, in favor of an integrative philosophy that can be seen as more in concert with the so-called information highway and ecology movement. One recent direction, referred to as "folding," is being described with such terms as "pliancy, continuous and heterogeneous systems, fluid transformations, and smooth mixtures of disparate elements." While some of this dialogue seems to suggest a renewed sympathy for the organic architecture of Frank Lloyd Wright, the actual manifestations in built and model form (unlike Wright) tend to treat the adjacent environment as an alien territory. As an afterthought, the surroundings are usually populated by those ubiquitous grids of trees that have little relationship to the centerpiece building. Folding in architecture is typically characterized by formal exercises in the use of warped planar surfaces to alter conventional relationships between exterior and interior. Whatever its claims for "pliancy and fluidity," the folded building still remains an isolated object that can be readily

∧ **Saudi Arabian Pavilion**
SITE
Seville, Spain
1992

Life is right, and the architect is wrong.
LE CORBUSIER

photographed apart from its context, without a loss of meaning. It is also heavily influenced by the organic shape-making characteristics of 1950s sculpture—a formal strategy that is regarded as hopelessly old fashioned in the art world; but, for some reason, has been resurrected in architecture as the cutting edge.

While some of the propositions of folding in architecture appear to be in accord with the new eco-sensibility, there is no real earth awareness or any particular intention to fuse structure with context (as implied by some of its stated objectives). In fact, there are no references to even the most elementary responsibilities of conservation technology and sustainable design. Instead, like the appropriation of deconstruction as the hypothesis for neo-Constructivism, folding seems to be one more extension of 20th century formalist orthodoxy. Its representative examples are very much a part of the traditions of early Constructivism and the notion that a building must always qualify as some form of abstract sculpture—in this case, comparable to a kind of architectural origami.

This tendency to cling to Constructivist traditions brings up the tangential question of why the most sophisticated mechanisms of the Information Age—most notably, Computer Aided Design—are used primarily to describe buildings that are stylistically rooted in the early Machine Age? Why, instead, isn't the entire phenomena of electronic communications (as well as the influence of earth sciences) utilized as the main inspirational resource for a new visual language? Part of the answer is obviously because 1920s Russian Constructivist architects did not have the luxury of software to articulate their complex formal innovations—so designers today feel somehow obliged to finish the job. Unlike the early Constructivists' work (which remained mostly unrealizable for the lack of computerized calculations and advanced construction technology), the CAD equipped architects now can easily describe and erect the most exotic configurations. Still, it seems oddly regressive to resurrect ideas from the 1920s, simply because they can be built in the 1990s. This leads to one central question. Why should the sources of formal influence remain early industrial, while the means of conception are cybernetic? Also, why have so few architects made the obvious conceptual and aesthetic connections between the integrated systems of the Internet and their ecological parallels in nature?

Returning to the concept of folding in architecture, an interesting linguistic contribution of this concept is an expansion of the meaning of "information" to "in-formation," which implies a fusion of both the transmission of data and the developmental process of shaping ideas. This thought leads directly to the main focus here, which is the interpretation of architecture as a system of "passages." It is a concept that links buildings, landscape, and elements of social/contextual/environmental communication. An edifice designed on strictly formal terms and then plunked down to await a bracelet of vegetation tends to remain static and insular. A building conceived as a fusion of structure and landscape is mutable, metamorphic, and evolutionary— constantly conveying new levels of information.

One way of looking at the integration of architecture and landscape architecture might be based, in part, on an observation about television. The TV set in one's living room is seldom regarded as anything more than a generic artifact for receiving and disseminating electronically generated images. Usually a viewer does not even notice the physical receptacle as an example of good or bad design, nor as an important object of furniture (although it can obviously be both). Instead, the importance of the ubiquitous box is its capacity to process information. Applying the same principles to a building in relation to its context, this comparison offers a way of breaking free from the strictly formalist interpretation of architecture. It is more consistent with the Age of Information and Ecology to shift the aesthetic focus of a building to its capacity to absorb and transmit messages. This suggests that walls, instead of being seen mainly as barriers for enclosure or compositional elements in the partitioning of space, can serve as information-filtering membranes (or points of passage) that fuse and dissolve traditional inside/outside relationships and incorporate narrative commentary. There is nothing new about the idea of walls delivering messages—all of the Medieval and Renaissance churches and civic buildings of Europe were based on this objective. Its radical appeal today derives from an opposition to conventional architectural geometry and the rich potential for establishing landscape and environmental awareness as leading forces of change in response to the spirit of a new millennium.

The interpretation of passages is infinitely variable and should not be considered as any kind of design formula. Basically, the concept proposes that walls and floor planes in a building should be seen as fluid, contextually responsive layers, converting the measure of aesthetic quality in architecture from formal design to how well a structure reflects and engages various aspects of landscape, regional identity, topography, and cultural references. In conventional Modernist/Constructivist architecture, walls are usually treated as functional/sculptural elements that respond to a clearly defined floor plan. Walls, interpreted as passages, can appear to defy the plan and range in physicality and purpose from indeterminate ribbons of transition in space to monitors of social/environmental change.

^ **Avenue Number Five**
SITE
Seville, Spain
1992

In terms of architectural construction, the concept of passages proposes that plant life and earth elements should be incorporated into the physical substance of shelter as readily as conventional building materials. From an aesthetic standpoint, the objective is to treat structure and landscape as a kind of interactive and biographical dialogue. When translated into a visual imagery, this fusion can describe their mutual origins in nature. This entire direction in design suggests the development of new paradigms for the building arts, based on ecological models.

There are also here obstacles to this integrative mission. Since our society has no collectively shared cosmology or religious associations with nature—of the kind, for example, that built the Celtic monuments of Wiltshire or rock cut temples of Ajanta—designers of today's environment cannot rely on a consensus iconography for communication. At the same time, the earth and sun are still universal symbols and the global awareness of ecology has become a motivating psychological force in the development of a post-industrial version of Jung's "collective unconscious." In this context, landscape still remains one of the world's most potent sources of symbolism.

Whereas the term folding in architecture seems to suggest a design process of methodical, geometry-driven, formal strategies, the notion of passages is intended to describe a mutational, organic, and informal set of connections between buildings and landscape. For example, this concept might take the form of a series of lateral, informational walls that can be distributed over a land parcel in both an orderly and random way, allowing roof structures and the surrounding context to casually bridge and/or penetrate the spaces between the partitions. This approach creates great flexibility in the orientation of sheltered services, as the covered areas can be distributed arbitrarily. Taken to its potential artistic extreme, it can completely break down the established definition of where architecture begins and landscape leaves off.

One major problem is trying to apply the theory of passages to a standard formula for high rise architecture. When the cost of real estate is the determining factor in ecological and aesthetic decisions, the idea of an office tower as the product of such nature-oriented design features as "fluidity, indeterminacy, and chance" is hard to sell to the cost-conscious developer. On the other hand, there is the possibility of interpreting large civic structures as heavily vegetated microcosms of their regions—taking cues from the Japanese concept of "borrowed scenery"—where gardens become tableaux of other places—or perhaps even contemporary equivalents of the Gardens of Babylon. As a footnote to this issue of high rise construction, there is now a question of the viability of skyscrapers, since this building type has generally proven to be the most anti-ecological in terms of its use of resources and choice of construction technology. Also, after the destruction of the World Trade Center on 9/11, the construction of trophy buildings and signature towers is becoming a less attractive option. In fact, environmental protection and new standards of anti-terrorist security may ultimately prohibit all high rise development in favor of lower height and clustered buildings, or even a preference for underground architecture.

The theory of passages seeks to chart a cartographic route through new and sometimes conflicting territories. While there is plenty of design world rhetoric now advocating integrated systems, the evidence on a vast majority of architects' and landscape architects' drawing boards reflects the familiar scenario of two cautious protagonists. They publicly profess sympathy for collaboration; but, behind the scenes, they continue to jockey for a position of aesthetic supremacy. Hopefully, the idea of passages can be used as a critical tool and premise for revised thinking about the relationship between architecture and landscape. It is intended as a means of reversing more than 100 years of anti-ecological and anti-communicative conventions in the building arts.

As part of this revised thinking, there are broad based and disturbing questions that have gnawed at the roots of cultural and theological development since the birth of the world's dominant religions. For example, how are we expected to evaluate and reconcile the environmental success of so many pantheistic ancient and aboriginal civilizations, where each element of nature was identified by its own divine spirit? At the opposite extreme, the dominant monotheism of today embraces a strictly male God—proclaimed in the human image. As a consequence, the destruction of the earth is viewed as a privilege of Man's sovereignty over nature. There is substantial evidence that a distribution of responsibility among multiple gods (of both male and female gender) related to the sun, rain, soil, rivers, crops, etc has been a far more successful theological vision. It has proven to be both ecologically and agriculturally superior to the despotic ego-centrism associated with a single deity and the myopic delusions of "nature for Man's convenience."

Another question asks why 20th century philosophy and linguistic studies have produced so few persuasive voices whose sources of signs and symbols have been drawn from the natural environment? Instead, the majority of leading theoreticians have scavenged through the cacophony of pop billboards, the fetishes of fast-food psychology and the digitalized rituals of consumer culture (actually, the shallowest elements of surface structure) that block access to nature, while ignoring the richness of an earth-centered symbolism that lies behind this junk world detritus. Where, one asks, are the theoreticians and interpreters of an evolving eco-language? Where is the Baudrillard, Lacan, Foucault, Levi-Strauss, Barthes, Saussure, or Lyotard of a new "terrestrial signification?"

Rather than address such broad-based philosophical questions, much of the ecologically motivated and so-called "sustainable" work today is nothing more than a catalogue checklist of routine environmental technology and land conservation programs tacked onto otherwise conventionally designed buildings and landscapes. The green mission is essential, the intentions are admirable; yet, the results are boring. A more convincing approach to the fusion of architecture and vegetation should demonstrate an aesthetic commitment to the translation of nature's integrative model into persuasive visual realizations. The secret now in the building arts is to recover those fragile threads of unity, which Heidegger called "connectedness to the earth," that have been lost for most of this century. The archetypal precedents for this approach can be found in all of those contextually harmonious ancient cities of the Middle East, Africa, and Asia. The value of these precedents is the construction of shelter in concert with nature, which has maintained its beauty and symbolic presence over the centuries by converting a combination of sustainability, landscape, and communicative iconography into high art. In the 21st century these examples have never been more relevant. Clearly, the interactive dialogue between architecture and landscape is an art, as well as an ecological imperative.

The present Age of Information and Ecology is, like the spirit of passages, a critical point of transition and connection. It has arrived for some architects and landscape architects like a plague on the conscience, threatening entrenched beliefs, stylistic preferences, and routine work habits. For others, it has become the revolutionary and resource-saving opportunity to develop new technologies in the name of environmental advocacy. For more contemplative designers, it has been seen as the beginning of a deeper awareness of the earth and a cause for re-thinking the relationships between architecture and landscape by blending art, philosophy, technology, and the lessons of nature's integrated systems. While this third group is potentially the most productive, the challenges it faces are daunting. It means confronting—and probably having to ultimately embrace—concepts that endanger the institutional frameworks of religion, economy, and politics, not to mention most things the building arts have been about for the last 100 years.

∧ **Horoscope Ring**
SITE
Toyama, Japan
1992

^ **Aerial View of Rue de la Federation**

^ **Aerial View from Quai Branly**

The Japan Cultural Center in Paris is designed as a fusion of references from French and Japanese architecture and landscape. The purpose of the building is to celebrate the arts of Japan, with a special focus on the history of symbolic artifacts and horticulture identified with the Oriental garden. This semi-circular museum (responsive to the configuration of an adjacent intersection) is an example of "narrative architecture," absorbing visual clues from the surrounding French neighborhood. The structure is designed as a series of fan-like platforms, which support a metamorphic sequence of architectural fragments. When circling the building (viewed from the street level) this imagery gradually changes from Parisian classicism and formal gardens, based on principles of logic, to a Japanese environment of horizontality and inside/outside relationships, based on a ritualized interpretation of landscape. Each level of the six-story museum is shaped like a Japanese fan, which allude to a radiating sun, the layered plates of a Samurai armor, the fusion of nature and architecture, and the spirituality of the Zen garden. The fan-shaped floor planes start at the top of the building with a geometric consistency and then gradually evolve into random layers of cantilevered balconies with overhanging projections. The thermal walls of glass are recessed to allow shade and exterior garden spaces. To accent the iconographic transition from France to Japan, a series of freestanding window frames and doorways (abstracted from Western and Eastern archetypes) are mounted on the edges of the platforms and gradually diminish in number as vegetation takes over. The interior spaces conform to the fan-shaped plan and all of the blade-like segments converge at the rear of the center to create a five-floor atrium. In a number of areas, the exterior landscape penetrates the offices and galleries, bringing a special emphasis to the inside/outside theme of the Japan Cultural Center.

The concept for Shinwa Resort hotel and
conference center is based on the classical
Japanese image of the sun and its expanding
rays. The combined entertainment facility,
shopping center, parking area, and hotel are
contained within a fan-shaped plan, enclosing a
semi-circular plaza space. In addition to its
inherent symbolic shape, the structure is totally
responsive to existing topography. This
configuration offers the additional advantage of
a centrifugal merchandising area, which
encourages people to assemble at a focal point
and then gravitate outward to other parts of the
complex. In order to respond to the magnificent
mountainous terrain and integrate the resort
with its context, each section of the building
grows organically out of the landscape and the
roof structures are completely covered with
earth and regional vegetation. When viewed
from approach roads and parking lots, the
entire complex appears to have grown like a
plant out of the surroundings. These
landscaped roofs have the additional advantage
of helping to control the interior temperature by
retaining warmth in the winter and deflecting
heat in the summer.

^ **Kisokoma-Kogen**
Japan
1991

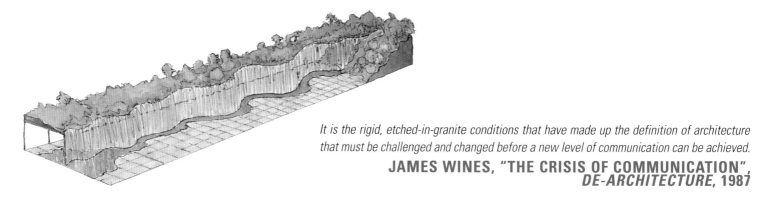

It is the rigid, etched-in-granite conditions that have made up the definition of architecture that must be challenged and changed before a new level of communication can be achieved.
JAMES WINES, "THE CRISIS OF COMMUNICATION",
DE-ARCHITECTURE, 1987

This public space and restaurant facility project was originally designed for one of the five main pedestrian corridors, providing access to national pavilions at Expo 92. During the exposition, it housed a series of five restaurants and their adjacent outdoor dining spaces. After the exposition, this project became the centerpiece of a new Columbian Park and contains Columbus-related exhibitions. The SITE concept is designed as a narrative experience, celebrating the Guadaquivir River in Seville and its history as the route to the sea for 15th century nautical explorers. For the exposition period it represented the general theme of "Discovery," and the technological/ecological emphasis of the entire event. The ribbon-like shape of Avenue Five is a microcosmic representation of the basic topography of the Guadaquivir and, from an environmental standpoint, architecture used as a system of climate control. In the summer heat of Seville, this project represents an ideal example of natural cooling by means of water and vegetation. Consistent with the river image, the west part of the Avenue Number Five relates to the source of water from the mountains, the center is the river itself, and the east end suggests the exit to the sea. A 300-meter-long, six-meter-high undulating water wall of glass achieves this effect by running the entire length of the site. A massive "lifted landscape" (vegetation planted in the recessed pockets of an inverted waffle-grid roof system) covers the entire length of the processional. The water wall encloses the restaurant/exhibit areas and the monorail station. Each facility is shaded by a combination of landscaped roofs, tall trees, vegetated columns, and a vine-covered trellis.

^ Greenroof Planting

Expo 92's intention is crediting all nations' participation in the international environmental initiative. The premise for the pavilion was based on a view that one of the major world issues during the 21st century will be the protection of natural resources. In order to reflect this concern and express Expo 92's theme of "Discovery," the World Ecology Pavilion is proposed as a celebration of the value of terrain, atmosphere, bodies of water, vegetation, crops, and minerals. The 75,000-square-foot pavilion is designed as a microcosm of typical landscapes, associated with the seven continents of the world—North America, South America, Africa, Asia, Europe, Australia, and Antarctica. The building is defined by a row of parallel, undulating ribbon-like structures in concrete that support the regional plant life and characteristic terrain of each continent. These verdant canopies function as roof shelters, enclosures for exhibitions, shade cover for plazas, and as an acoustical band shell over an outdoors theater. They also create a context where visitors can relate to both the surface and interior geology of the earth. The undulating canopies are designed as seven inverted, deep-joist, concrete structures with honeycomb coffers to contain the landscape elements. The interior provides a 10,000-square-foot theater, 48,000-square-foot thematic exhibition space, 250,000-square-foot art gallery, a 10,000-square-foot restaurant with terrace, and a 5,000-square-foot office and V.I.P. lounge.

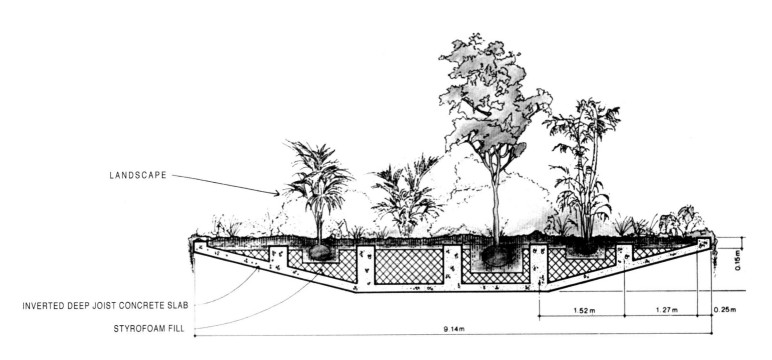

LANDSCAPE

INVERTED DEEP JOIST CONCRETE SLAB

STYROFOAM FILL

0.15m

1.52 m   1.27 m   0.25m

9.14 m

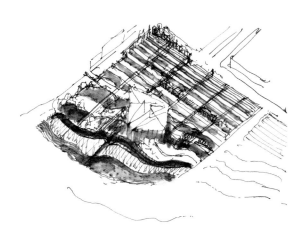

^ **Pedestrian pattern along promenade by waterfront**
Chattanooga, USA
1800s

Ross's Landing Park and Plaza is part of a riverfront revitalization program, associated with a $100 million mixed-use development project on the Tennessee River in Chattanooga. This area is both an important historic center in the community, as well as the site of the Tennessee Aquarium, designed by Cambridge Seven Architects. This facility is the world's only aquarium dedicated to fresh-water aquatic life. The surrounding park and plaza is intended to soften the effect of this imposing architectural mass and integrate it more effectively with the heavily vegetated riverfront. The SITE-designed park is treated as a microcosm of the entire city and region—including its urban grid and flowing landscape. To create a metaphorically readable and visually appealing equivalent for the township, the site is articulated by a series of 35 longitudinal ribbons of paving, tile, water, and vegetation. To further emphasize the cityscape/landscape metaphor, these ribbons compose a rich tapestry of color and texture in the form of 20-foot-wide reflections of the urban grid.

Gradually, as these bands approach the aquarium, they lose their geometric definition and become increasingly organic in profile—finally, metamorphosing into lush water, stone, and landscape environments that surround the aquarium and extend down to a riverfront boat dock and small performance amphitheater. These bands of paving proceed chronologically through the park and, in certain locations, they rise above the surface to form undulating bridges, performance spaces, and water features. Since each band is assigned a period of years, the ground surface becomes a time-line history of the founding and settlement of Chattanooga. Through the use of artifacts, artworks, landscape features, and quotations embedded in the paving surface, the city's rich legacy of events—for example, the Civil War, Civil Rights Movement, formation of the railroad, beginning of blues music, first Coca-Cola bottling, and formation of the Tennessee Valley Authority—gradually unfolds for park visitors.

After the completion of the Tennessee Aquarium and Ross's Landing Park and Plaza in 1992, SITE was asked by the regional development authority to propose an environmentally related center that would explore aspects of water-related science, other than aquatic life. This concept, entitled "AQUATORIUM," is dedicated to the history, science, culture, and preservation of water. The purpose is to inspire a profound appreciation of humanity's relationship to the earth's most precious resource. By means of sight, sound, and touch, the building and its exhibition spaces are designed to tell the story of water and people. Located on top of Kirkman Hill, adjacent to the SITE-designed Ross's Landing, this new facility is integrated with its circular site as an over and underground experience. The structure also connects to the earliest origins of cosmology, when shelter and ceremonial monuments were constructed as reflections of people's debt to the sun, moon, and earth. The building configuration is composed of a series of lateral information walls (inside/outside structures) that carry the exhibitions from interior to exterior and fuse with the hillside topography. These animated walls divide the sections of the museum into culture, science, habitat, technology, and agriculture, using such exhibit devices as video, water events, virtual reality, gardens, natural phenomena, and hands-on displays that explain the value of water to all cultures. In addition to these narrative environments, the AQUATORIUM also provides several grand spaces for special shows and conferences, a theater, study center, library, administrative offices, a restaurant specializing in aqua-culture cuisine, and a health center featuring water therapies.

< **Bathing Child**
Varanasi, India
1997

Ancient Roman Aquaduct
SITE Archives

Stonehenge
SITE Archives

Moby Dick
SITE Archives

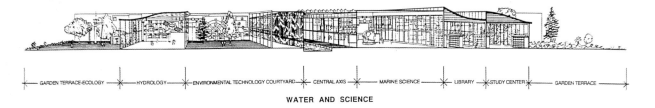

GARDEN TERRACE-ECOLOGY | HYDROLOGY | ENVIRONMENTAL TECHNOLOGY COURTYARD | CENTRAL AXIS | MARINE SCIENCE | LIBRARY | STUDY CENTER | GARDEN TERRACE

WATER AND SCIENCE

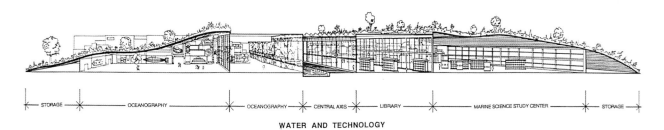

STORAGE | OCEANOGRAPHY | OCEANOGRAPHY | CENTRAL AXIS | LIBRARY | MARINE SCIENCE STUDY CENTER | STORAGE

WATER AND TECHNOLOGY

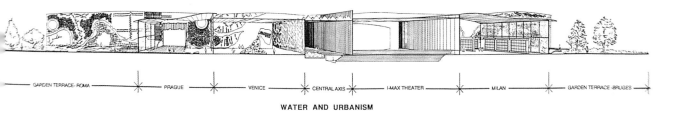

GARDEN TERRACE-ROMA | PRAGUE | VENICE | CENTRAL AXIS | I-MAX THEATER | MILAN | GARDEN TERRACE-BRUGES

WATER AND URBANISM

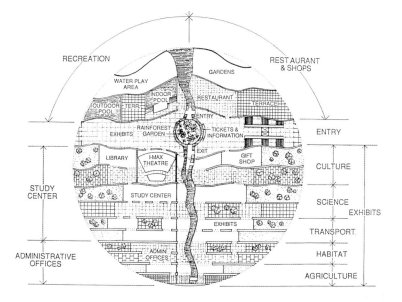

Ancient cultures understood that humanity's final destiny lay in the balance between the structure of the universe and the resources of the earth and that the only role for art was to pay homage to these decisive forces.

JAMES WINES, *DE-ARCHITECTURE*, 1989

This Japanese commercial complex surrounds a children's park in the mountainous town of Toyama. At the request of the municipality, the project is based on the symbolism of the horoscope. The shape of the enclosure is a circular plaza with imagery connections to the constellations and orbits of the planets. The totemic wall structure suggests a relationship between the traditional Japanese garden—with its allusions to a non-terrestrial landscape in Paradise—and the mountainous topography of the region. The enclosed sections are designed around a central plaza, to provide shelter for a variety of commercial enterprises. A series of fragmented, wedge-shaped, parallel walls slope toward the center of the park and each unit is filled with the regional vegetation. Against Toyama's backdrop of surrounding mountains, the Horoscope Ring appears to flow directly out of the adjacent hillside. There is a rock garden that conforms to the pattern of the stars between each vertical structure. Defined by strategically placed stones, graphic lines in the paving illustrate the traditional images of the Zodiac. The central public space is organized in concentric exhibition platforms, to accommodate a constantly changing display of children's entertainment facilities and play equipment. From a conceptual perspective, the Horoscope Ring offers an unusual interpretation of the classical Japanese concept of inside/outside. It establishes a relationship between the contemplative inner space of the Oriental garden, and the outer space associated with the Zodiac.

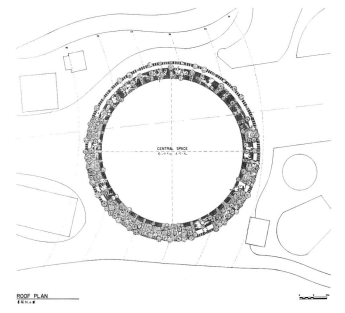

ROOF PLAN

∧ **Zodiac Signs**
SITE Archives

∧ **Typical Japanese Garden**
SITE Archives

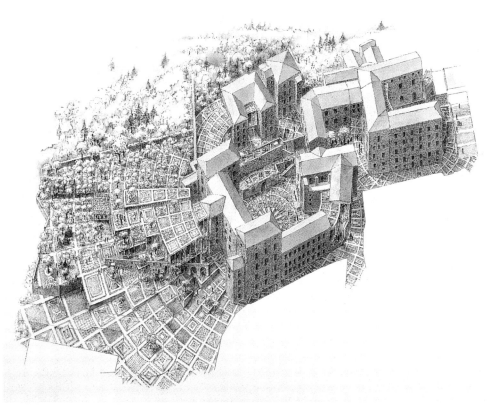

This competition winning proposal includes a master plan for the adaptive re-use of historic buildings and a civic center for the medieval city of Le Puy-En-Velay in the Haute Loire region of France. The purpose of the project is to revitalize the old center as a tourist attraction, create civic office spaces, and develop a new building for the state government of the region. In addition, there are provisions for a music and dance school, student housing, restaurants, public gardens, and underground parking. The basis of the plan is two intersecting circles—consistent with the original configuration of this 12th century city—that connect the town and state centers. Each circle is segmented into a series of radiating lines and concentric intersections, constructed from paving units in regional materials. The unifying function of these expanding circles provides a thematic matrix for a great variety of landscape, public space, and architectural situations. They form a ground plan for the hillside gardens, define the terraces for the deputies' restaurant, give shape to the new civic building, translate into public rooms, become elevated bridges between edifices, create an amphitheater for outdoor concerts, and define the centerpiece plaza for the state offices. Existing buildings are adaptively renewed for their various programs and minimally altered in order to preserve the city's historic character. In the public garden areas, the new state center literally grows out of a terraced hillside site. This concept is designed to unify a number of old functions and accommodate new ones. It proposes a contemporary version of the garden city by extending this theme throughout the new building—primarily as terrarium with vegetation, situated inside and outside the glass walls in each part of the state office center.

∧ **Medieval Radial Plan**
SITE Archives

∧ **Le Puy-En-Velay**
SITE Archives

This concept for the Saudi Arabian Pavilion at Expo 92 is based on a composite of elements that are characteristic of the Kingdom's architecture and landscape. The building is defined by a rectangular steel grid enclosure—reflecting the geometric origin of Saudi arts, crafts, astrology, and Islamic patterns—which also functions as a matrix to support a variety of archaeological fragments, regional artifacts, and a group of energy-conservative cooling towers. The general configuration of the pavilion is based on a generic Saudi structure, with its exterior masonry enclosure surrounding an internal, open-air atrium. However, whereas these typical buildings are completely enveloped by dense walls to isolate inhabitants, this Expo pavilion opens up its façade to welcome the world. This has been accomplished by designing the building as a series of overlapping partitions in space—with an exterior volume built of mud-brick and stucco—then cut away to reveal successive layers of structure, vegetation, and architectural features. A massive tent, fabricated from hundreds of Bedouin blankets, shelters the interior courtyard. When viewed from the adjacent monorail train and the pavilion's V.I.P. terraces, this vast collage of woven fabrics and brilliant colors serves as a visual tribute to the regional diversity of Saudi Arabia and its richly varied cultural legacy.

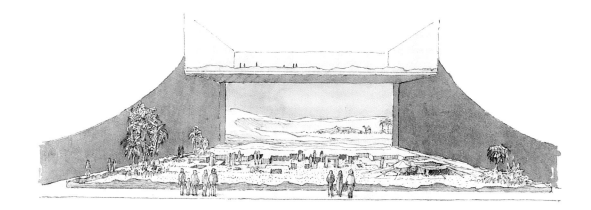

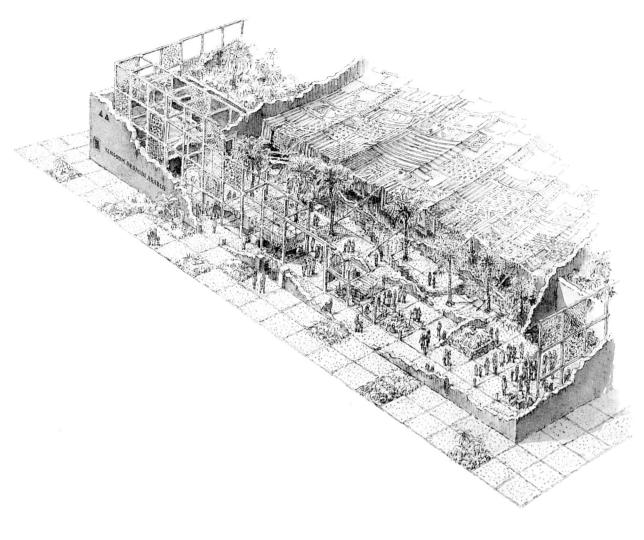

Geological Terrarium
to display oil
technology

Tie-down Cables and
tent supports for display

^ **Beduin Textiles**
SITE Archives

TRAWSFYNYDD INTERNATIONAL ENERGY COMMUNICATIONS CENTER

BRITISH BROADCASTING CORPORATION AND THE CITY OF TRAWSFYNYDD   TRAWSFYNYDD, NORTH WALES

1994

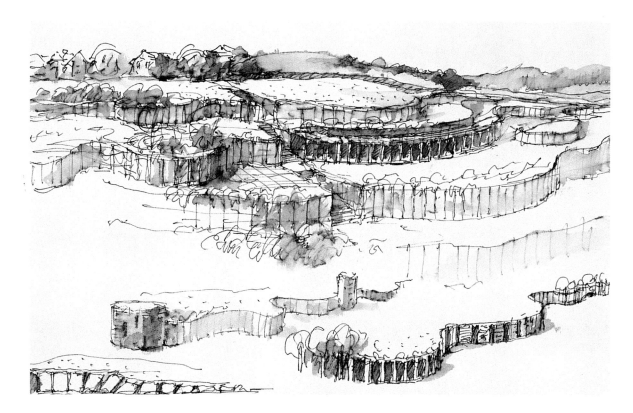

In the fall of 1994 SITE was asked to develop a proposal for the British Government's planned decommissioning of a nuclear power station in Trawsfynydd, North Wales. This resulted in a two-part concept. Firstly, a proposal for the use of robotics and phyto-remediation in the decommissioning of the existing facility and its conversion to safe storage for nuclear wastes. Secondly, the plan suggested the design of an International Energy Communications Center for the study of decommissioning and alternative energy sources in the future. The new center is located on a magnificent hillside site, just below the town of

Trawsfynydd and overlooking a nearby valley, lake, and the dormant power station. On physical and aesthetic terms, the building is intended to integrate with its majestic North Wales environment and, at the same time, signal the dangers of the nuclear age. The configuration of the center is based on a combination of a Celtic cross and the typical layered mounds of Neolithic monuments. The building physically fuses with its context by cutting the structure into the hillside and using sections of the local landscape to cover the roof. The existing slate and stone walls on the site are extended to integrate with the glass partitions of the architecture.

The communications center contains facilities for education, exhibition, and transmission of information on all aspects of alternative energy concepts and the disposal of nuclear wastes. It is equipped with many design features related to environmental technology and sustainability, which establish the T.I.E.C.C. as a functioning and continuously evolving example of energy research and conservation. Since the center is designed with landscape as an intrinsic part of the architecture, it is anticipated that the structure will become increasingly metamorphic in physical appearance and less and less visible as the natural context absorbs the building.

^ Short-Term Green Storage

< Trawsfynydd Landscape

< Regional Neolithic Monument
Trawsfynydd, North Wales

A nuclear archaeology is in the process of being created.

STAN OPENSHAW, *POWER TO CHANGE*

Our world is strewn with the detritus of the dead epoch. The great task incumbent upon us is that of making a proper environment for our existence.

LE CORBUSIER

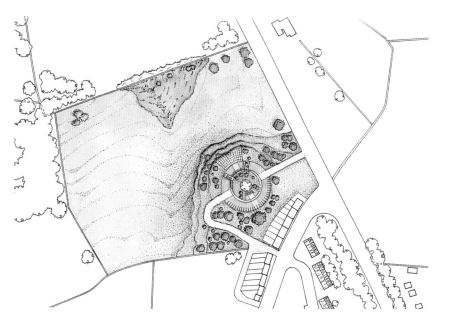

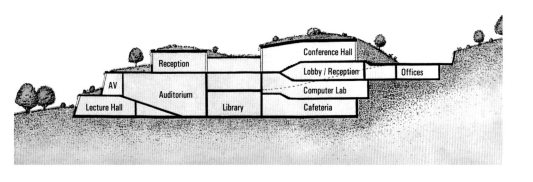

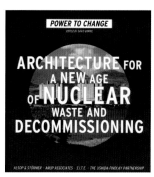

^ **Nuclear Power Station**
Trawsfynydd, North Wales

< **Longitudinal section—Upper levels to house auditorium, classrooms, research libraries, and computer libraries**

^ Recyclable junk as building materials

The purpose of the Prince William County Environmental Education Center is to tell an ecological story—demonstrating the vast disparity between the methods that humanity and nature use to recycle waste. The aesthetic purpose is to integrate the entire site area surrounding the new building by means of nature paths and interpretation trails. The major route includes a narrative exhibit that describes mankind's ineffective means of waste management (landfills, garbage dumps, incinerators), versus the ways that nature handles this task so much more efficiently. The Environmental Education Center occupies a 3,000-square-foot site on the crest of a hill, surrounded by a forested terrain. The interior space is 2,145 square feet, including an exhibition area, open study lab, one administrative office, bathrooms, and storage. Architecture, in this case, is interpreted as an information station along the Prince William Park trail system. The trail itself is proposed as a narrative artery that emerges from a nearby landfill and cuts through the woodland to integrate with the center. As the pathway approaches the building, it gradually converts into wall sections that rise out of the earth in the form of compressed industrial waste blocks, composed of various metal products and other discarded materials. Near the environmental center, this undulating waste wall changes into an increasingly higher structure, with information windows that explain recycling technology. At the point where the wall intersects with the building, it illustrates how waste materials return (or resist the return) to nature. On the east side of the center, the wall becomes a series of vertical wood forms—metaphorically suggestive of the surrounding trees—that gradually dematerializes into the earth and becomes a wetlands overlook platform.

^ **Existing Condition**
  Riyadh, Saudi Arabia
  1996

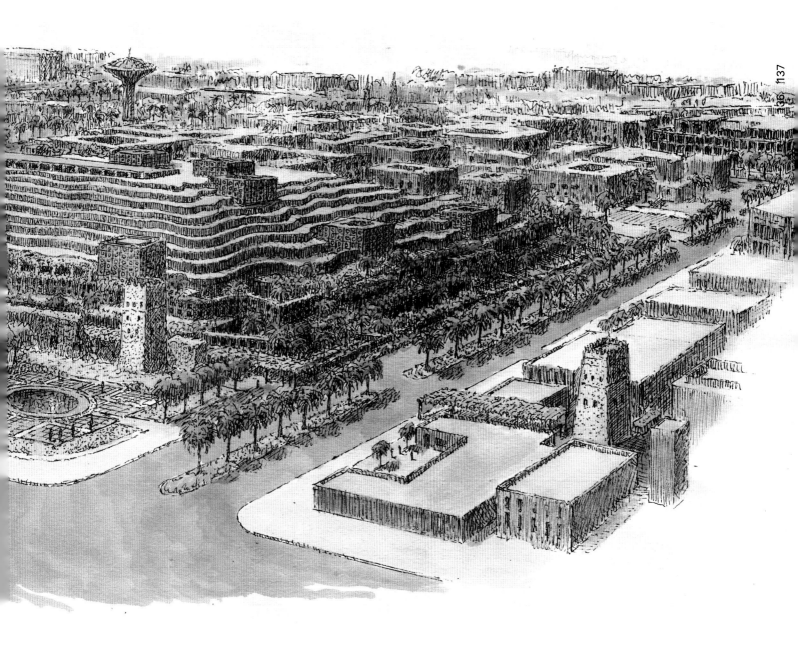

This museum is designed as a celebration of the legacy of King Abdul Al-Aziz, the founder of modern Arabia, and the symbolic significance of his achievements as they relate to the land and people of the Kingdom. The structure is an integration of surrounding terrain (part of a natural desert wadi), the original mud-brick city of Riyadh, and regional vegetation. The main structure is a multi-layered series of undulating tiers that recall the landscape of the Azir region, the tradition of ziggurat buildings in ancient Mesopotamia, and the ribbon-like striation of the nation's many glacier-carved wadis. The building is conceived as an 'inside/outside experience; including terraced "dry" gardens and a massive "wet" garden, contained within an open grid extension and maintained by computerized irrigation. For reasons of energy conservation, the roof planes are equipped with photovoltaic panels and evaporative cooling towers. The museum interior is covered by the giant, shell-like, undulating roof, which shelters a collection of historic adobe dwellings. This "building-within-a-building" is fused into the exhibition, becoming the matrix for exhibitions, displays of historical artifacts, video presentations, and a wide range of hands-on exhibits.

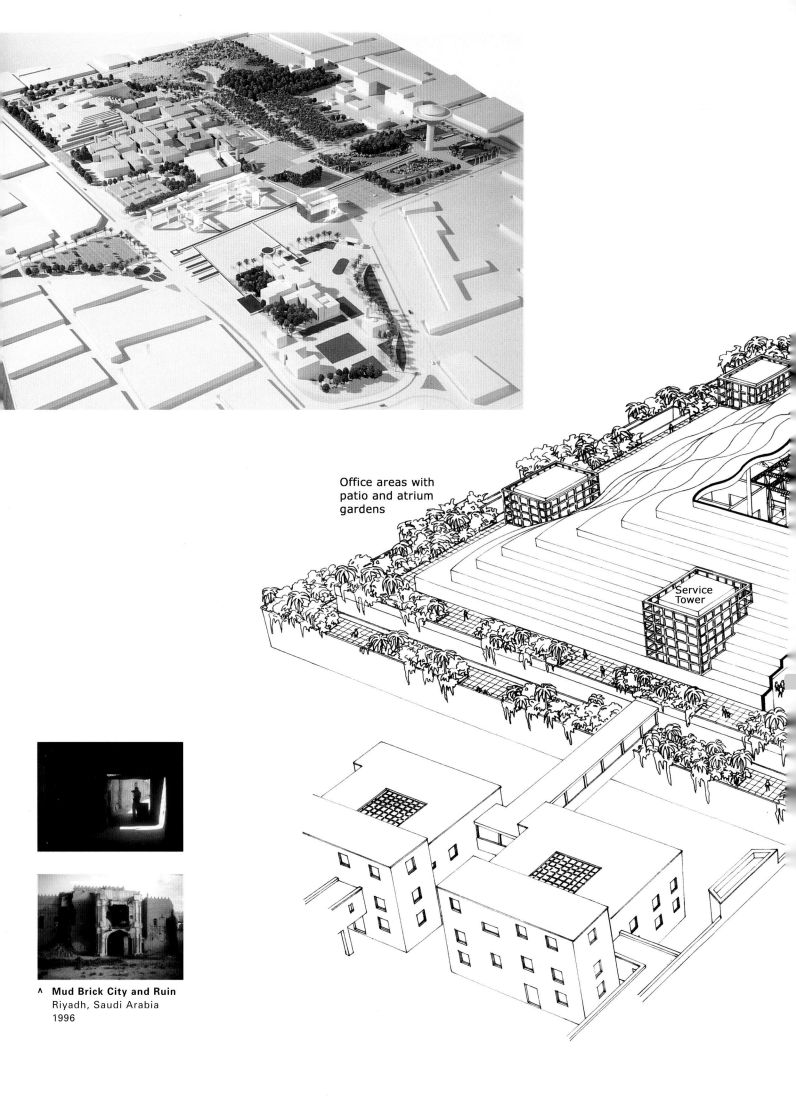

Office areas with patio and atrium gardens

Service Tower

^ **Mud Brick City and Ruin**
Riyadh, Saudi Arabia
1996

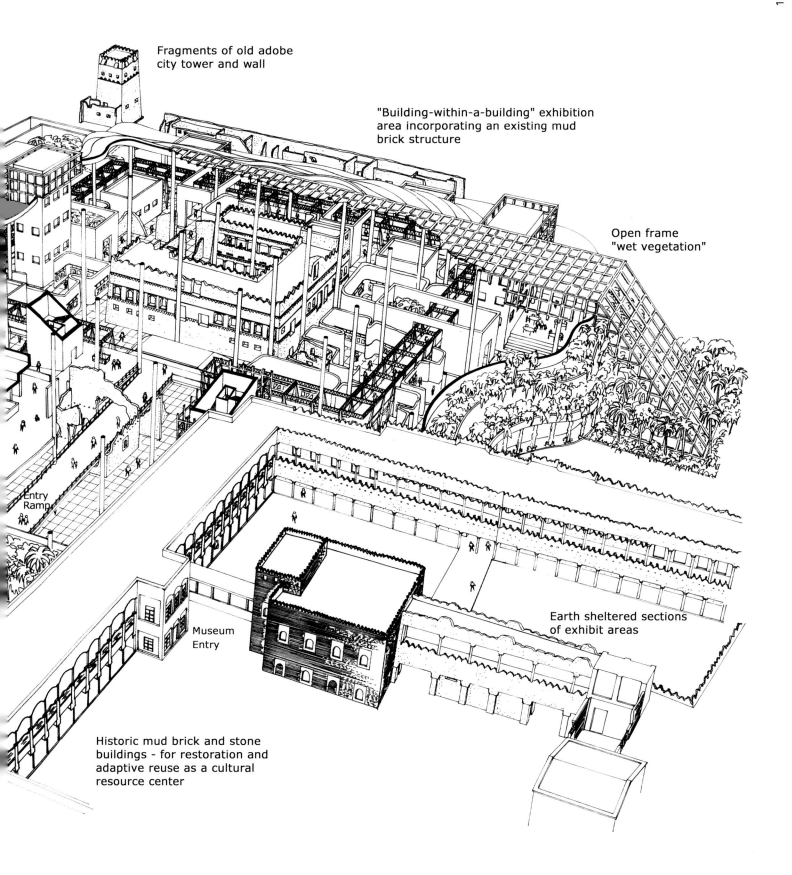

Fragments of old adobe
city tower and wall

"Building-within-a-building" exhibition
area incorporating an existing mud
brick structure

Open frame
"wet vegetation"

Entry
Ramp

Museum
Entry

Earth sheltered sections
of exhibit areas

Historic mud brick and stone
buildings - for restoration and
adaptive reuse as a cultural
resource center

^ **Existing Mud-Brick City**
Riyadh, Saudi Arabia
1996

^ **Terraced Landscape of Azir Region**
Saudi Arabia
1996

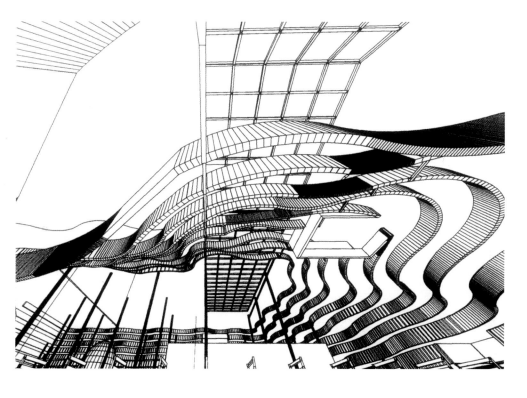

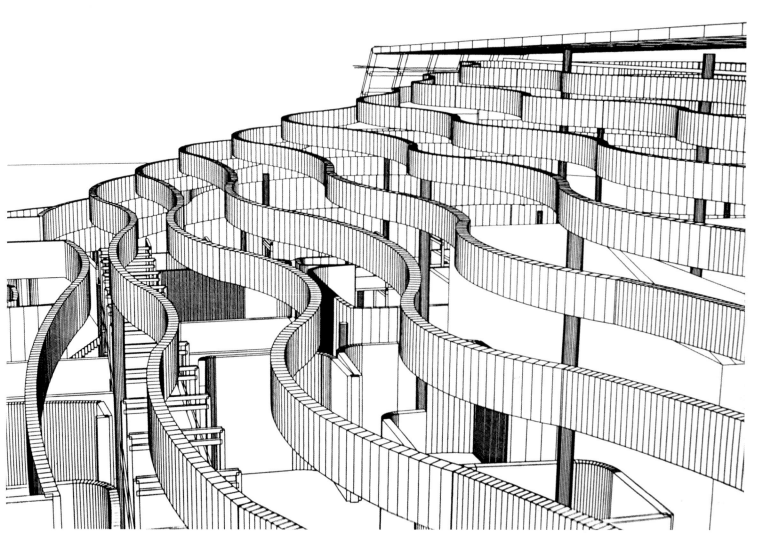

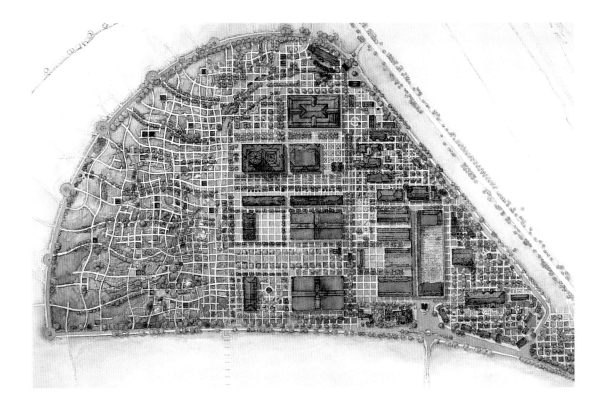

The IGA Island, located in Dresden's Elbe River, was originally occupied by the meat packing industry in the early 1900s. This master plan project is intended to transform the massive site to a large public park. It establishes the home base for an annual international flower exposition, converts a series of existing warehouse buildings into cultural facilities and includes an ecology study center, aviary, science museum, art gallery, youth hostel and experimental enclave for the demonstration of responsible environmental practices. Since all of the masonry buildings are part of the historical register, they must be preserved and integrated into the park plan. Also, the regional government wants the island to serve as a working model for water preservation research and advances in "blue/green" technology. The IGA project responds to the dual challenge of preserving the past, while reflecting the present Age of Information and Ecology—proposed as a metamorphic transition between old and new. This is achieved by treating the site plan as a microcosm of the city and a demonstration of the cyclical process of hydrology in nature. The park is composed of a 25-meter-square grid (defined by walkways), based on the original plan of the meat packing buildings. A geometric grid surrounds the industrial structures and then gradually dematerializes to become a series of undulating pedestrian arteries in the garden areas. In the sections surrounding the meat packing warehouses, the grid is used to define small plazas, formal gardens, and ecological exhibitions. As the walkways fan out over the site, they become increasingly organic and evolve into a ribbon-like labyrinth of plants, trees, and flowers. In the ecological section, visitors encounter the entire cyclical process of nature—precipitation, runoff, retention, purification, and the storage of water supplies. The environmental program is sculpturally interpreted in the form of earth depressions, paved water channels, ponds, rivers, aquatic marshes, and expansive sections of protected wetlands.

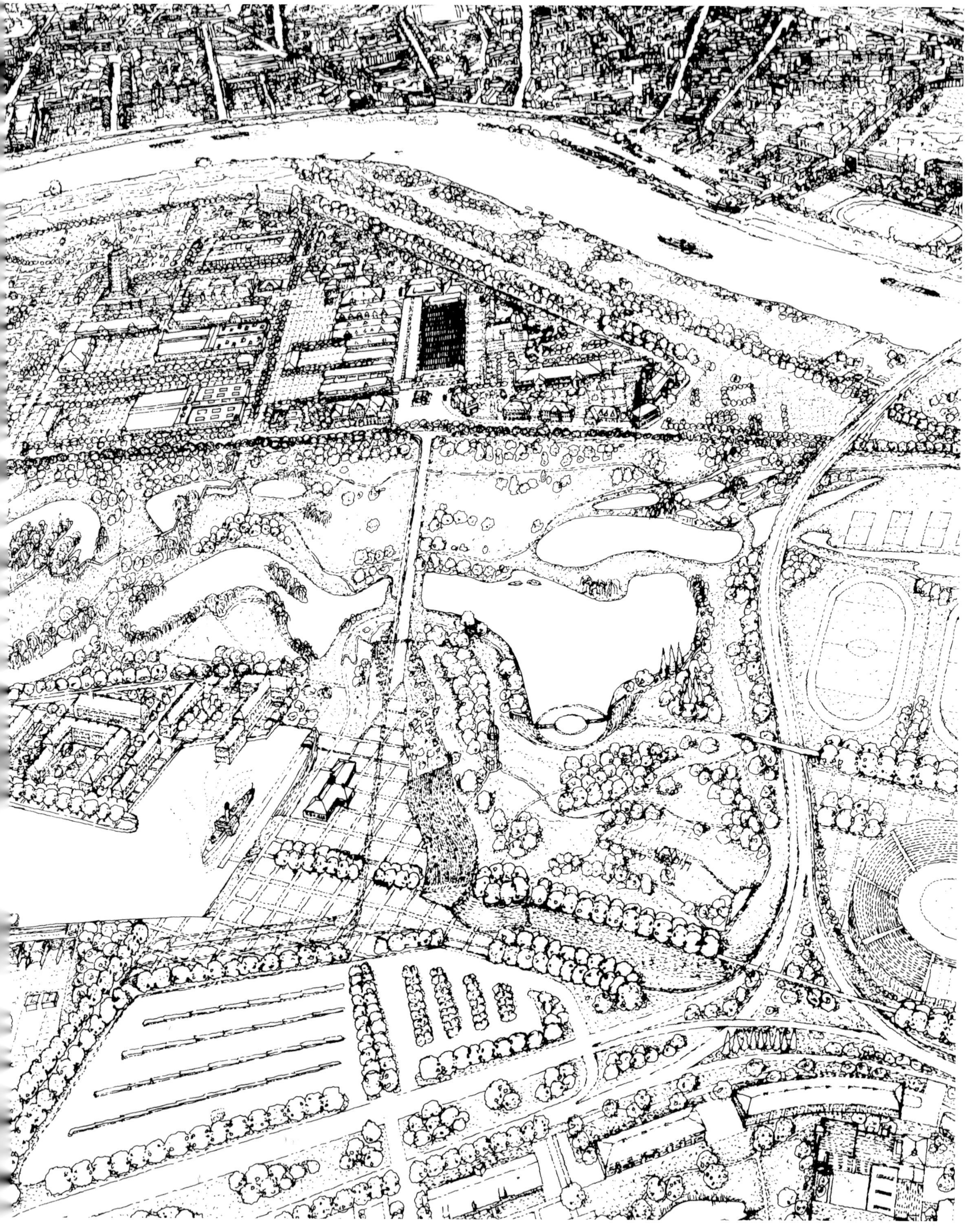

The new Museum of Islamic Arts in Doha, Qatar is designed as a total fusion of architecture, exhibition spaces, environmental technology, electronic communications, and the surrounding context. Confirming SITE's belief that architecture should reflect the integrated systems governing nature, this project is the result of an unusually close collaboration of architects, artists, and technicians. The team started with the premise that this cultural facility should express the spiritual unity of Islam by means of three organizing features— 1. a 12-meter grid plan that "de-materializes" on the exterior to create the undulating pathways of a public garden, 2. a series of lateral walls that pass from inside to outside and become a support structure for the exhibitions, 3. a sequence of undulating roof planes that create dramatically sculptural interiors, with varied ceiling heights and sources of daylight. When viewed from the adjacent neighborhood, the museum is intended to appear as though the building is the garden and the garden is the building. The architectural imagery is a response to sources associated with Doha. These features include Islamic culture, the rolling desert, the sea, nautical commerce, and the specific topography of the site area. In this sense the building's configuration is "biomorphic"—meaning that its form and content are a visual reflection of the evolutionary processes of nature. It is also "geomorphic"—suggesting that the structure is a microcosm of the surrounding area and its wider geographical hemisphere. The museum is intended to suggest a vast desert landscape, punctuated with architectural features and an occasional oasis of greenery. Conceived as a layered ensemble of walls, the façade starts as a processional colonnade, framed by a massive glass water wall that filters light and cools the lobby area. Directly inside, there is a grid structure showcasing fragments of Islamic architecture, followed by a succession of walls with different degrees of opacity and transparency. The interior spaces include the latest video and computer technology to help explain the artifacts on display. Most of the exhibits are designed as an intrinsic part of the wall system. Consistent with its integrative design concept, the museum combines the symbolic presence of the wall in Islamic culture, climate-related architectural elements, and a digital communications program, with an outreach to other museums internationally.

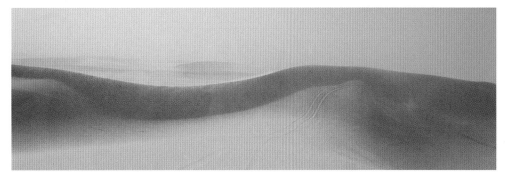

^ Sand Dune Desert
Doha, Qatar
1997

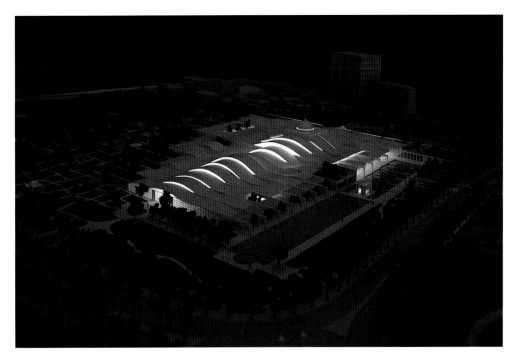

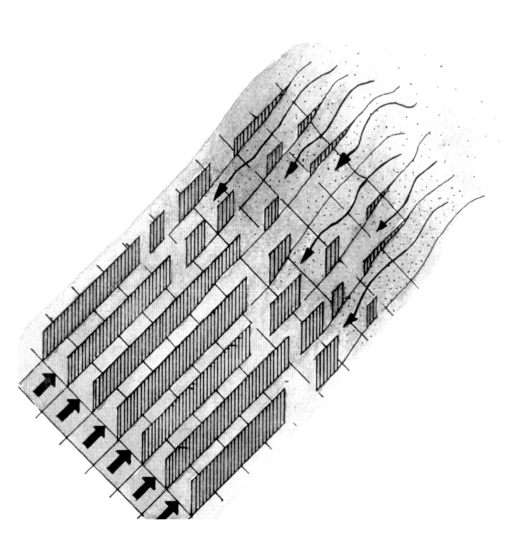

^ **Site Location Existing Condition**
Doha, Qatar
1997

^ **Landscape Partii**
SITE Archives

< **Inside/Outside Diagram**

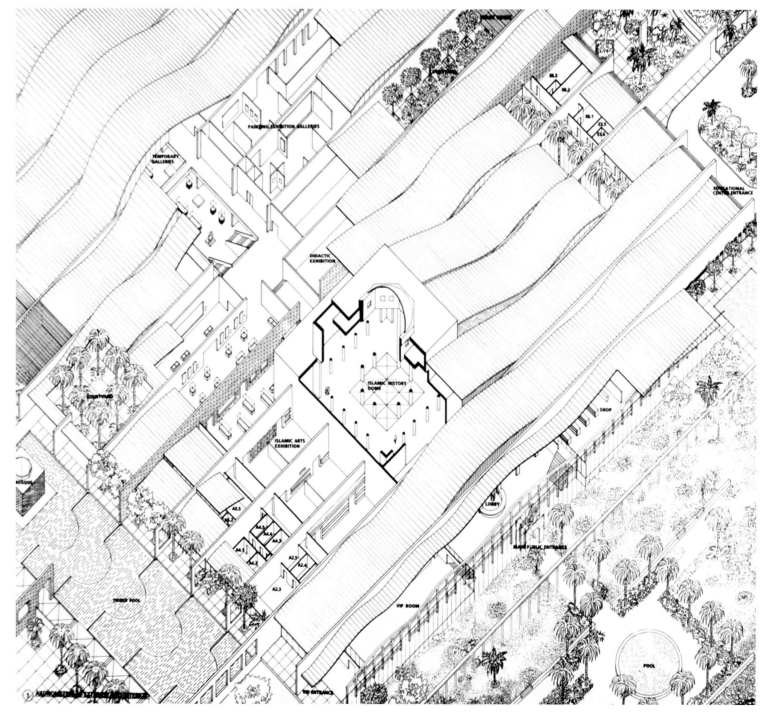

The CHILI'S Grill and Bar Restaurant in Aurora, Colorado has been designed as a composite of the pop culture iconography identified with traditional Southwestern roadhouses during the 1950s. Certain of these elements have been converted into a contemporary version of false-front highway architecture. The restaurant is built as a commentary on the imagery identified with CHILI'S from its earliest origins—including the chili pepper logo, wood frame construction, and profusion of Americana artifacts that decorate the bar and seating areas. The entire building is composed of a series of five intersecting board and batten façades, plus three wood frame trellis walls. These vertical elements start at ground level (as partially buried fragments) and grow upward in a successive layering of iconic partitions.

CHILI'S front and back façades are constructed in red brick, locked between these lateral sections. The contour of the masonry wall is roughly the shape of a giant chili pepper; but the effect is abstract, so visitors become aware of the image gradually, through a process of subliminal recognition. To add a feeling of "second story" height to the restaurant, the upper edges of the brick walls are fragmented and include window frames, which are open to the sky—creating the impression of fenestration that has remained from a once higher building. The inside of the restaurant is designed as an extension of the identical materials, false front panels, and window frames used on the exterior. The glass panes in these windows exhibit a wide range of objects and photographic images (as transparencies), drawn from the history of CHILI'S and Southwestern roadway culture. To present this visual material in a more evocative way, many of the artifacts combine illusion and reality. Part of a two-dimensional image is reproduced on the window glass, while its physical presence outside the frame is the actual object. For example, the frame of a bicycle is presented as a photo within the window, while the wheels occupy real space. The main objective is to create a totally integrated visual experience, where every architectural feature on the outside reappears on the inside.

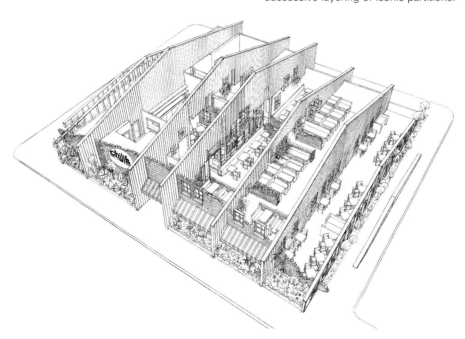

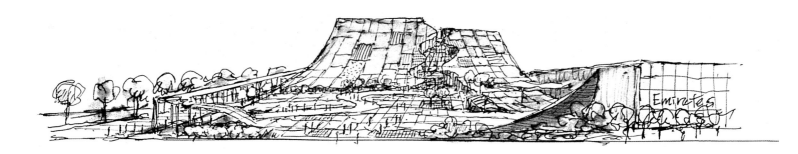

In April of 1998 SITE was selected by the US State Department to design the USA Pavilion for Expo 2000 in Hannover, Germany. The building was never realized for lack of government support and a failure of the American commissioner to raise funds from private corporations. The American Pavilion is a celebration of the themes of diversity and opportunity in the United States. In response to this mission, the building and its public spaces are designed as a microcosm of the country— a tapestry of America—where the plaza level and roof plane fuse together in a patchwork collage of varied materials and landscapes. In order to translate the country's distinctive terrain into architecture, the pavilion's mosaic-like plaza and gardens start at grade level and incline upward to integrate with the roof plane of the main exhibition areas. This design approach takes advantage of the building's dramatic aerial visibility from the exposition cable car system. For a visitor standing in the main esplanade, the entire pavilion appears to be a fluid, sweeping microcosm of the United States, tilted upward toward the sky. As an expansion of this concept, the collage roof surfaces are separated by an undulating 10-meter-wide walkway (inspired by the famous Route 66 built in 1926 to link Chicago to California). This pedestrian artery cuts diagonally across the site and carves out a processional in the center of the building, similar to a roadway passing through a canyon. The facilities located along this arcade include a main entrance to the exhibitions, shops, a restaurant, a theater, a variety of kiosks, and a series of electronically controlled information walls. In compliance with the Expo 2000 environmental policies, the building also includes demonstration exhibits of photovoltaic panels, solar collectors, fuel cells, wind power, and rammed earth construction. Theme-related exhibits extend the tapestry references throughout the interior spaces and exhibitions.

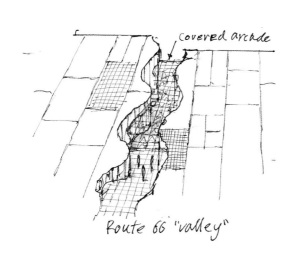

Route 66 "valley"

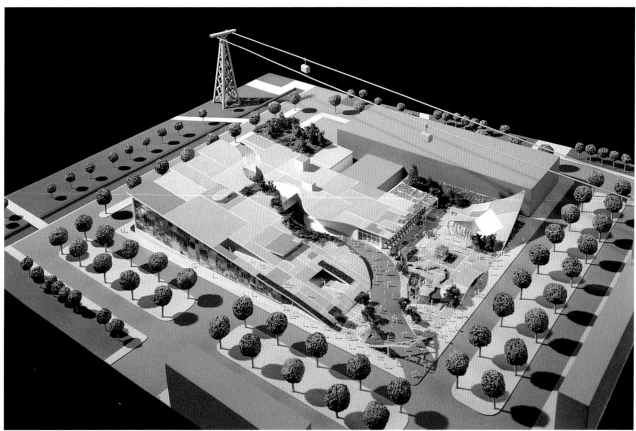

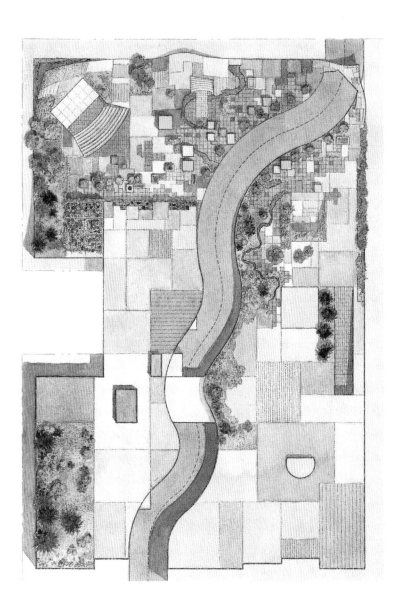

Route 66

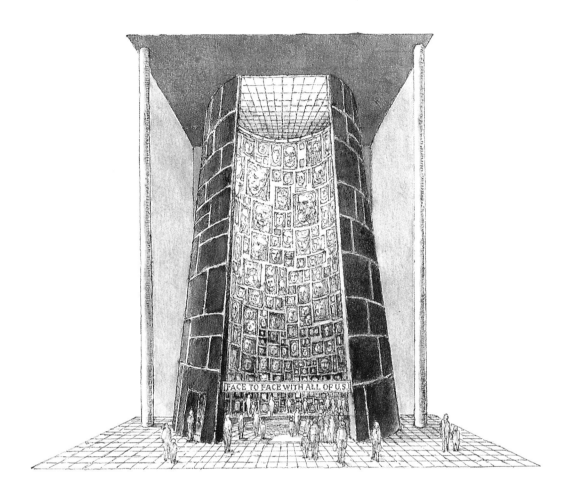

Metamorphosis – Flag becomes landscape

^ **Face to Face with all of U.S.**
Interactive American Rotunda.
The interior walls of this soaring
cathedral-like space are covered with a
grid of 2,000 photographs, film projections,
and video images of American faces, past
and present—representing all of the races,
professions, and countries of origin. Via
electronic communications and animation,
the images engage in conversations or
make personal statements about American
life. This people wall also includes
fragments of famous inspirational oratory.

> **James Wines, Gianni Pettena and Denise M C Lee**
Arsenale, Venice, Italy

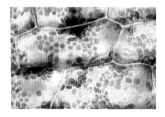

< **Kapok Tree**
Osa Peninsula, Costa Rica
2002

< **Graffiti**
New York City, USA
2003

< **Chlorophyll cell**
SITE Archives
2000

< **Home Depot**
Tampa, Florida, USA
2004

< **Suburbia Traffic and Billboards**
New York City, USA
2000

< **Vastu Purusha Mandala—Energy Grid**
SITE Archives

< **People**
Hong Kong, China
2002

< **The Great Stupa**
Sarnath, India
1997

> **Straight Line**
> Nazca, Peru
> 900 B.C. and 600 A.D.

> **Monkey**
> Nazca, Peru
> 900 B.C. and 600 A.D.

> **The Hanging Gardens of Babylon**
> Euphrates River Bank, Ancient
> Mesopotamia
> circa 600 B.C.

> **Cargo**
> SITE Archives
> 1990s

> **Target**
> Stripmall, Florida, USA
> 2003

> **Boot Shelter Signage**
> Stripmall, Florida, USA
> 2003

> **Egg Vendor**
> Hong Kong, China
> 2002

> **Starbucks and FedEx Reflections**
> New York City, USA
> 2004

> **Beverage Display**
> Hong Kong, China
> 2002

ON SITE'S DELIGHT

MICHAEL J. CROSBIE

In 1987, shortly after my wife and I moved to Connecticut, we went on a little shopping expedition at a stripmall in the town of Hamden, just north of New Haven. As I pulled into the parking lot of the Hamden Plaza, off to the left, in a corner of the lot facing the main drag, I spied a collection of about a dozen 1960s-era cars, slowly sinking into the pavement. They were covered completely with tar and asphalt—dark, mysterious, bulbous hulks that had once gleamed with chrome were now one with the lot. "SITE!" I chirped to my wife, "It's the Ghost Parking Lot!"

I quickly swung our car over toward the silent sentinels of the shopping mall to inspect SITE's 1978 piece of sculpture in the environment. The Ghost Parking Lot was littered with cigarette butts and broken beer bottles. It had obviously become a hang-out for kids, who I imagined squatting on this SITE landmark, just passing time with friends. My wife, who had grown up in the area, reported that these heaps were actually the remnants of car wrecks, or at least that's what she'd heard. Each one stood as a mock headstone to the teens who had perished in auto accidents.

In fact, the cars were from a junk yard, and Jim Wines and his collaborative SITE cohorts had placed them there not as a temperance lecture about the evils of drinking and driving. It was just the Ghost Parking Lot. It was cool. It made you stop and look and think. What you thought about it was your business, but it was important to SITE that you did not just cruise by and ignore it. The fact that the Ghost Parking Lot was now a hang-out made it even better. And it had become part of the local folklore. This, for SITE, has always been a hallmark of victory: creations that people get excited about, muse about, walk about—that make folks see their environment in a new way, like it or not.

I'm sorry to say that the Ghost Parking Lot is no more. In September of 2003, as part of a sprucing up of the Hamden Plaza, the piece was destroyed despite the efforts of an art history professor to raise funds for its restoration. Now there is nothing to challenge consumer sensibilities, no distractions to keep shoppers from going directly into the mall and getting right down to business. For that, it's a poorer place. The Ghost Parking Lot had such rich associations: the dominance of the car culture, the defiling of these shiny chariots under black grime, the wrecking of the environment with acres of asphalt and tons of pollution, even the creepy connection between these sinking autos and the comically macabre scene in *Psycho*, as Tony Perkins briefly panics when the car in which he has entombed the body of Janet Leigh halts its descent into a swamp, only to gurgle and finally slip beneath the reeds. It's the Ghost Parking Lot.

As an architect, James Wines expresses a brittle impatience with the navel-gazing of his fellow designers, who believe that architecture is all about formalism and paying daily homage to the canon of architectural ideas. Modernism is a solid piece of that canon, and the sorriest scene today is how Modern Revivalism masquerades as the avant-garde. Wines can watch the parade not far from his office window in lower Manhattan at 25 Maiden Lane, where SITE shares the second floor with the Modern Nails salon. A few blocks away, it's business as usual on the site of Ground Zero, where a Retro-Modern tower of indeterminate parentage is rising to prove to the world, once and for all, that we haven't learned much. Fireballs, anyone?

In his studio, above the hustle of Maiden Lane, the gregarious Wines holds forth. He and his chief collaborator, Denise M C Lee, are just finishing up a delightful little food kiosk for Madison Square Park, which blurs the lines between landscape and hardscape, architecture and agriculture. For this project, SITE has somehow distilled Daniel Burnham's towering Flatiron building and the garden setting, together, to create a hot-dog stand that looks as though it's being devoured by English Ivy.

∧ **Ghost Parking Lot**
SITE
Hamden, Connecticut, USA
2003

∧ **Highway 86 Processional**
SITE
Vancouver, British Columbia, Canada
1986 World Expo

∧ **Shake Shack**
SITE
New York City, USA
2004

∧ **BEST Terrarium Showroom**
SITE
South San Francisco, California, USA
1978

Wines' torrent of ideas, appraisals, and observations is punctuated by a deliciously villainous laugh (which you have already heard about from Tom Wolfe). Wines leans forward, slaps the table, and roars from behind a façade of Teddy Roosevelt teeth. His machine-gun patter riddles every conventional wisdom in sight. The M.O. of most artists is to question what they have just done, rip it up, and move in another direction, while architects pretty much lumber along in a linear fashion, moving on to the next logical step from project to project. While the so-called avant-garde wallows in an orgy of form-making, Wines sees a fascinating future in "non-volumetric" architecture—an architecture of electronics, media, and bytes—which he is still struggling to define.

"The building as sculpture has been the big idea," says this one-time sculptor, and it's a dead idea. Instead, Wines believes that you should experience something about a building that changes your perception of it. Maybe it's not a building at all. If architecture can possess the power to alter the way we perceive the environment around us, why can't it do that without creating volumes. The space it creates is inside our heads.

Wines mentions SITE's Highway 86 project for the 1986 World Expo in Vancouver as one that would mean nothing without the engagement of the observers. "Without the people, the project didn't exist. It had to be encrusted with people. It was architecture as a theatrical event. It's what it provokes—people doing their own thing. It's not a static object. It's like a stage-set." It fails, Wines notes proudly, what he calls "the pedestal test." You can't put it on a pedestal and call it sculpture. It's too complex, demanding, funky, unbridled. "If it looks like sculpture, get rid of it."

The biggest problem with architecture as sculpture, especially in the city, is that it doesn't age very well. Within the first 15 minutes of being finished, the building is already getting trashed, says Wines. The photographers move in and take their shots while the paint is drying, before the humans descend upon it and screw it all up. What kind of architecture is this?

It doesn't work for SITE. "We're interested in how people interact with the architecture," says Wines. "If they don't do something to it, it doesn't work. I prefer environments that don't disrupt everyday activity, that fit into the way people work and flow. How it inserts itself, how it evolves, and is interacted with. Architecture is far more interesting as a social act—how it displaces and brings things out of people. That's the neat stuff."

MICHAEL J. CROSBIE

Nothing communicates that messy engagement with the world as it exists as well as Jim's squiggly sketches. Wines is the Edward Koren of the architecture world. If Koren were an architect, instead of a cartoonist for *The New Yorker*, he'd draw like Wines. One of my favorite books of Wines is his sketch riff on Edward Lear's Nonsense. It's never clear in Jim's sketches where the project ends and the rest of the world begins, and that's just what he's after. No pristine reliquaries of the architectural canon here. SITE's creations put down roots, and they grow all over the place. Even in SITE's earliest work (the early-1970s) like the Peekskill Melt and a school courtyard in New York City, the projects are eroded, merging with the landscape. Others, like the Binghamton Dock and the Platte River Rest Stop heave surfaces into the air and twist them around. The BEST showrooms from the 1970s had all sorts of erosions, intrusions, fractures, peels, tilts, and rubble. Bridging the 1970s and 1980s, the Hialeah Showroom (best known as the "Rainforest Building") and the Forest Showroom reveal a decisive new direction of blurring the edges further and merging the building completely with the landscape. These buildings were an outgrowth of the BEST Terrarium Showroom that was never built—a project from 25 years ago that is as fresh, inventive, and brilliant today as it was then. Flip through any architecture fashion magazine today, with their projects converging architecture and landscape, and you will see echoes of that 1978 opus. It becomes more complex in the Ansel Adams Center, a 1985 competition-winning project, and leads right into such creations as Ross's Landing Park and Plaza and Avenue Number Five, SITE's creation for Seville's Expo 92.

The past decade has seen SITE's focus on sustainable architecture become sharper. Wines is right to complain that most green architecture today is too heavy on the engineering and too light on the poetry. No matter what the time, or the project, SITE has never shortchanged the poetry or the humor in its work. Those early BEST showrooms had both, and so does a new project for a house in Mumbai, India. Working along with Wines and Lee, Sara Stracey is the genius behind this project. It is a wonderful cross between the High-rise of Homes and the Hanging Gardens of Babylon, blooming on a stalk of steel cables. Just like the Ghost Parking Lot, it makes you smile, and it makes you think.

Michael J. Crosbie is an architect, critic, and the author of more than a dozen books about architecture.

∧ **Private Residential Tower**
SITE
Mumbai, India
2004

These two projects are interrelated examples of critical commentary on the post-industrial era of architecture, one positive and the other negative. United under the general title of "La Ville Radieuse," these proposals have been inspired by Le Corbusier's visionary city and his C.I.A.M. declarations of the 1930s. He rightfully appreciated the power of the sun as a motivating influence in urban design, but failed to foresee the consequences of fossil fuel (the sun's most over-exploited product), including the destructive impact of urban expansion and toxic waste pollution. Looking at "La Ville Radieuse" from a revised perspective, this project approaches "the sun as a source" through duel interpretations. The first proposal utilizes an existing cargo crane in the city's Arsenale property to mount a critique of the world's dependence on fossil fuels and the problems of congestion, health affliction, and physical entrapment in the contemporary city. A cargo net, hanging from the crane, is filled with black, oil-covered mannequins. This petroleum-soaked icon drips slowly and sporadically onto the mirror surface of an oil basin, installed at the base of the crane. The dark silhouette of the cargo net, suspended against the sky and reflected below, serves as a kind of "Ville Radieuse redux"—a microcosmic reminder of the industrial era and its ominous legacy of resource abuse. The second project provides a more optimistic sun theme—in this case, a celebration of urban agriculture. One of the primary deficiencies of most contemporary cities is their lack of integrated vegetation, in the form of roof gardens and farmlands. For health reasons, it is anticipated that this greening process will become more prevalent in the future. In Venice (as the ultimate water city) it seemed appropriate to create a moving garden that can travel throughout the canal system. Since the vaporetto is universally recognized as the primary means of Venetian transportation, it seemed appropriate to take advantage of its iconic presence as a support structure for the garden. The project is realized by filling exterior and interior sections of the vaporetto with soil and a variety of indigenous plants and crops. The environmental commentary of these projects is intended to draw attention to some of the urban issues that will inevitably challenge architects over the next decade.

^ Existing crane and docking area
Arsenale, Venice

...Man is in danger of being shown ultimately by nature who, in reality, is the conqueror, and who is conquered.
JOHN EAPS BROWN, *THE SPIRITUAL LEGACY OF THE AMERICAN INDIAN*

LA VILLE RADIEUSE

Project by SITE + I-Beam Design + Gianni Pettana Consortium, based on the Theme: "The City - More Ethics, Less Esthetics"

LA BIENNALE D' ARCHITETTURA • VENEZIA

L'Arsenale di Venezia - 15 Guigno a 15 Novembre, 2000

^ **Tree branches collected from hallway deforestation to be reused in exterior wall modules**

This master plan and Visitors Pavilion is designed for a 35-acre sculpture garden located on an island in the Chesapeake Bay. The purpose is to provide an exhibition environment for outdoor artworks, utilize the regional landscape, respect existing sculpture installations, and incorporate an earlier master plan as part of a new unified concept. The park is also planned as a matrix of varied spaces that will inspire artists to add site-specific works in the future. By engaging the forest, meadow, and waterfront the plan proposes a dramatic series of forest arcades and meadow-linked passageways. These processional-like features are the result of orchestrated planting, trimming bushes, and a clearing away of certain existing trees as part of the deforestation of the over-grown wooded area. This process opens up a

series of new exhibition spaces and sculpturally reconfigures the present topography with various mounds and surface markings. The Visitors Pavilion, inserted as an axial extension of one of the forest arcades, is designed to accommodate exhibit spaces, a lecture hall, a library, and executive offices. Various collections of branches, gathered from surrounding trees, are incorporated as an intrinsic part of the exterior walls. This "horizontal forest" effect is achieved by suspending the branches between a double layer of exterior glass and interior metal scrim partitions. In this way, all of the major innovations pertaining to architecture, exhibition facilities, and landscape are conceived as a single integrative work of environmental art.

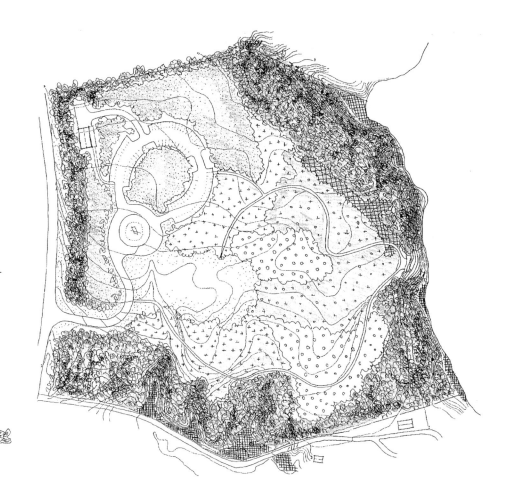

Site Analysis: Vegetation

Virginia Pine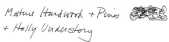

Pure Pine

Pine + Young Hardwood

Hardwood + Pine

Hardwood

Wetlands

Mature Hardwood + Pines
+ Holly Understory

Layers of vegetation and
trees along walkways

New Acquisition
– P.540, P.556 and P.316

Annmarie Garden
– Existing Parcel

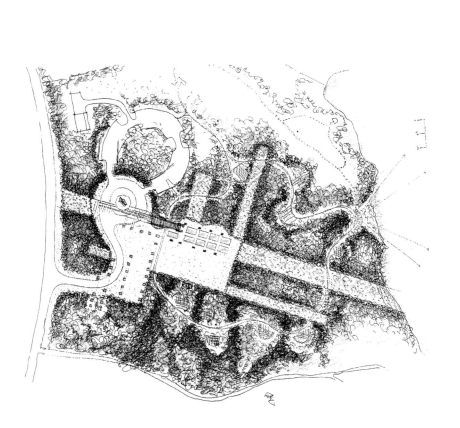

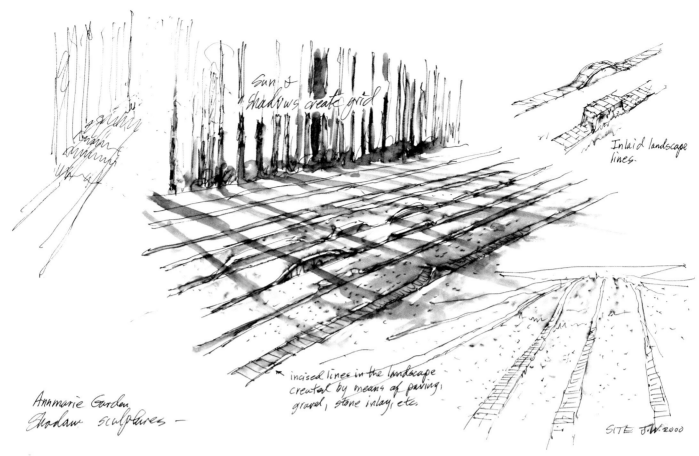

Sun & shadows create grid

Inlaid landscape lines.

incised lines in the landscape created by means of paving, gravel, stone inlay, etc.

SITE J.W. 2000

Annmarie Garden
Shadow sculptures —

Cathedral-like Forest rooms cut out of the tree canopy

Trellis enclosure

< **Donato Bramante Tempietto**
Little Temple
Rome, Italy
1508

< **Shadows**
Annmarie Garden

< **Hallway as Sculpture Room**
Annmarie Garden
2003

< **Juan Munoz, Marquette
Storage at Hirshhorn Gallery**
Washington D.C., USA
2002

< **Giocometti, Marquette
Storage at Hirshhorn Gallery**
Washington D.C., USA
2002

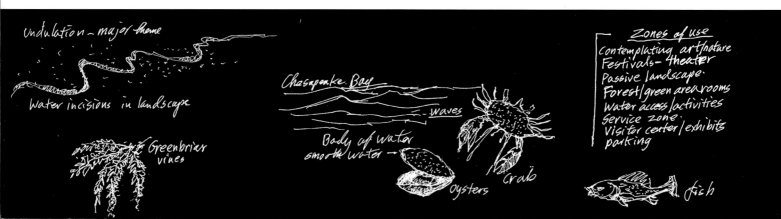

The Garden Pavilion is an example of integrative architecture—a fusion of art, building, landscape, and exhibition space—commissioned by Fondazione Rossini. Located on a hillside site, this structure is part of the master plan for a 150-square-meter sculpture garden. The concept includes a series of walls, used as a means of unifying the property and visually connecting various land parcels and artworks. The building design is a response to the surrounding landscape and characteristic topography of Briosco. Constructed out of stone, brick, glass, recycled metal, and other locally available materials, the wall system and Pavilion are bonded together by a network of cast stone T-shaped columns. These vertical units articulate a continuous ribbon-like structure, which flows along the crest of the hillside and evolves into the circular configuration of the building. The "T" columns offer a modularized means of exhibiting sculpture, providing rest areas, defining the functions of separate territories and establishing a unified scale reference for the entire property. For support purposes in the Pavilion, these vertical units are placed at strategic load-bearing points. Additional columns enclose the building with irregular and tilted clusters, which accent the "inside/outside" relationships and frame views of the distant mountains. In order to integrate the Pavilion with the hillside site and provide a year-round assurance of climate control, an earth-sheltered roof covers the entire structure.

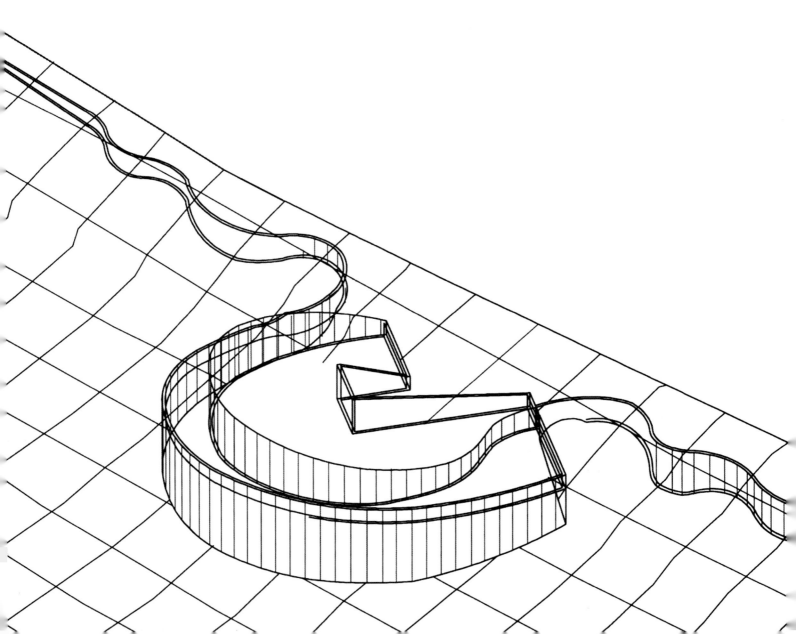

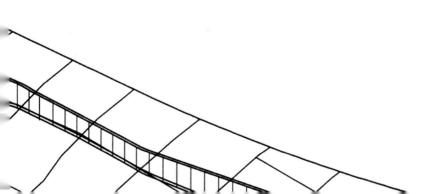

^ **Built Condition vs Design Model**

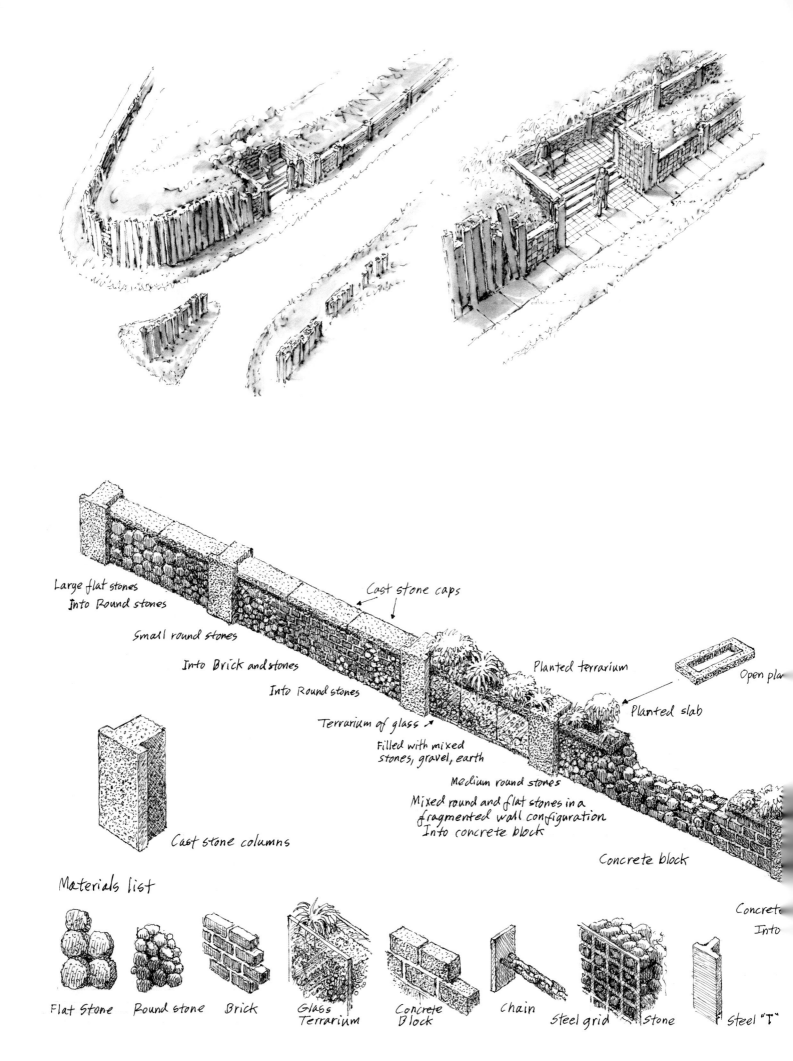

Large flat stones
Into Round stones

Cast stone caps

Small round stones

Into Brick and stones

Into Round stones

Planted terrarium

Open pla

Terrarium of glass

Planted slab

Filled with mixed
stones, gravel, earth

Cast stone columns

Medium round stones

Mixed round and flat stones in a
fragmented wall configuration
Into concrete block

Concrete block

Concrete

Into

Materials list

Flat Stone   Round stone   Brick   Glass Terrarium   Concrete Block   Chain   Steel grid   Stone   Steel "T"

typical configuration

Double "T" posts as a sculpture base

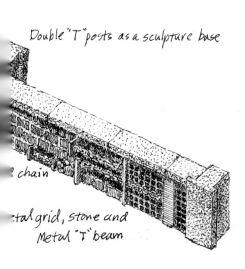

chain

tal grid, stone and
Metal "I" beam

^ **A Dream of Remembrance**
Juan Leal-Ruiz
2000

The Fabiani villa is situated on the crest of a mountain, overlooking Lake Maggiore and the Swiss Alps. The center of the property is covered with grass and low planting, while the north, south and west edges are enclosed by pines and evergreens. The orientation of the plan is intended to take advantage of east and southeast panoramic views. This 2,000-square-meter villa is designed in response to the client's vision of a place full of air and light—a house that seems perched for flight on the edge of the hillside. For this reason, the roof is composed of a series of undulating, wing-like structures in concrete that emerge from the

ground surface (partially covered with landscape) and then fan outward over the canyon below. While the client wants his residence to include the most advanced structural, environmental, and digital technology he also sees it as totally integrated with the agrarian characteristics of the surrounding community—including regional building materials and typical vegetation. Functionally, the Casa Fabiani includes very large social areas, an indoor swimming pool, sweeping deck space, guestrooms, a self-sufficient apartment, a state-of-the-art computer office, and ample guest parking.

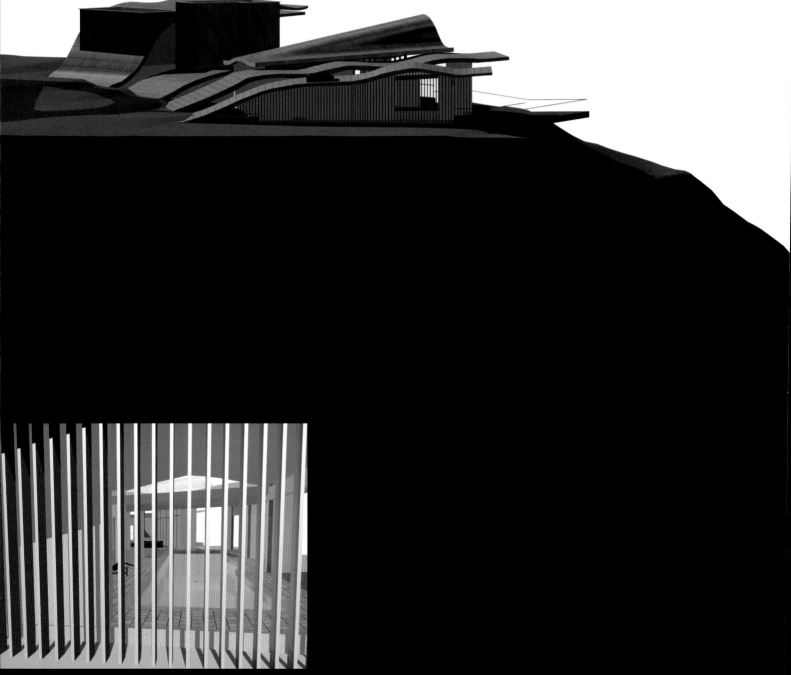

∧ **View through vertical louvre system into indoor swimming pool**

^ Partial view of site facing Lake Maggiore

^ Building elevation looking north

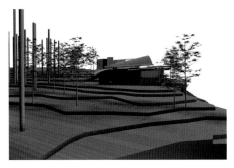

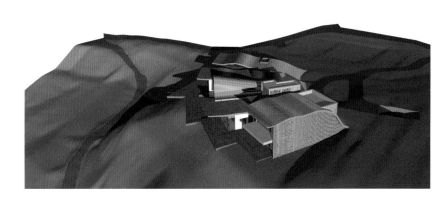

^ View from entrance vestibule at rolling
seatscape/fireplace as part of the living
environment

^ View from dining area with retractable wire mesh partition

FIRST FLOOR PLAN.dgn   08.27.2001   17.00

N

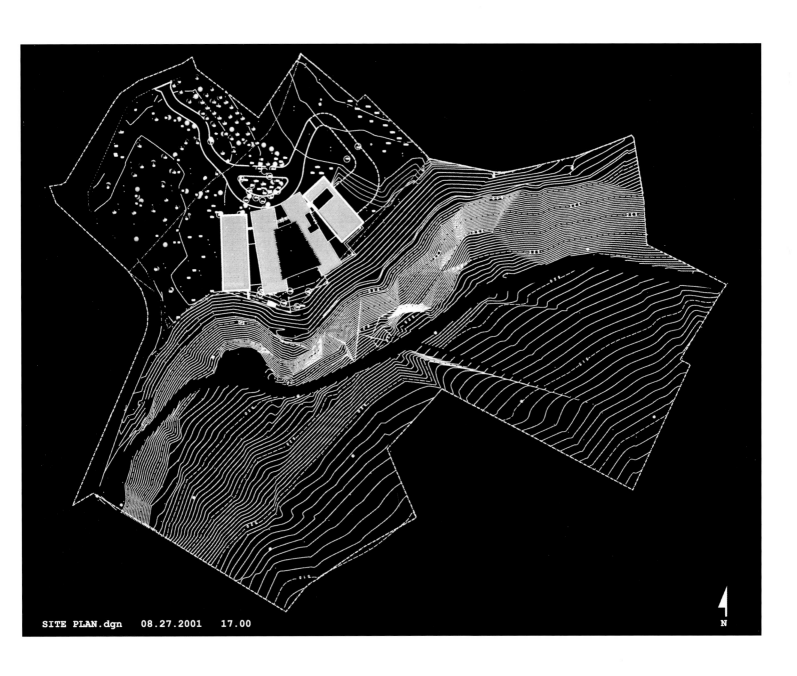

SITE PLAN.dgn   08.27.2001   17.00

N

182 183

The purpose of this master plan is to create an infinitely flexible matrix for varied uses and community enjoyment of the historic Railyard Park site. The intent is also to honor the railroad tradition, respect ecological and water shortage concerns, and provide an appropriate image for the City of Santa Fe. To accomplish these goals, the plan is designed as a microcosm of the regional landscape, as a model of a waffle garden system for the collection of the Park's rainwater, and as a graphic representation of the impact of the railroad on the history of the city. A 40-foot-square grid of various permeable paving materials and vegetation, articulated by eight-foot-wide walkways, defines the area surrounding a regional art museum and its adjacent public spaces. As the grid expands in a southwesterly direction, the walkways gradually lose their geometric configuration and become a series of fragmented ribbons—similar to railroad tracks leaving a city. The dematerializing grid provides areas for botanical displays, ecological demonstrations, historical exhibits, children's playgrounds, and commercial enterprises. In honor of the railroad history, all of its associated artifacts—track sections, wooden ties, box cars, passenger cars, seating units, engines, undercarriages, wheels, couplings, cargo handling equipment, remnants of trestles, etc—are converted to exhibition facilities, performance stages, bandstands, playground equipment, restaurants, and cafes. This is accomplished by the adaptive re-use of train cars and track sections — dissecting them for various purposes and creating collage interventions out of the fragments.

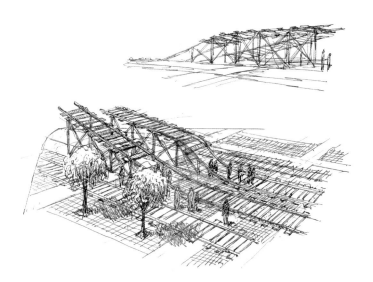

∧ **Aerial perspective of the park connecting with the various neighborhoods**

> **SITE Santa Fe team researching neighborhood**
> **connections to the site**

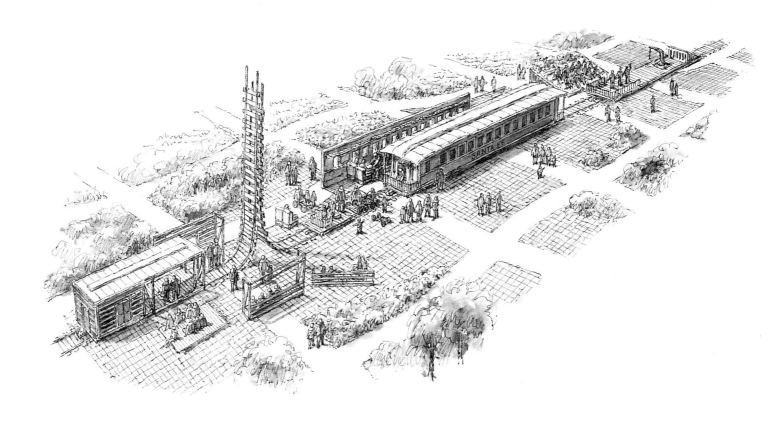

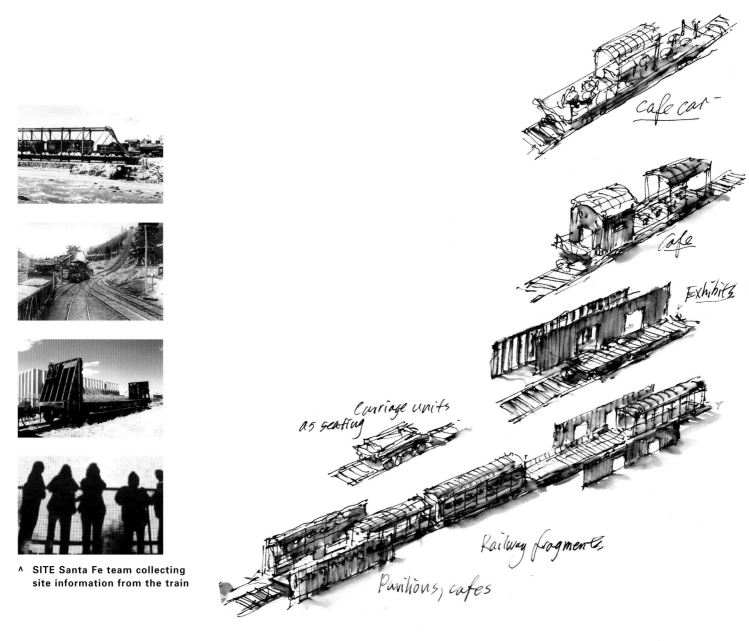

^ SITE Santa Fe team collecting
site information from the train

cafe car

cafe

Exhibits

Carriage units
as seating

Railway fragments

Pavilions, cafes

Rail ladder

∧ Rail ladders as central beacon
Lifted rail-lines forming shade structures for cultural
corridor. De-constructed rail cars (in background) as
shade structure and entry to children's play area

Ivy covered trellis

Ponderosa forest   stage   stone wall   grass mound
Section

^ Acequia Madre runs through City of Santa Fe
Santa Fe, New Mexico, USA
2002

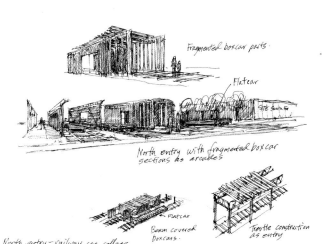

Fragmented boxcar parts.

Flatcar

SF Santa Fe

North entry with fragmented boxcar
sections as arcades

Flatcar

Beam covered
boxcars.

Trestle construction
as entry

North entry - railway car collage
elements as covered walkways

> Adaptive re-use of a watertower found in nearby scrap yard to house Blue-Blood by James Turrell, 1988—a pyramidal structure reminiscent of ancient celestial monuments built by Egyptian, Mayan, and Celtic peoples (as well as those by artists Michael Heizer and Nancy Holt). From the SITE Santa Fe collection located adjacent to park

^ Model showing waffle water collection system and rail car siding forming retaining wall to the bicycle and pedestrian pathway

> Model of shade structure along existing railway as connecting device between park and plaza

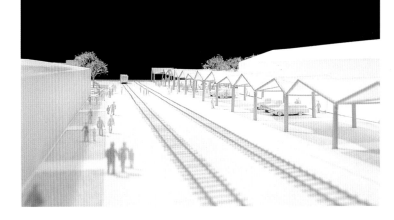

New World Trade Center - Memorial Areas

Thin laser beams of light at night.

Waterwall and pine forest Memorial.

SITE's proposal for a New World Trade Center was part of a special exhibition at the Max Protetch Gallery in New York. In response to the tragic events of September 11th and the need for a re-birth of the community surrounding the terrorist attack, this concept is based on replacing the rigidity and lack of human scale in the original WTC plan with a more flexible alternative. The intention is to re-establish Lower Manhattan's highly successful patterns of organic neighborhood development, commercial variety, and cultural diversity. The features of the SITE project are:

- Resurrect the former Lower Manhattan east/west and north/south street connections as the basis of a new site plan (disrupted by construction of the original World Trade Center).

- Create an inherently flexible master plan for the site that invites evolution and change, allows for mixed-use development, and encourages a strong representation of New York's ethnic diversity.

- Eliminate the inflexible concept of mega-skyscrapers and vast open spaces in favor of a variety of closely spaced mid-rise story buildings.

- Encourage sustainable architecture and resource-saving green design principles in all new construction for the site.

- Provide a variety of parks, plazas, and roof gardens throughout the new WTC community.

- Place two memorial landscapes in the footprint areas where the WTC towers once stood—to commemorate the police officers and firemen who lost their lives.

- Create an illuminated water wall and reflecting pool that honors the names of all the WTC victims, celebrates the value of water during the rescue and cleanup operations, and recognizes the natural phenomena of the tidal movement.

- Plant seven memorial tree lines that radiate outward from the center of the New World Trade Center site toward Harlem, the Bronx, Queens, Long Island, Brooklyn, Staten Island, and New Jersey and encourage continuing participation on a global scale. These satellite memorials pay tribute to all of New York through the planting of one memorial tree along the seven lines for every civilian life lost.

< SITE Change of Address Announcement— sent prior to September 11th
25 Maiden Lane (looking west towards Cortland Street), New York City, USA

> Memorial Detail
Water wall with illuminated names inscribed. Tree memorial beyond and reflecting pool. Water channeling from the Hudson River will dictate the flow rate of water according to the tidal pattern. Here marks the center of origin of the Satellite Tree Memorial.

PROPOSED FUNCTIONS :

- Green Plaza Area
- Tree of Life Memorial
- Water Wall Memorial
- Mixed Use Buildings
- Multi-Use Blocks
- Cultural/Recreational
- Commercial Retail
- Hotel Facilities
- Residential Buildings

> **SITE master plan**

^ **Postings of missing persons at Rays Pizza**
West Village, New York City, USA
September 13, 2001

^ **Connecting Building Overpass**
Duane Street, New York City, USA
2001

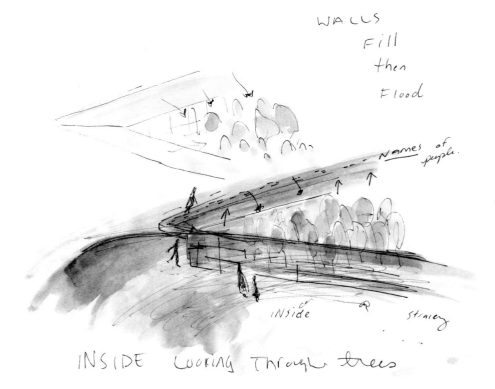

WALLS
Fill
then
Flood

Names of people.

inside   stairey

INSIDE Looking Through trees

September 11 is being described as "the day that changed the world forever." If our nation really means to take this statement seriously, then a period of profound evaluation of priorities is due in all fields of human endeavor, not just the building arts. At the heart of this revolution there is a need for the questioning of everything we Americans have always assumed was good for the people, good for the economy, good for the country and good for the world. This re-thinking initiative, particularly as applied to the design of the New World Trade Center, is a very good place to start.

SITE

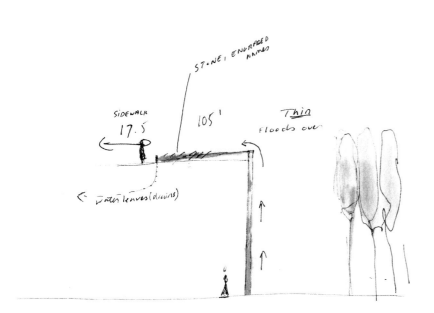

∧ Street level approach—proposed skywalks
as connectors between buildings

To commemorate the destruction of the World Trade Center, the Staten Island community sponsored a competition for a memorial, to be located in an existing park area of the island overlooking downtown Manhattan. At the time of this competition, SITE had already created a proposal in 2001 for the WTC area, honoring the loss of human lives by means of water walls, pine forests, and a satellite system of seven radiating pine tree plantings in each borough of the city (one tree for every victim of 9/11). For this reason, it seemed appropriate to use the Staten Island competition as the first satellite memorial. The reason for the pine forest choice is based on public opinion—since more than 80% of Americans prefer a 9/11 commemorative park to a monument or a real estate development. Also, trees and water provide a living, evolving tribute that engages all of the human senses. Applying the satellite tree concept to Staten Island, the SITE concept proposes 267 memorial pines to represent the lost community members. In addition, there is the same number of vertical glass columns, bearing names and family inscriptions for each

victim. These columns, in terms of placement and variable height, are intended to recall the lost reflection of the Twin Towers on the Hudson River and Lower Bay. The height of each column varies according to the age of the person being commemorated. Also, 78 columns stand five feet higher than the rest, as a tribute to the uniformed personnel of the NYFD, NYPD, and PAPD. At night, the colonnade becomes a radiant forest, with a single beam of light emanating from each column penetrating the night sky and illuminating the name of each 9/11 victim. This sea of light creates an ephemeral vision on the horizon and, in the spirit of the memorial pines, constantly changes with the passage of night and day. A windbreaker marks the point of entry and anchors the memorial site to Staten Island. Two steel plaques honor the Borough of Staten Island and announce the adjacent memorial. A series of flanking, rough-hewn, wood walls allow family members and visitors to leave behind their own inscriptions and personal artifacts at the memorial site.

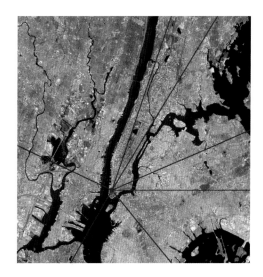

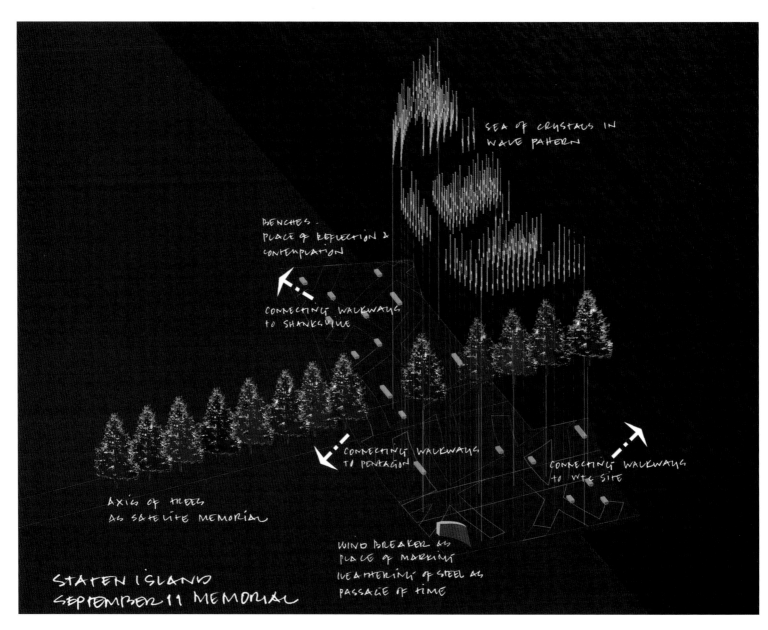

SEA OF CRYSTALS IN
WAVE PATTERN

BENCHES.
PLACE OF REFLECTION &
CONTEMPLATION

CONNECTING WALKWAYS
TO SHANKSVILLE

CONNECTING WALKWAYS
TO PENTAGON

CONNECTING WALKWAYS
TO WTC SITE

AXIS OF TREES
AS SATELITE MEMORIAL

WIND BREAKER AS
PLACE OF MARKING

WEATHERING OF STEEL AS
PASSAGE OF TIME

STATEN ISLAND
SEPTEMBER 11 MEMORIAL

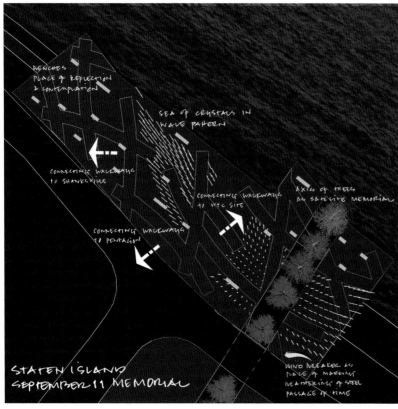

BENCHES.
PLACE OF REFLECTION
& CONTEMPLATION

SEA OF CRYSTALS IN
WAVE PATTERN

CONNECTING WALKWAYS
TO SHANKSVILLE

CONNECTING WALKWAYS
TO WTC SITE

AXIS OF TREES
AS SATELITE MEMORIAL

CONNECTING WALKWAYS
TO PENTAGON

WIND BREAKER AS
PLACE OF MARKING
WEATHERING OF STEEL AS
PASSAGE OF TIME

STATEN ISLAND
SEPTEMBER 11 MEMORIAL

as I move closer, the soft glow crystallizes.
a sea of reflection and refraction shimmering
in harmony with the rippling water

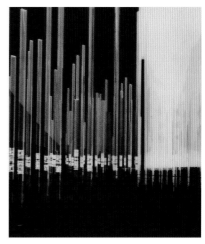

^ Satellite Memorial

^ Conceptual Sketch

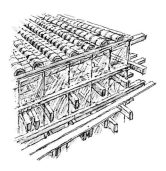

The client for this family house in Rome requested a spacious living environment and swimming pool to be placed on a relatively small (5,000-square-meter) property in the Olgiata section of Rome. In order to provide the desired size of the residence on a restricted site, the design is conceived as an integrated, above and below ground experience with various inventive means for bringing light into the lower sections. Since the orientation of the land parcel is not ideal for sunlight penetration, the pool is located in a lateral position (relative to the front of the property) as a means of minimizing cast shadows and taking advantage of the southern exposure. To accommodate this innovation, the house is split apart in the center—with separate units connected by a bridge—allowing the pool to pass through the middle of the building. In this way, the main social space of the villa becomes a piazza-like centerpiece, as opposed to a backyard appendage. To create an integrative image for the building, forest-like walls of bamboo columns pass from outside to inside in an undulating continuum of clustered, tilted and irregularly spaced vertical units. The windows, situated behind this arbitrary rhythm of columns, provide floor to ceiling illumination. Large bamboo trees and lush regional vegetation define the edges of the property, hiding the house from public view in front and opening it up in the back for a lawn, patio, and panoramic views of a golf course, framed by distant woods.

^ **Two Roofscapes—**
Typical Chinese Siheyuan roofs found in Beijing and typical Roman tiled roofs and traditional Japanese vernacular architecture—wall composition

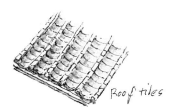

Roof tiles

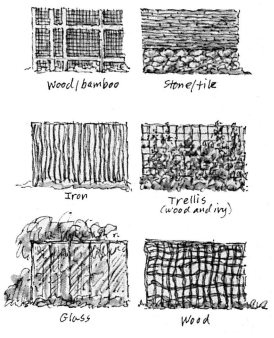

wood/bamboo   Stone/tile

Iron

Trellis (wood and ivy)

Glass   wood

INSIDE/OUTSIDE WALLS

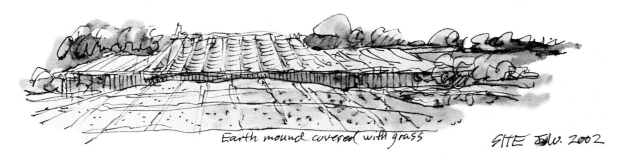

Earth mound covered with grass   SITE Jan. 2002

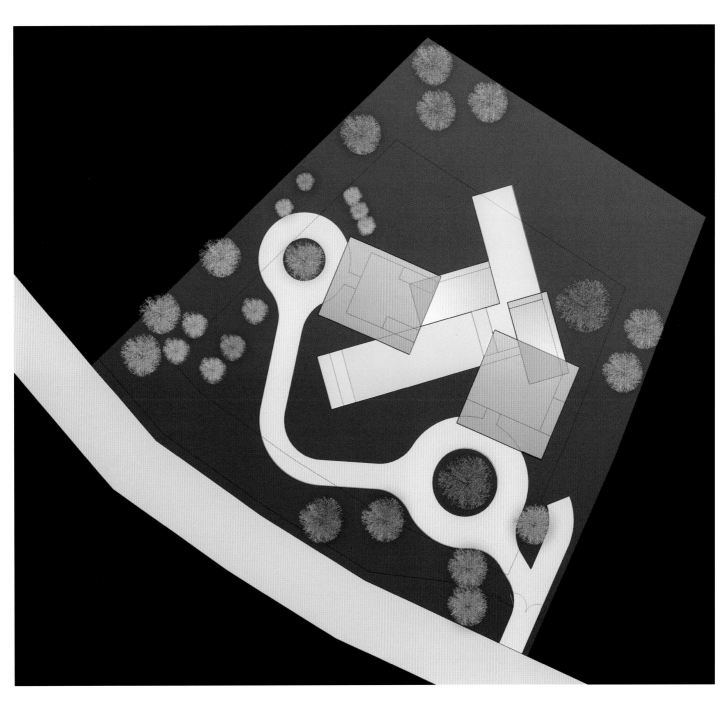

> **Wild Bamboo Grove**
> Olgiata, Italy
> 2003

> **Bamboo Scaffolding**
> Hong Kong
> 2003

> **Location of pool determined by sun/shade study for receiving maximum sunlight. Buildings shown sided with bamboo brise soleil for cooling and shading of the structure. Transparent bridge above pool, connecting the guest and private wings**

^ **Plant life reference for mosaic tiling**
Rajasthan, India

^ **Existing condition showing ventilation
ducts along retaining wall**

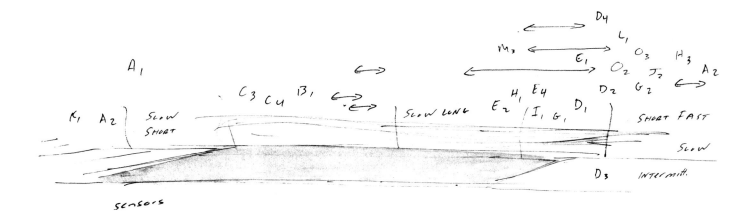

This permanent installation project acts as a vitalizing remedy to the existing condition of a stagnant and static subterranean swimming pool environment. It is also to disguise an exposed ventilation ductwork system that invades the interior pool area of a private residence. The solution uses semi-translucent plastic strips to construct a woven, fabric-like wall of interlocking ribbons. These modules of undulating strips are mounted over a series of pistons that are activated by motion sensors along the lap pool. This movement of the translucent ribbons creates a kinetic (breathing) wall, which is similar to the ripple effects on the surface of the water. The bottom of the pool is covered with a rich pattern of mosaic tiles, which suggest a tropical garden by catching refractions of light and shadow from the ribbon wall. This ensemble of elements transforms a dark and rather oppressive recreational area into a facility full of light and movement.

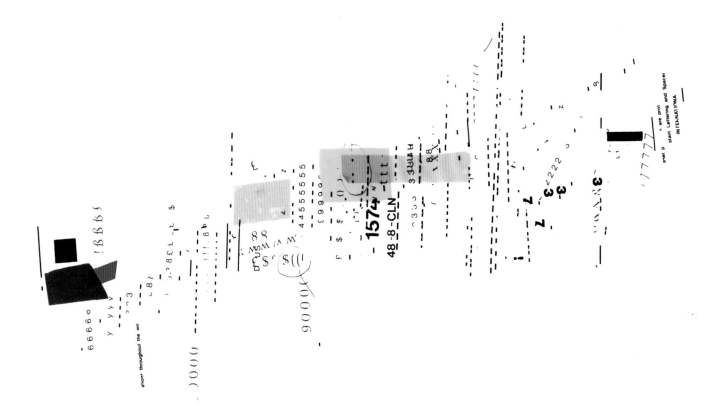

This Manhattan office space has been created for the hedge fund that emphasizes transparency and communication in its investment process. The space was planned to facilitate and aesthetically reflect these values. A series of glass walls define the space, with one 55 foot by 9 foot lateral division spanning the length of the interior on a slight angle allowing for an open passageway between the front and back rooms. The central focal point is a large holographic projection on glass showing moving financial information.

By definition, Xerion is the "elixir of life," an alchemist's material that transforms common unappreciated or unrecognized bases. Along both sides of the long glass wall a deeply shadowed, nonlinear, crystalline tide ascends. The layered signs and symbols are formed from traces of feedback loops, food chains, bubbles, channels, self-references, price points, growth charts, currency, etc—a financially fabled, timeless economy-scape at once converging and swarming, rising, and falling—oceanic and tide-like; it is witness to its cyclical and infinite nature.

All the people that love the great-simplified dream, in front of a sky that is nothing but the world of "transparency," will understand the vanity of "apparition." For them, "transparency" will be the most realistic appearance. It will give them the intimate lesson of lucidity.

YVES KLEIN

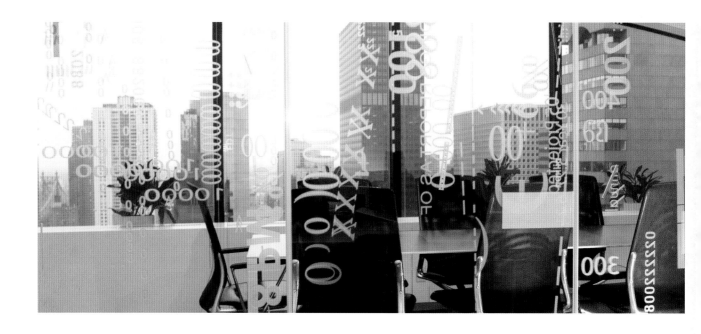

Simply I thought of the idea of a projection of an invisible fourth dimension, something you could not see with you own eyes.

MARCEL DUCHAMP

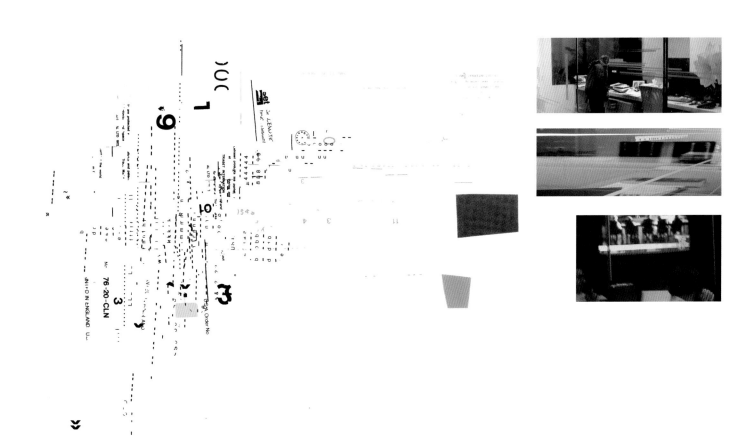

This small food kiosk is designed for the historic Madison Square Park in New York City. The concept responds to several important features of the surrounding community—the triangular shape of Daniel Burnham's Flatiron Building, the plan of the historic park, the profusion of vegetation, and the festive atmosphere that prevails during all seasons. The kiosk is designed to serve typical American hot dogs, hamburgers, milk shakes, and other simple lunch items. A large shade trellis, with English ivy that also covers an inclined roof and the entire back wall, unifies the 486-square-foot building. Since the image of a fast food stand is indelibly associated with American commercial strip architecture, it seemed logical to create a kiosk that combines this popular culture reference with the elegance of Burnham's nearby skyscraper and pastoral atmosphere of the park. To give the kiosk a feeling of lightness, the service counters and kitchen areas are completely enclosed by glass. This feature makes the top sections of the structure appear to float in space—opening up views of the surrounding trees, seen through the building. The corrugated zinc façade material is intended to reflect the color and rib-like surfaces of the Flatiron Building. The general intention of this design is to provide a food kiosk for Madison Square Park that becomes a miniature park in itself.

^ **Ivy covered façade**
West Village, New York City, USA
2004

^ **Taylors Refresher**
Napa Valley, California, USA

^ **Flatiron Building**
23rd Street & 5th Avenue, New York City, USA
2003

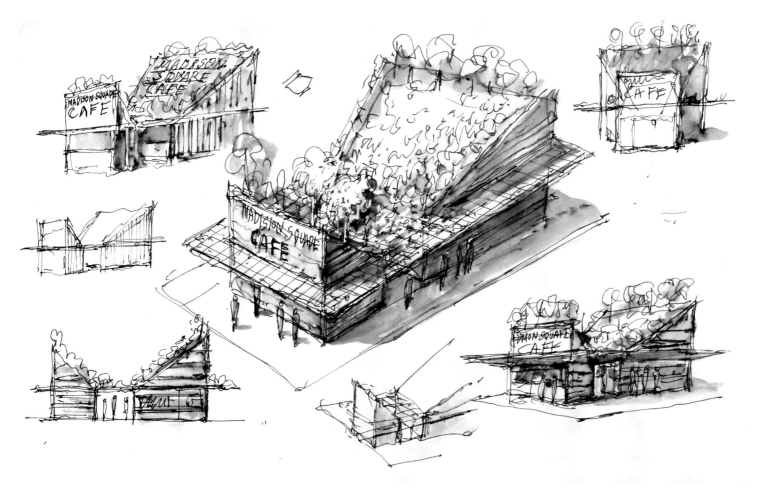

The Human Body and mind are complex instruments, which communicate, absorb, expand and get consumed in nature. Nature, Man and Vastu are the natural evolutionary extensions of one another, forming a complete whole.

PROF. B.B. PURI, *APPLIED VASTU IN MODERN ARCHITECTURE*

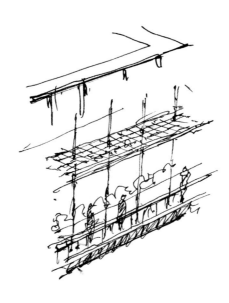

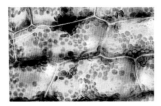

^ Water and Air Plants
SITE Archives

^ Photosythesis Diagram
SITE Archives

This Residential Tower in Mumbai, India is designed as a garden in the sky. The concept is based on an ancient and continuing tendency among cultures internationally to free landscape from its earthbound confinement. The structure also reflects SITE's long-standing interest in the celebrated Hanging Gardens of Babylon, built in 600 B.C.

In developing a design approach, our team responded to the principles of historic Vedic architecture of India—particularly, the classic relationships between science, landscape, and the human body—which translate into the treatment of buildings as extensions of the natural environment. We acknowledged that the Vastu-purusha mandala (Hindu symbol of creation) has traditionally been designed to express the connections between dwelling space, planetary forces, and physical/spiritual energy within the body.

The tower is based on a stratified structural spine, reinforced by a series of steel cables that support five "floating" floor planes and a variety of interim garden tiers, terraces, trellises, viewing platforms, water features, and recreational facilities. In addition to stabilizing the floor planes, the cable system can also be utilized as a matrix for various species of

vegetation, protective monsoon screens, and festive lighting apparatus. The visual effect is intended to appear as if the floor planes and their interim strata are suspended in space. All of the horizontal elements emerge from an axial structure, like the vertebrae of a spinal column. This vertical core provides a thematic point of reference—offering an infinite variety of projections for artistic, horticultural, recreational, and practical uses, which include seating, storage, shade vestibules, light filtration, weather protection, multi-level planting, and private areas for contemplation. While the spine serves as the main source of support, it also acknowledges the Vastu-purusha concepts of enlightenment and the connections between structure, nature, and spirituality.

Within the main residence, on the top floor, the vertebrae and stratification themes are interpreted as a series of inside/outside elements—sunscreens, canopies, suspended ceilings, scrim-like walls, etc—each contributing to a more intimate human scale. Located on a 4,000-square-meter plane, with helipad, the surrounding garden is intended as a showcase of botanical variety in India.

The interior includes a large, glass-enclosed living area that takes advantage of the most spectacular panoramic views of Mumbai and the sea. In keeping with Vastu-purusha, the central atrium (as the Brahma, or genesis of life) is oriented on a precise north/south and east/west axis, which also allows light to penetrate all floors from above.

The structural system is based on a concrete backbone, supporting a series of cantilevered concrete-encased steel-frame slabs. High strength cables, hanging from a steel mega-truss under the residential platform, support these slabs. When the concrete core is complete, this truss is assembled at ground level and elevated by crane to the top tier, where it is then used as a platform from which to lift the intermediate floors into their final location. This innovation simplifies the building process and eliminates the need for an on-site crane during the major part of construction.

The form and configuration of the tower maximizes the potential for energy conservation and environmental responsibility. In response to various hot/humid climate issues, the construction materials are chosen, treated and encased to maximize the longevity of their life cycle and prevent deterioration.

The project incorporates a series of prototypical solutions, for example: light shelves providing reflected sunlight and reducing the need for artificial illumination during the day; double glass skins with air cavities for cooling; ventilation tubes to capture rising warm air and exhaust it to the outdoors; moveable southwest and northeast roof louvres as protection from midday and late afternoon sunlight; solar and photovoltaic panels for supplemental power and hot water.

According to the Chakra meanings of architecture, the zones of a building are symbolically linked to earth, water, fire, air, sound, light, and knowledge. For this Residential Tower, these seven elements are thematically orchestrated as; KNOWLEDGE (top level—residence and formal gardens); LIGHT (level six—blooming flower gardens); SOUND (level five—family garden and play areas); AIR (level four—garden of the senses and botanical study center); FIRE (level three—private entertainment area and dining); WATER (level two—swimming pool and health club); EARTH (level one—entertainment areas and gardens of delight).

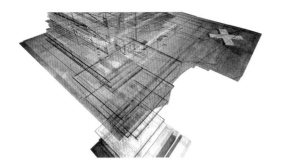

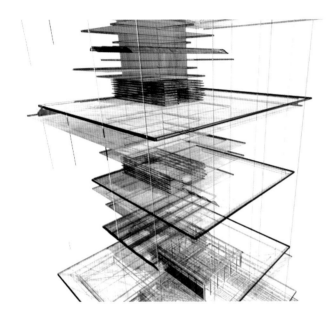

> **Munich's Crystal Palace**
> SITE Archives

> **Cable Detail**
> SITE Archives

> **Water Level/Landscape Terrace 2 Reference**
> SITE Archives

From an aesthetic standpoint, the parallel partitions of the floor planes create a "mille feuille" effect against the sky. They reduce the thickness of the individual floor slabs and provide a means of capturing the most advantageous qualities of light and shade during all hours of the day. The horizontally of the strata—in counterpoint with the verticality of the tower—can be seen as a 21st century interpretation of the "tiers of life" imagery found in ancient Hindu architecture.

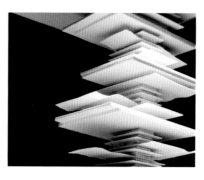

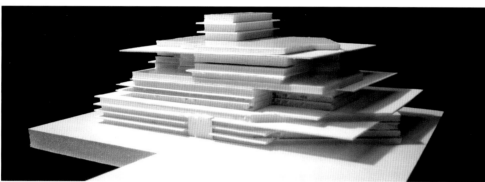

Mille Feuille/concentric banding
Concept for floor planes to form a harmonic landscape, and from this folded and layered topography fluid spaces for vegetation and living

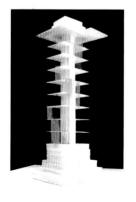

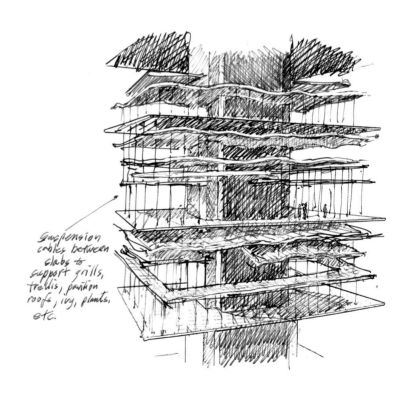

suspension cables between slabs to support grills, trellis, pavilion roofs, ivy, plants, etc.

Hoyaleswara Temple—Banding Detail
Halebid, India

Vertical Section of Hindu Temple
Similar to that of the tonic and a musical composition

Building with Water
Water being channeled for collection; heaviest after seasonal monsoons

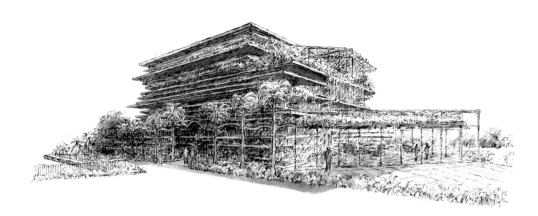

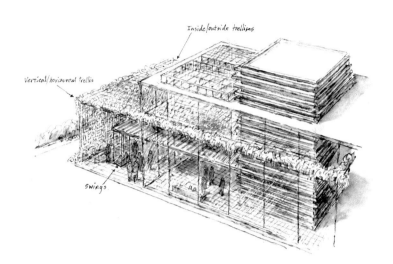

Inside/outside trellises

Vertical/horizontal trellis

Swings

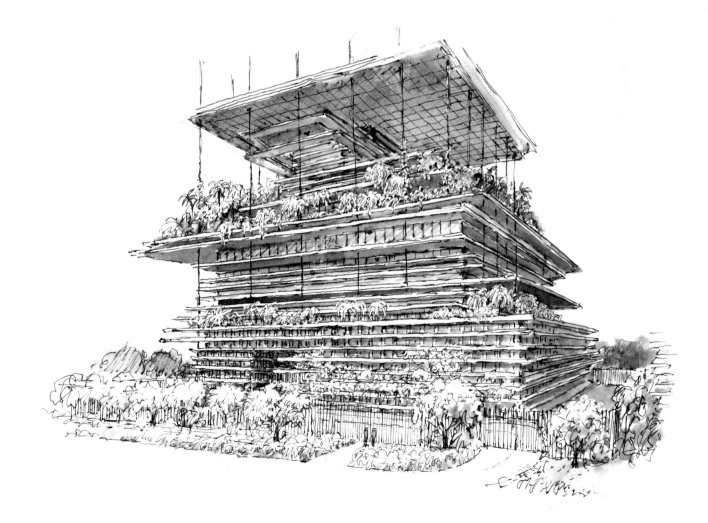

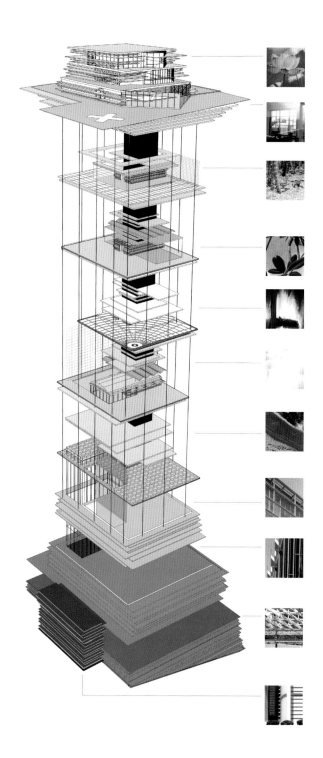

The spine is a long downward extension of the subconscious. At the base of the spine, the outward-flowing energy becomes locked at its south pole, where it is referred to as kundalini. The north pole, at the top of the cranium, is the sahasrara ("thousand petaled lotus").

SWAMI KRIYANANDA

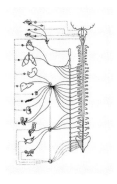

^ **Axonometric—Garden Themes and Environmental Studies**

< **Vertical Spine/Organ Diagram**
SITE Archives

Vastu Purusha Mandala is the clearest model of the universe. In Vedic language, it is called Shunya, meaning absolute void—and Bindu, the seed, the source of all energy. Square means the earth, while circle denotes the universe. Vastu means environment, matter, or a building.

PROF. BAL SAINI, LECTURE ON VASTU PURUSHA MANDALA, BRISBANE 1998

Trellis Structure

Outdoor Dining area —vista

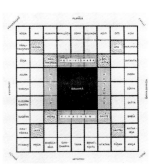

∧ **Vastu Purusha Mandala
the Vedic Building—
Energy—Diagram**
SITE Archives

♢ ——— SPACE
☽ ——— AIR
△ ——— FIRE
⊖ ——— WATER
⊡ ——— EARTH

∧ **Lord Ganesh/Elephant God is formed
with the stacking of the vertical
corresponding element symbols**
SITE Archives

The construction of a domestic building is something like the birth of a human being—who according to the time and place of birth will come under certain astrological influences throughout life.

At the time of construction the place and position of the structure are all important factors for the future of the building.

STELLA KRAMRISCH, *THE HINDU TEMPLE*

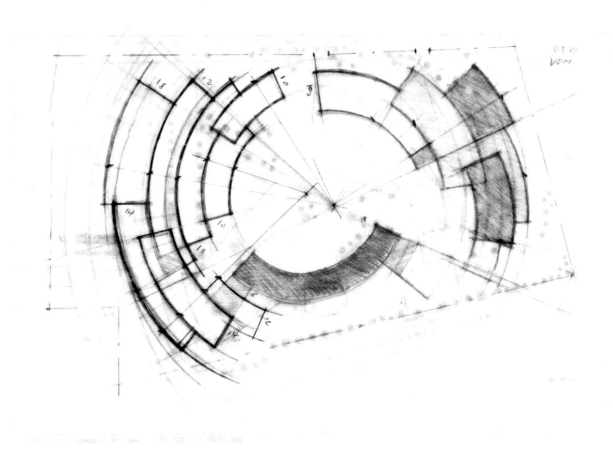

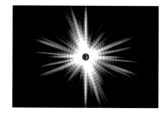

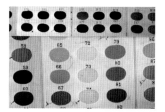

This corporate headquarters is proposed as a garden city for an industrial corporation in India. The plan includes offices and apartments, accommodates an existing curvilinear office building and responds to the client's intention to preserve all of the major trees on the site. The company also requested a complex that reflects the message of its corporate mission; "Growth is Life."
In response, the structure will be built as a green (LEED standard) headquarters, utilizing regional materials and energy efficient technology. The buildings are designed as a series of curved structures, surrounding a central garden. This public space also serves as a division between the working and living environments. The entire area in front of the existing building and the south section of the site are proposed as large parks, with heavily forested sections and a lush pattern of ground cover. The multi-tiered composition of the buildings provides outdoor terraces, roof gardens, and courtyards for the penetration of light. The façades of the buildings include a variety of shade devices—trellis structures, sculptural protrusions, canopies, awnings, and tile-covered arcades—that create a pattern of horizontal ribbons. These tiered elements also produce aesthetically pleasing light and shadow patterns on the walls. The corporate headquarters side of the complex is higher on the southwest elevation as a way of providing additional protection during the monsoon season. Also, the residential building steps downward toward the northeast to take advantage of more daylight. By developing the five-acre site as a fusion of gardens and buildings, these new headquarters reflect SITE's philosophy of "integrative thinking." This concept refers to architecture as a response to the parallels between the interdependent elements found in nature and the reciprocal structure of today's communication systems and digital technology.

< **Visual arts such as painting found in India use Mandalas with three basic elements namely, a dot, a square, and a circle. The dot is constant and represents the dead center of the Energy vortex. Square means the Earth, while circle denotes the universe.**

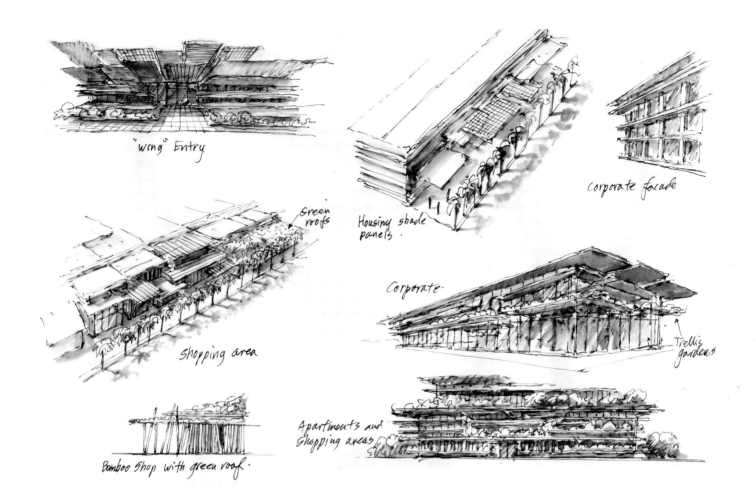

"wing" Entry

corporate facade

Green roofs

Housing shade panels.

Corporate.

Trellis gardens

Shopping area

Apartments and shopping areas

Bamboo shop with green roof.

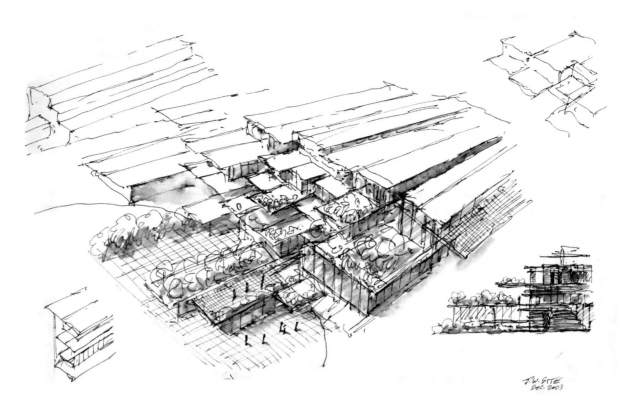

वनोपान्तनदीशैलनिर्झरोपान्तभूमिषु ।
रमन्ते देवता नित्यं पुरेषूद्यानवत्सु च ॥

The gods always play where groves are near, rivers, mountains and springs, and in towns with pleasure gardens.
BRHAT SAMHITA, I. V. 8, BHAVISYA PURANA, I. CXXX. 15, STELLA KRAMRISCH, *THE HINDU TEMPLE*

A man who does a work of architecture does it as an offering to the spirit of architecture—a spirit which knows no style, knows no techniques, no method.

There is architecture, and it is the embodiment of the unmeasurable.

LOUIS KAHN, 1969
ON ENERGY: ON SITE PUBLICATIONS 1974

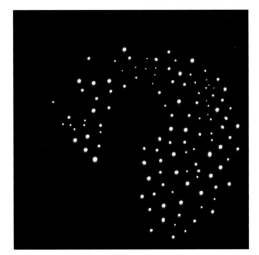

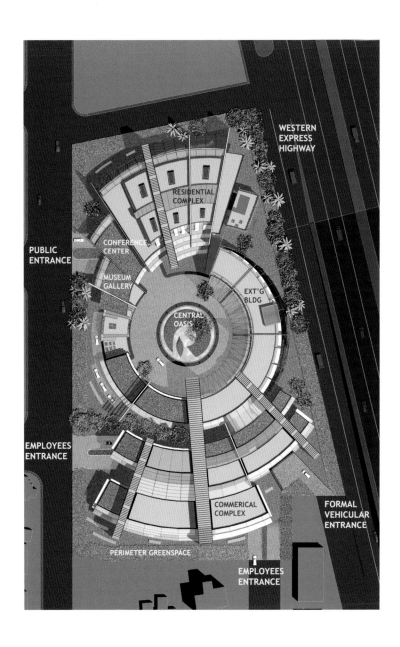

^ **LED Type Lighting**
The company logo to come into clear form when viewed from air and land. The lights appear to be woven as part of the building both artificial and natural.

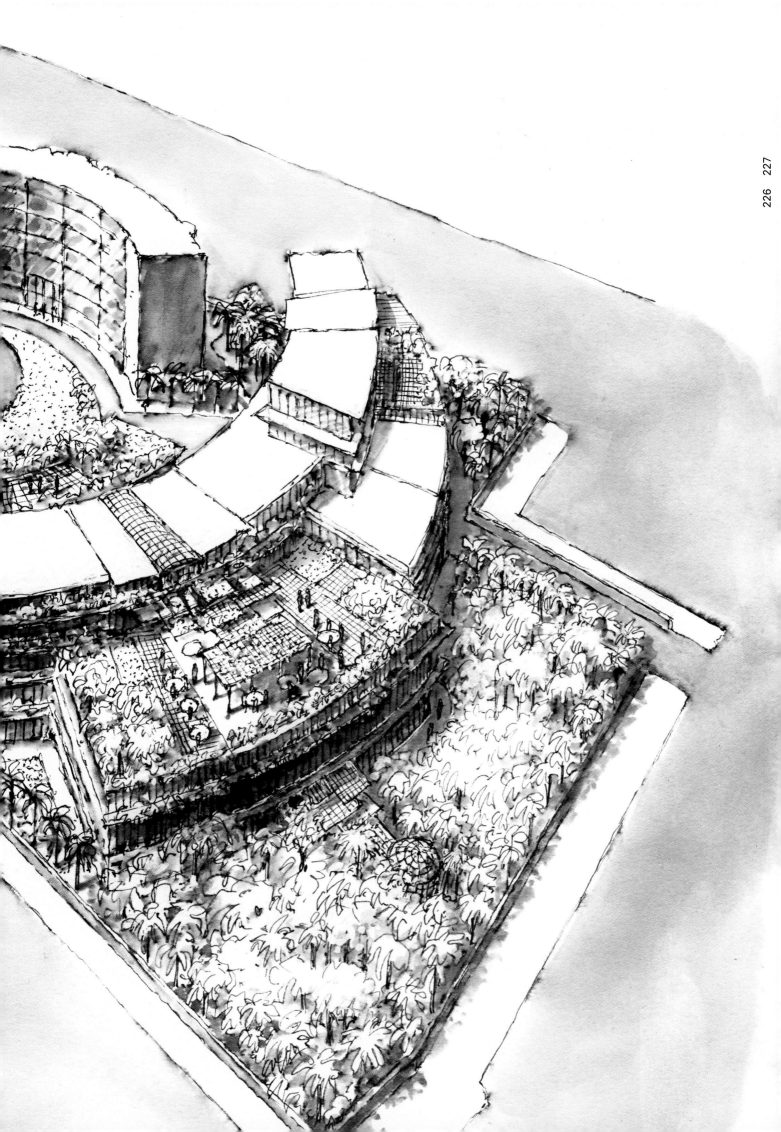

CURRENT ORGANIZATION

DENISE M C LEE 1992 -
STOMU MIYAZAKI 1983 -
SARA STRACEY 2001 -
JOSHUA WEINSTEIN 1982 -
JAMES WINES 1969 -

Founding Members
CYNTHIA EARDLEY 1969–1972
DANA DRAPER 1969–1973
NANCY GOLDRING 1969–1973
MARC MANNHEIMER 1969–1971
JUDITH SCHWARTZ 1969–1970
JAMES WINES 1969–

Original Partners
ALISON SKY 1969–1991
EMILIO SOUSA 1972–1982
MICHELLE STONE 1969–1997
JAMES WINES 1969–

Past SITE Members
CAROLYNN ABST
MARY BARBOUR
GLEN COBEN
DONNA CONLEY
SETH CORNELL
JOHN DE VITRY
KIM DOGGETT
JUAN DOWNEY
DAVID DOWNS
JOAN DURRAND
AMY EGGERTSON
LYNN ELMAN
TERESA ENGLE
MARCY FEURSTEIN
LEAH GOLDMAN
HARLAN EMIL GRUBER
PATRICK HEAD
TOSHI ICHIKAWA
ALFREDO JARR
ALICE JARRARD
DARREN KAHNAU
PETER KINCL
BRYAN LANGLANDS
ALISON LEAHY
MICHAEL MCDONOUGH
HORATIO MERCADO
VICTORIA MOHAR
EMILY MOSS
ANN O'DELL
PATRICIA PHILLIPS
CHRISTINE PIETRUCHA
NAOTO SEKIGUCHI
PEG SHEA
MARC SOKOL
KATSUYUKI TAKEMATA
JAQUELINE TATOM
QUENTIN THOMAS
WENDY TIPPETTS
LI WEN
ROBERT WERTHEIMER
SUZAN WINES

TIMELINE FOR SITE 1968–2005

1956 to 1965

SITE founder James Wines worked primarily as a sculptor, living in Rome, Italy, and New York City, where he produced a series of Constructivist-influenced works in concrete and steel. During this period, he exhibited with the Marlborough Gallery in New York and was commissioned to create several large public artworks in bronze for architectural settings in New York, New Jersey, and Wisconsin. His individual works were purchased by 30 museums in North America and Europe, including the Museum of Modern Art in New York, the Tate Gallery in London, the Whitney Museum in New York, the Neuberger Museum in Purchase, New York, the Los Angeles County Museum in California, and others. During this period, Wines won a Rome Prize in 1956, a Guggenheim Fellowship in 1962, and a Ford Foundation Grant in 1964.

1965 to 1968 SITE

As James Wines became more involved with environmental art, he produced six "landsite" sculptures, which were integrated with surrounding terrains. This shift to "situational" ideas evolved into his concept of public art as the environment, as opposed to in the environment. From 1968 to 1970, he gradually expanded the scope of his interests to include the fusion of buildings and public spaces. The work of this period anticipated his increased commitment to architecture and the formation of a multi-disciplinary organization (SITE) to re-think the relationships between art and architecture.

1968 to 1970

The environmental art projects of James Wines became increasingly architectural in feeling and concept—exemplified by plaza proposals for the Everson Museum in Syracuse, New York and the south wall of the Metropolitan Opera House in New York City. This change of emphasis led to the formation of SITE (originally an acronym for Sculpture in the Environment) for the purpose of designing site-specific art in public spaces. The original members were James Wines, Cynthia Eardley, Dana Draper, Nancy Goldring, Marc Mannheimer, and Judith Schwartz with Alison Sky as the coordinator for SITE and SITE/SVA (School of Visual Arts). An inclination toward the integration of architecture and context distinguished the group from artists who, at that time, were producing public sculpture, process art and earthworks. In the beginning, the organization functioned somewhat like an architectural office, with members contributing collectively and individually to various projects. In order to preserve individual autonomy, each member worked alone on a project and then reported progress during group dialogue. During this period, SITE began organizing lectures and conferences at colleges and universities internationally.

S.I.T.E. - LECTURES

∧ **Landsite Model V, James Wines and SITE—Architecture in Context**
Musée des Beaux-arts d'Orléans and Fonds Régional d'art Contemporain du Centre (FRAC) at the 4th annual Archilab Conference, Orleans, France, Exhibition
2002

∧ **Dana Draper, Marc Mannheimer, Cynthia Eardley, Judith Schwartz, James Wines and Nancy Goldring**

∧ **Dana Draper, Alison Sky, Nancy Goldring, Michelle Stone, Lynn Elman, Cynthia Eardley, and James Wines**
SITE Lecture Brochure

∨ **Landsite Model—Rock Bed Site**
James Wines
1969

SITE is united by the philosophical conviction that sculpture, conceptually realized to involve a total site, is preferable to the decorative placement of object art in public circumstances.

SITE, ART AND ARTISTS, 1970

1970 to 1972

With the official charter of SITE in 1970, its founding partners—Alison Sky, Emilio Sousa, Michelle Stone, and James Wines—started developing architecture and public space projects. Some of these works included critical commentaries on the formalist traditions of Modernism and Constructivism—proposing that buildings and public spaces should reject these pervasive stylistic conventions and, instead, be treated as the subject matter for art, rather than the objective of a formulaic design process. In 1971, two environmental art projects by James Wines won awards from the Design in Steel Institute and the Envirovision exhibition at the Everson Museum of Art in Syracuse, New York. In 1972, the Peeling Project for BEST Products Company was completed, under the direction of original SITE member Cynthia Eardley.

1972 to 1978

This period marked the completion of two seminal projects in SITE history—The Indeterminate Façade Building for BEST Products Company in Houston, Texas (1974) and the Ghost Parking Lot for National Shopping Centers in Hamden, Connecticut (1977). These early structures demonstrated the group's interest in working with the subliminal implications of context, using buildings as a form of architectural critique, and drawing ideas from social and psychological references. This period also marked the beginning of the ON SITE series of books and publications, dealing with environmental art and architecture. Alison Sky and Michelle Stone published *UNBUILT AMERICA* as a Bicentennial book (McGraw-Hill 1976), and *ON ENERGY* (Scribners 1974) focused on environmental concerns. In 1978 the first monograph on SITE, edited by Bruno Zevi, was published under the title of *SITE: Projects and Theories* (Dedalo Libri, Italy). The group participated in the Venice Biennale of International Architecture (Molino Stucky project) in 1975 and, during the same year, the group had its first retrospective exhibition of work spanning the years from 1970 to 1975 at the Wadsworth Atheneum in Hartford, Connecticut. SITE projects were also shown at the Whitney Museum and the Museum of Modern Art in New York, the Louvre and Centre Pompidou in Paris, the CAYC Museum in Argentina, and the Australian National Gallery in Sydney.

1978 to 1982

In total, SITE designed and constructed eight merchandising buildings for BEST Products Company, which expanded the range of possibilities in treating architecture as a subject matter for art. By using these ubiquitous stripmall structures as filtering zones for contextually related ideas, the aesthetic objective was based on inversions of meaning in a junk culture environment. The BEST Buildings included the Hialeah Rainforest Showroom and the Cutler Ridge Showroom, both in Miami, Florida (1979). This period marked the beginning of interior design work for the WilliWear fashion design company, furniture design in Italy, and the publication of a series of architectural essays by James Wines for international magazines. Three monographs on SITE were published: *SITE—Architecture as Art* (Academy Editions, London, 1980), *SITE Buildings and Spaces* (a museum catalogue associated with a 10 year retrospective), and *Gehry, SITE, Tigerman* (Editions du Moniteur, France, 1981). SITE won awards from *Progressive Architecture* magazine and the American Society of Interior Designers. An exhibition of SITE's BEST Products Buildings was given at the Museum of Modern Art in New York (1979). The Virginia Museum of Fine Arts staged a retrospective, entitled SITE—Buildings and Spaces, (1980). Various projects were shown at the Palazzo Grassi and Palazzo Strozzi in Venice, the Cooper Hewitt Museum in New York, the Staakichen Museen Preussiocher in Berlin, the Ronald Feldman Gallery in New York, the Vancouver Art Gallery in Canada, and the Los Angeles Institute of Contemporary Art in California. In 1981 SITE designed a major exhibit, Disney Animation, for the Whitney Museum of American Art in New York. Joshua Weinstein R.A. joined SITE as a partner in 1982.

1982 to 1984

In this period, SITE changed the name of the organization to SITE, Environmental Design (later, to just SITE) and increased its involvement with environmentally responsive projects that included the High-rise of Homes (1982), Bedford House (1983), plus a variety of context-oriented structures, like the Frankfurt Museum of Modern Art (1983) and the Inside/Outside Building for BEST Products in Milwaukee (1984). A monograph entitled *High-rise of Homes* was published by Rizzoli International (1982) and an exhibition of this same project was presented at the Architecture Association in London. SITE moved its headquarters to an 8,000-square-foot space in Louis Sullivan's famous Bayard-Condict Building on Bleecker Street, where the group designed the interiors. While working in this location, SITE completed two WilliWear showrooms in New York and London, won two first awards for interior design from *Interiors* magazine, and exhibited projects at the Neuer Berliner Kunstverein in Berlin, Columbus Art Museum in Ohio (a SITE retrospective), the Berkshire Museum in Massachusetts, the Whitney Museum and the Museum of Modern Art in New York, and the Victoria and Albert Museum in London.

What kinds of space do people enjoy, what brings them together?
CYNTHIA EARDLEY, URBAN ARTS CONFERENCE, 1971

^ **Cynthia Eardley and Emilio Sousa**
ON SITE Membership/Subscription form
1970s

^ **Emilio Sousa, Alison Sky, Michelle Stone and James Wines**

1984 to 1990

During this period, SITE produced a number of interior design projects, including Glen-Gery Brickwork Design Center (1984), the Museum of the Borough of Brooklyn (1985) and the Laurie Mallet House (1985). This era also initiated a greater commitment to public space design. With Highway 86 for the Vancouver World Expo (1986), the firm completed its first major plaza project incorporating a fusion of the surrounding context, narrative content, and people interaction. SITE continued its focus on interactive public spaces in Japan, with the construction of the Isuzu Space Station, a children's park in Yokohama, and the Four Continents Bridge in Hiroshima, celebrating humanity's relation to global environmentalism (both in 1989). James Wines expanded his personal commitment to architectural education by becoming the Chairman of Environmental Design at Parsons School of Design in New York City (1984 to 1990) and publishing his book *De-architecture* (Rizzoli International, 1987). SITE won a competition for the design of Ansel Adams Center in Carmel, California (1985) and another first award for Pershing Square in Los Angeles (1987). The firm completed two interiors for the ALLSTEEL Corporation in New York (1986) and showrooms for Swatch Watches in New York and Zurich (1989). Environmentally oriented projects were proposed for the Japan Cultural Center in Paris and a concept entitled Cosmo World for the waterfront of Yokohama, Japan (1987). A retrospective of SITE was held in Florence, Italy at the Comune di Fiesole Museum (1989), with an accompanying book entitled *SITE—Architetture 1971–1988*. Other monographs included *SITE* (Rizzoli International, 1987), *SITE* (A+U Publishing Company, Tokyo, 1986), *SITE—American Visions* (Champion

Paper Company, 1989), and *James Wines, Dessins d'Architecture* (Les Editions du Demi-Cercle, Paris, 1989). Additional exhibitions included the Institute Francais d'Architecture in Paris (1990), the Whitney Museum in New York (1989), the Comune di Trieste Museum in Italy (1990), and a retrospective of James Wines' drawings for SITE at the Cour de Mai Gallery in Paris (1988) and Ville Gillet Museum of Contemporary Art in Lyon (1990).

1990 to 1994

SITE became increasingly involved with the creation of public spaces and green design projects, including the Horoscope Ring Park in Toyama, Japan (1992), the World Ecology Pavilion, the Saudi Arabian Pavilion, and Avenue Five for the 1992 Seville World Expo, Ross's Landing Park and Plaza in Chattanooga (1992), the Aquatorium project for Chattanooga (1993), and the winning competition entry for a civic center in the French Haute Loire town of Le Puy-en-Velay (1994). Each of these projects was developed from social, cultural, regional, and ecological sources, with the intention of creating hybrid structures based on a fusion of architecture and various elements of context. Exhibitions during this period took place at the Comune di Torino Gallery in Italy (1993) and the Comune di Trieste Gallery (1990). Denise Lee joined SITE in 1992 and became the Associate Director of the New York studio in 1999.

1994 to 1998

The office increased its involvement with large-scale urban projects, which reflected SITE's philosophy of integrated systems in architecture and planning. These works included the Trawsfynydd International Energy Communications Center for North Wales (1994) and competition entries for the Saudi Arabian National Museum in Riyadh (1996) and the Museum of Islamic Arts in Qatar (1997). SITE's project for the decommissioning of a nuclear power station in North Wales was the subject of a documentary film by the British Broadcasting Company in England, as well as an exhibition at the Royal Institute of British Architects in London (1995). The firm was chosen by the United States Information Agency to design the USA National Pavilion for the Hannover 2000 World Expo (1998). James Wines received a Chrysler Award for Innovation in Design (1995) and was included in an exhibition of the award winners at the San Francisco Museum of Modern Art (1995). SITE works were exhibited at the Joan Miró Foundation in Barcelona (1996) and a retrospective of James Wines' drawings for SITE was presented at the University of California Gallery (1996). A book, entitled *James Wines and SITE* was published by Korea International Publishers in Seoul, Korea (1996).

1998 to 2005

SITE increased its projects in Europe—including the Rossini Sculpture Garden and Pavilion in Briosco, Italy (1998), the Gianluca Fabiani Villa in Nebbiuno, Italy (2000) and the Giandomenico Fabiani Villa in Rome (2002). Sara Stracey joined SITE in 2001 to work on a New World Trade Center and continues to develop projects and publications. Books published were James Wines' exploration of environmental design, entitled *Green Architecture*, for Taschen Verlag Publishers (2000) and the catalogue for a retrospective exhibition of SITE at the Musée des Beaux-Arts in Orléans, France, entitled *James Wines & SITE—Architecture dans le Contexte* (2002). This period saw James Wines' re-engagement in architectural education, as head of the Architecture Department at Penn State University, from 1999 to 2002, followed by a professorship in 2002. Publications include an interview book—*Ventidue Domande a James Wines*—released by CLEAN Edizone in Italy (1999). There were SITE works exhibited at the Marlborough Gallery in New York (1998), the Rocky Mountain College of Art and Design in Colorado (1999), the Museo d'Este in Padua, Italy (2001), Denver Art Museum (USA Design—1975 to 2000) in Colorado (2002), the Venice Architecture Biennale in Italy (2002), Max Protetch Gallery (New World Trade Center Exhibition, 2002), the Museum of Modern Art in Queens (2002), and the National Building Museum in Washington, D.C. (Big and Green show of international ecological design, 2002). In the summer of 2003, SITE began work on two large-scale buildings in Mumbai, India for a major corporate client.

< Snowman Prototype
Built and melted 2003
New York City, USA

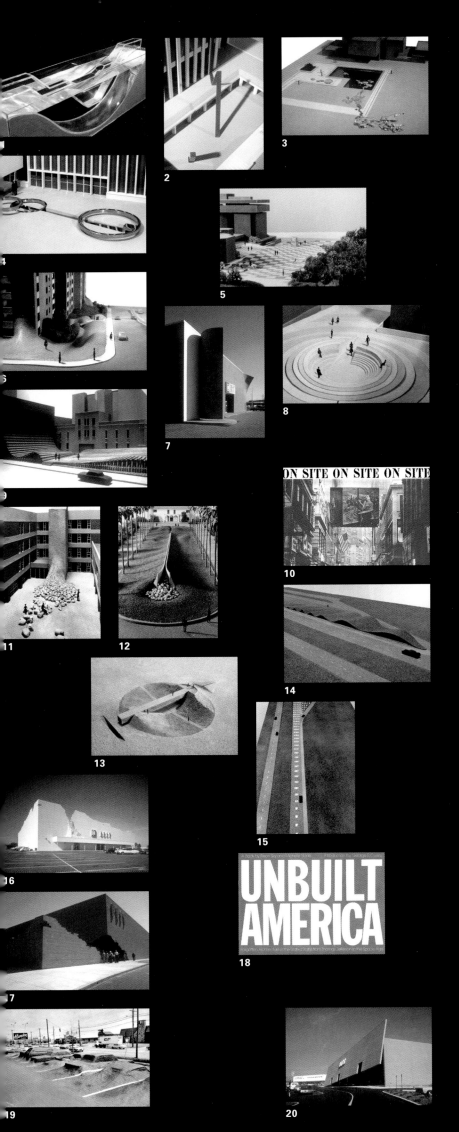

CATALOGUE

21 MOLINO STUCKY—Project for the adaptive re-use of a 19th century grain mill—Venice Biennale, Giudecca Island, Venice, Italy—schematic design phase, 1978

22 BEST TERRARIUM SHOWROOM—Catalog showroom for a retail merchandising chain store corporation—BEST Products Company, South San Francisco, California, USA—schematic design phase, 1978

23 341 MADISON AVENUE—Environmental art façade project for an office building—Vector Real Estate Corporation, New York City, USA—schematic design phase, 1978

24 BEST-ANTI SIGN—Distribution center for a retail merchandising chain store corporation—BEST Products Company, Ashland, Virginia, USA—built, 1978

25 SITE PROJECTS AND THEORIES 1969–1978—Monograph book on the work of SITE, Edited by Bruno Zevi, Dedalo Libri, Milan, Italy—published, 1979

26 BEST PRODUCTS HIALEAH SHOWROOM—Catalog showroom for a retail merchandising chain store corporation—BEST Products Company, Miami, Florida, USA—built, 1979

27 CUTLER RIDGE SHOWROOM—Catalog showroom for a retail merchandising chain store corporation—BEST Products Company, Miami, Florida, USA—built, 1979

28 BEST FOREST SHOWROOM—Catalog showroom for a retail merchandising chain store corporation—BEST Products Company, Richmond, Virginia, USA—built, 1980

29 GHOST HOUSES—proposal for a neighborhood of illusionary houses constructed in deceptive materials—Summit, New Jersey, USA—schematic design phase, 1980

30 PROTOTYPE BANK—Branch office for a regional bank—Perpetual Savings and Loan Association, Rapid City, South Dakota, USA—schematic design phase, 1980

31 BUILDINGS AND SPACES—Traveling Retrospective Exhibition of SITE Projects—Sponsor, Virginia Museum of Fine Arts, Richmond, Virginia, USA—exhibited, various USA museums and galleries 1980–88

INDEPENDENCE PLACE—Apartment building plaza—Independence Place Apartments, Philadelphia, Pennsylvania, USA—schematic design phase, 1980

32 PROTOTYPE STORE—Levi products merchandising store façade and interior—The General Store, Washington, D.C., USA—schematic design phase, 1980

33 FAMOLARE SHOES—Shoe store interior—New York City, USA—schematic design phase, 1981

34 DISNEY ANIMATION EXHIBITION—Exhibit design for Walt Disney Studios animation history—Whitney Museum of American Art, New York City, USA—built, 1981

35 VIRGIN RECORDS STORE—Entranceway wall for corporate offices—Virgin Records, New York City, USA—schematic design phase, 1981

36 HIGH-RISE OF HOMES—High-rise housing proposal—multiple urban locations throughout the USA—schematic design phase, 1981

37 WILLIWEAR BOUTIQUE—Retail fashion design store—Harrod's Department Store, WilliWear, London, England—built, 1982

38 WILLIWEAR WOMEN'S SHOWROOM—Wholesale fashion design showroom and corporate offices—WilliWear, New York City, USA—built, 1982

39 WILLIWEAR MEN'S SHOWROOM—Wholesale fashion design showroom—WilliWear, New York City, USA—Built, 1982

40 SPACE STATION—NASA exhibition center—National Aeronautics and Space Administration, New York City, USA—schematic design phase, 1982

41 GREENHOUSE SQUARE BEST PRODUCTS BUILDING—Catalog showroom for a retail merchandising chain store corporation—Best Products Company, San Leandro, California, USA—schematic design phase, 1982

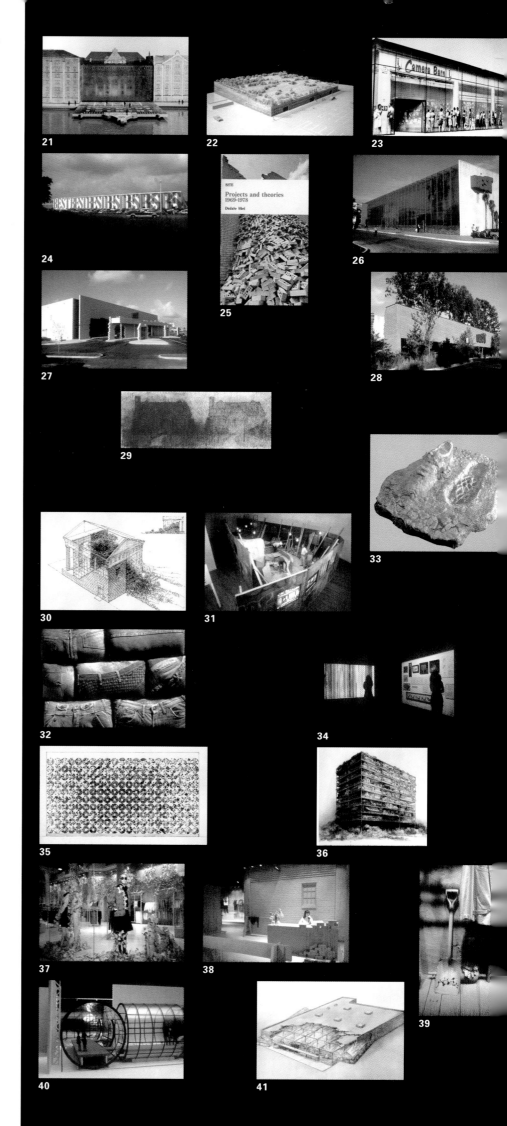

42 HOUSE WITH FLOATING WALLS—Loft apartment interior—private client, New York City, USA—schematic design phase, 1982

43 BEDFORD HOUSE—Private home in a heavily wooded area—private client, Bedford, New York, USA—construction documents phase, 1983

44 THE FRANKFURT MUSEUM OF MODERN ART—competition entry for a museum of visual arts—Municipality of Frankfurt, Germany—schematic design phase, 1983

45 WILLIWEAR EXECUTIVE OFFICES—Fashion design executive office—WilliWear, New York City, USA—built, 1983

46 APOCALYPSE/UTOPIA—Exhibition based on invited designers' personal interests—"l'Affinitá Elettive Exhibition" at the Milan Triennale, Milan, Italy—built, 1984

47 FLOATING MCDONALD'S—Restaurant for a fast food chain—McDonald's Corporation, Berwyn, Illinois, USA—built, 1984

48 SITE PROJECTS OFFICE—Offices, work studio and gallery space for architectural design—SITE, New York City, USA—built, 1984

49 PAZ BUILDING—Adaptive re-use of an existing building for a commercial and office complex—Paz Corporation, Brooklyn, New York, USA—design development phase, 1984

50 NEW YORK BRICKWORK DESIGN CENTER—Masonry products showroom—Glen-Gery Corporation, New York City, USA—built, 1984

51 BEST INSIDE/OUTSIDE BUILDING—Catalog showroom for a retail merchandising chain store corporation—BEST Products Company, Milwaukee, Wisconsin, USA—built, 1984

52 UNIQUE CLOTHING WAREHOUSE—Retail clothing store—New York City, USA—built, 1984

53 FORMICA DOOR—Special door design for a traveling exhibition of laminate products—Formica Corporation, Cincinnati, Ohio, USA—constructed, 1985

54 DOOR WITHIN A DOOR WITHIN A DOOR—Limited edition door series in wood—SITE, New York City, USA—constructed, 1985

55 ANSEL ADAMS CENTER OF PHOTOGRAPHY—Winning competition entry for the Friends of Photography museum, Carmel, California, USA—schematic design phase, 1985

56 LAURIE MALLET HOUSE—Private Residence and restoration of a Greenwich Village historic building—Ms. Laurie Mallet, New York City, USA—built, 1985

57 HIGHWAY 86 PROCESSIONAL—Winning competition entry for a Transportation Pavilion and Plaza for the Canadian 1986 World Exposition—Expo 86, Vancouver, Canada—built, 1985

58 THE MUSEUM OF THE BOROUGH OF BROOKLYN—Interior architecture for a regional museum, support space and executive offices—Brooklyn, New York, USA—built, 1985

59 MELTING CANDLESTICK—limited edition product design in silver—Swid/Powell, New York City, USA and Baleri Associati, Milan, Italy—manufactured, 1985

60 FROZEN ARCHEOLOGY—Exhibition of innovative uses of terracotta tiles—Ludowicki Celedon Corporation, New York City, USA—built, 1985

61 "ICEBERG" BOTTLE—Product design for a commercial water company—Vittel Corporation, Vittel, France—manufactured, 1986

62 DENISON PARKWAY—Urban revitalization project for existing buildings in a rural community—Corning Glass Works, Corning, New York, USA—schematic design phase, 1986

63 ALLSTEEL ARCHAEOLOGY—Temporary installation for a furniture manufacturing company—ALLSTEEL Corporation, Interior Design Center of New York, Long Island City, New York, USA—built, 1986

64 DE-ARCHITECTURE—Book on contemporary art and architecture theory, by James Wines—Rizzoli International Publications—published, 1987

65 THE LUBE COMPANY—Automobile service station— The Lube Company, Parsippany, New Jersey, USA— schematic design phase, 1987

66 WEST HOLLYWOOD CIVIC CENTER—Competition entry for a government building—City of Los Angeles, California, USA—schematic design phase, 1987

67 COSMO WORLD—Waterfront development project, based on a 20th century transportation theme—Cosmo Petroleum Company, Yokohama, Japan—schematic design phase, 1987

68 PERSHING SQUARE—Winning competition entry for a downtown public park and plaza—City of Los Angeles, California, USA—schematic design phase, 1987

69 WILLIWEAR RETAIL STORE—Retail fashion design store—WilliWear, New York City, USA—built, 1988

70 ALLSTEEL SHOWROOM—Showroom for a furniture manufacturing company—ALLSTEEL Corporation, Interior Design Center of New York, Long Island City, New York, USA—built, 1987

ALLSTEEL FABRIC EXHIBITION—Display of new fabric coverings for furniture—Interior Design Center of New York, Long Island City, New York, USA—built, 1987

71 LOADING ZONE RESTAURANT—Casual dining restaurant, utilizing a former auto repair garage—Loading Zone Company, Boston, Massachusetts, USA—built, 1989

72 HEARTTHROB CAFE AND RESTAURANT—Restaurant and night club—Heartthrob Corporation, New York City, USA—schematic design phase, 1989

73 ISUZU SPACE STATION—Public space and exhibition center for children—Isuzu Corporation, Yokohama, Japan—built, 1989

74 THE FOUR CONTINENTS BRIDGE—Bridge for the 1989 Japan Exposition—Expo 89 Corporation, Hiroshima, Japan—built, 1989

75 THE WORLD ECOLOGY PAVILION—Pavilion for the 1992 Seville World Exposition—Expo 92 Corporation, Seville, Spain—schematic design phase, 1990

AUTO MALL—Automotive specialty store for Mt. Olive Shopping Center, New Jersey—Ardleigh Development Corporation, Roselle, New Jersey, USA—schematic design phase, 1989

76 PEPSI REFRESHMENT ISLAND—Recreation center and plaza—Pepsi Cola Company, Universal City, California, USA—schematic design phase, 1990

77 SHINWA RESORT—Ski resort complex—Yutaka Tanaka, Kisokoma-Kogen, Japan—schematic design phase, 1990

78 OMAN PAVILION—National pavilion for the 1992 Seville World Exposition—Expo 92 Corporation, Seville, Spain—schematic design phase, 1990

ARTS PARK LA—Competition entry for a public park and outdoor amphitheater—City of Los Angeles, California, USA—schematic design phase, 1990

79 SUNSET BOULEVARD—Mixed-use apartment and commercial complex—Raleigh Corporation, West Hollywood, California, USA—schematic design phase, 1990

80 ALGERIAN PAVILION—National pavilion for the 1992 Seville World Exposition—Expo 92 Corporation, Seville, Spain—schematic design phase, 1990

81 MAISON DE LA CULTURE DU JAPON—Competition entry for a museum of Japanese culture—Japanese National Government Agency, Paris, France—schematic design phase, 1990

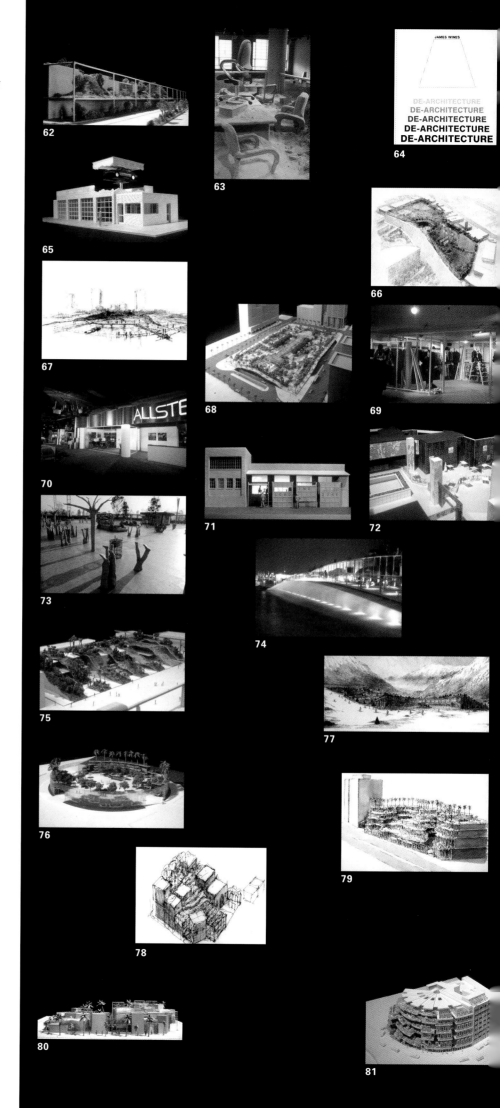

82 SWATCH—Prototype retail store concept for watch sales—Swatch Watch Company, Zurich, Switzerland—built in Nantucket, Massachusetts, USA, 1987; New York City, USA, 1988; Swatch Building, Zurich, Switzerland, 1988; Macy's Department Store, New York City, USA, 1989; Macy's Department Store, Paramus, New Jersey, USA, 1990

ROOF GARDEN—Corporate headquarters roof garden—Komatsu Construction Company, Tokyo, Japan—schematic design phase, 1990

83 ROCKPLEX—Entertainment center and corporate offices—MCA Development Corporation, Universal Studios, Los Angeles, California—schematic design phase, 1990

84 HANDS OF THE WORLD DISPLAY—Supermarket display and racking system—Frito-Lay, Dallas, Texas, USA—built, 1992

A DECADE OF LITERARY LIONS—Temporary Installation—New York Public Library, New York City, USA—built, 1990

85 BLACK LIGHT—Venetian glass lamps, designed as a theme and variations series—Foscarini Italia, Murano, Italy—manufactured, 1991

86 SAN FRANCISCO EMBARCADERO—Competition entry for a series of bus shelters—Arts Commission of San Francisco, San Francisco, California, USA—schematic design phase, 1991

87 THEATER FOR THE NEW CITY—Center for the performing arts—Theater for the New City, New York City, USA—several phases built, 1992–95

88 WINDSOR RIVERFRONT DEVELOPMENT—Public park, science museum and exhibit center—City of Windsor, Windsor, Canada—schematic design phase, 1992

89 HOROSCOPE RING—Main pavilion and park for the 1992 Japan Exposition—Toyama Japan Exhibition Association, Toyama, Japan—built, 1992

90 ROSS'S LANDING PARK AND PLAZA—Riverfront park and plaza—River City Company, Chattanooga, Tennessee, USA—built, 1992

91 AVENUE NUMBER FIVE—Public plaza and restaurant complex for the 1992 Seville World Exposition—Expo 92 Corporation, Seville, Spain—built, 1992

92 MAK BOOKSTORE ENTRANCE—Environmental art project for a museum bookstore entrance—Museum für Angewandte Kunst, Vienna, Austria—built, 1992

93 CHATEAU DE BLOIS—Garden Plaza—City of Blois, France—schematic design phase, 1992

94 SAUDI ARABIAN PAVILION—National pavilion for the 1992 Seville World Exposition—Expo 92, Seville, Spain—built, 1992

95 FESTIVAL DES JARDINS—Garden design—Jardin de la France, Chaumont-sur-Loire, France—built, 1992

96 LE PUY—CIVIC SPACE AND ADAPTIVE RE-USE PROJECT—Competition winning urban design for State and City offices, public spaces and preservation of historic buildings—City of Le Puy-En-Velay, France—design development phase, 1992

97 INNER HARBOR LINK—Competition entry for a public space project—Baltimore, Maryland, USA—schematic design phase, 1994

98 TENNESEE AQUA CENTER AKA AQUATORIUM—A resource education center and museum for the history of water and civilization—River City Company, Chattanooga, Tennessee, USA—schematic design phase, 1993

AIR & SPACE MUSEUM—Competition winner for the adaptive re-use of an abandoned airport and public space—City of Paris, France—schematic design phase, 1993

99 IMAX THEATER—Competition entry for an educational theater and office building—River City Company, Chattanooga, Tennessee, USA—schematic design phase, 1994

100 ITALIAN TILE EXHIBITION—Temporary exhibit of ceramic tiles—International Tile Association, Anaheim, California, USA—built, 1994

101 VANCOUVER ARENA PARK—Competition entry for a public park—City of Vancouver, Canada—schematic design phase, 1994

102 RASH FIELD—Competition entry for a public space—City of Baltimore, Maryland, USA—schematic design phase, 1994

BALTIMORE CHILDREN'S MUSEUM—Museum and public space—City of Baltimore, Maryland, USA—schematic design phase, 1994

PORT OF FAME—Competition entry for an environmental art project—Liverpool, United Kingdom—schematic design phase, 1994

103 TRAWSFYNYDD INTERNATIONAL ENERGY COMMUNICATIONS CENTER—Research and communications center for nuclear energy—City of Trawsfynydd, North Wales, United Kingdom—schematic design phase, 1994

104 VIACOM ENTERTAINMENT PRODUCTS STORE—Entertainment industry supermarket for multiple locations in the USA—Viacom Corporation, New York City, USA—schematic design phase, 1995

105 MANCHESTER SHIP CANAL—Waterfront environmental art project and pedestrian promenade—Public Art Fund, Manchester, United Kingdom—built, 1995

106 THE OLIVE GARDEN—Prototype new restaurant and retro-fit for existing restaurants, to be built in various locations throughout the USA—Darden Corporation, Orlando, Florida—construction documents phase, 1995

107 ENVIRONMENTAL EDUCATION CENTER—Facility for waste recycling education—Prince William County, Maryland, USA—schematic design phase, 1995

108 COSTA COFFEE—Prototype coffee bar and restaurant, based on adaptive re-use of existing buildings and interior spaces—Costa Coffee, London, England, United Kingdom—built, 1996

COLUMBUS MILLS—Shopping center entranceways—Mills Corporation, Columbus, Ohio, USA—schematic design phase, 1995

109 MCA GARDEN—Landscape design and pedestrian promenades—Universal Studios, Orlando, Florida, USA—built, 1996

ZUZU RESTAURANT—Prototype restaurant design, including interior/exterior, furniture, signage, and product development for a Mexican food restaurant chain—Zuzu Corporation, Dallas, Texas, USA—built, 1996

110 SAUDI ARABIAN NATIONAL MUSEUM AND DARAT AL MALIK ABD AL-AZIZ—Competition entry for a museum and urban plan, including several new buildings and restoration of existing historic structures—City of Riyadh, Saudi Arabia—schematic design phase, 1996

111 DRESDEN URBAN PLAN—Competition entry for a new public park, including renovation of existing buildings—City of Dresden, Germany—schematic design phase, 1996

112 TÖÖLÖNHANTI PARK—Competition entry for an urban park master plan—City of Helsinki, Finland—schematic design phase, 1997

113 THE MUSEUM OF ISLAMIC ARTS—Competition entry for a new museum, with an adjacent park—City of Doha, Qatar—schematic design phase, 1997

114 CARRABBA'S RESTAURANT—Prototype restaurant design—Carrabba's Corporation, Orlando, Florida, USA—built, 1998

115 TERRA TAVOLA—Prototype table and chair line for Italian furniture company, Milan, Italy—manufactured, 1996, 1998, 1999

116 USA PAVILION—2000 HANNOVER WORLD EXPO—National pavilion for the United States of America at the Hannover World Exposition 2000—United States Information Service, Hannover, Germany—schematic design phase, 1998

LYON, PLACE DAUPHINE—Competition entry for urban development plan—City of Lyon, France—schematic design phase, 1998

CAPE MAY URBAN DEVELOPMENT—Landscape design and urban plan—City of Cape May, New Jersey, USA—schematic design phase, 1998

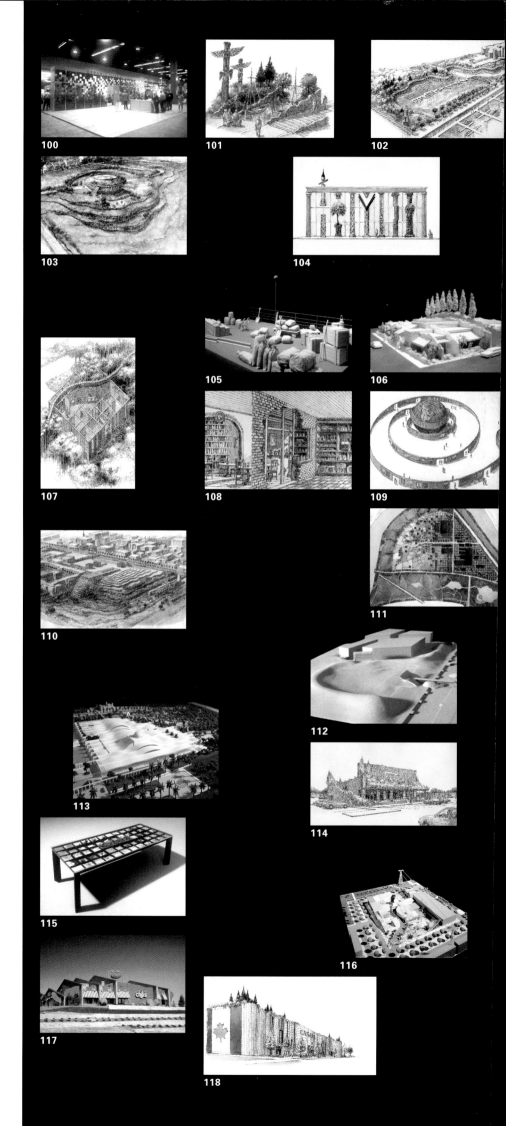

119

120

121

GREEN ARCHITECTURE

122

123

124

125

126

127

128

129

ACME STUDIO

130

131

132

133

134

135

PROJECT CREDITS

A NEW WORLD TRADE CENTER, 2001–04
Location: New York City, NY, USA (traveling exhibition)
Exhibitor: Max Protetch Gallery
Concept: SITE—Denise M C Lee, Sara Stracey,
Patrick Head, Stomu Miyazaki, James Wines
Status: Installed

ALLSTEEL ARCHAEOLOGY, 1986
Location: International Design Center of New York,
Long Island City, NY, USA and ALLSTEEL
Headquarters, Aurora, IL, USA
Client: ALLSTEEL, Inc.
Concept: SITE
Installation: Donna Brueger, John Gunnison-
Wiseman, New York City, NY, USA
General Contractor: Gordon Construction Corp.,
New York City, NY, USA
Status: Built

ALLSTEEL SHOWROOM, 1987
Location: International Design Center of New York,
Long Island City, NY, USA
Client: ALLSTEEL, Inc.
Concept: SITE
Structural Engineer: Geiger/KKBNA, New York City,
NY, USA
Mechanical/Electrical Engineer: Mariano D. Molina,
New York City, NY, USA
Lighting Design: Jules Fisher and Paul Marantz,
Inc., New York City, NY, USA
Artifact Installation: Architectural Sculpture Assoc.,
Lancaster, PA, USA
General Contractor: Gordon Construction Corp.,
New York City, NY, USA
Status: Built

**AMERICAN BICENTENNIAL
COMMEMORATIVE MONUMENT AT FOUR
CORNERS, 1974**
Location: Navajo Indian Nation, Shiprock, NM, USA
Client: American Bicentennial
Concept: SITE
Status: Schematic design (unbuilt)

**AMERICAN BICENTENNIAL PROJECT AT
YORK REST STOP—INTERSTATE 80, 1974**
Location: Various locations, NE, USA
Sponsor: State of Nebraska—the America
Bicentennial Project
Concept: SITE
Status: Schematic design (unbuilt)

**ANNMARIE GARDEN VISITORS CENTER
AND SCULPTURE GARDEN MASTER PLAN,
2003–04**
Location: Solomans Island, MD, USA
Client: Koenig Private Foundation, Inc.
Master Planning Concept: SITE—James Wines,
Denise M C Lee
Landscape Designer: Mark Battaglia and Dan Jones,
State College, PA, USA
Landscape Architect: James Urban Landscape
Architecture, Annapolis, MD, USA
Status: Under construction
Visitors Information Center + Formal Garden Design
Concept: SITE—James Wines, Denise M C Lee,
Patrick Head; team—Joshua Weinstein, Sara Stracey
Landscape Architect: James Urban Landscape
Architecture, Annapolis, MD, USA
Status: Design development

ANSEL ADAMS CENTER, 1985
Location: Carmel, CA, USA
Client: The Friends of Photography
Concept: SITE
Structural Engineer: Weidlinger Assoc., Inc.,
New York City, NY, USA
Status: Competition winner (unbuilt)

APOCALYPSE/UTOPIA, 1985
Location: Triennale, Milan, Italy (traveling exhibition)
Exhibitor: Triennale di Milano, Milan, Italy
Exhibition Title: Le Affinita Elettive
Concept: SITE
Status: Installed

ARCHITECTURE IN CONTEXT, 2002
Location: Musée des Beaux-Arts d'Orléans,
Orléans, France
Exhibitor: Fonds Régional d'Art Contemporain (FRAC)
Curator: Marie-Ange Brayer with Denise M C Lee
Concept: SITE—Sara Stracey, Denise M C Lee
Assistant: Nicolas Royer, Manuel Brillault; Orléans,
France
Coordination: Sophie Bellé, Orléans, France
Status: Installed

AVENUE NUMBER FIVE, 1989
Location: Seville, Spain
Client: EXPO 92—1992 Universal Exposition
Concept: SITE—Joshua Weinstein, Michelle Stone;
team—James Wines, Glen Coben, Ann O'Dell,
Horatio Mercado, Alison Leahy, John de Vitry
Associate Architect: CYGSA Control Y Geologia,
S.A., Seville, Spain
Landscape Architect: Signe Nielsen, P.C.,
New York City, NY, USA
Lighting Designer: Quentin Thomas Assoc.,
Brooklyn, NY, USA
Consulting Engineer: Saincosa, S.A., Seville, Spain
General Contractor: Ferrovial, Seville, Spain
Status: Built

BEDFORD HOUSE, 1980
Location: Bedford, NY, USA
Client: Private
Concept: SITE
Status: Unbuilt

BEST ANTI-SIGN, 1978–79
Location: Ashland, VA, USA
Client: BEST Products Co., Inc.
Concept: SITE—Alison Sky
Panel Fabricator: ERVITE Corp., Erie, PA, USA
Status: Built

BEST CUTLER RIDGE SHOWROOM, 1983
Location: 19600 South Dixie Highway, Miami, FL, USA
Client: BEST Products Co., Inc.
Concept: SITE—Alison Sky
Associate Architect: Johnson Assoc. Architects,
Inc., Miami, FL, USA
Structural Engineer: Weidlinger Assoc., Inc.,
New York City, NY, USA
General Contractor: Whiting-Turner Contracting Co.,
Fort Lauderdale, FL, USA
Status: Built

BEST FOREST SHOWROOM, 1980
Location: 9008 Quioccasin Road, Richmond, VA, USA
Client: BEST Products Co., Inc.
Architect: SITE
Structural Engineer: Weidlinger Assoc., Inc.,
New York City, NY, USA
Civil Engineer: LaPrade Brothers Engineers,
Richmond, VA, USA
Landscape: Watkins Nurseries, Inc.
General Contractor: Whiting-Turner Contracting Co.,
Fort Lauderdale, FL, USA
Status: Built

BEST GREENHOUSE SHOWROOM, 1982
Location: San Leandro, CA, USA
Client: BEST Products Co., Inc.
Architect: SITE
Structural Engineer: Weidlinger Assoc., Inc.,
New York City, NY, USA
Status: Unbuilt

BEST HIALEAH SHOWROOM, 1979
Location: 5310 West 20th Avenue, Hialeah, FL, USA
Client: BEST Products Co., Inc.
Architect: SITE
Associate Architect: Johnson Assoc. Architects,
Inc., Miami, FL, USA
Structural Engineer: Weidlinger Assoc., Inc.,
New York City, NY, USA
Consulting Engineer: Milton Costello, P.E.,
Amityville, NY, USA

Landscape: Fluker Lawn Care Service
General Contractor: Whiting-Turner Contracting Co.,
Fort Lauderdale, FL, USA
Status: Built

**BEST INDETERMINATE FAÇADE BUILDING,
1975**
Location: Alameda-Genoa Shopping Center,
Kingspoint and Kleckley Streets,
Houston, TX, USA
Client: BEST Products Co., Inc.
Concept: SITE
Associate Architect: Maple-Jones Assoc.,
Fort Worth, TX, USA
Structural Engineer: Weidlinger Assoc., Inc.,
New York City, NY, USA
General Contractor: Conceptual Building Systems,
Dallas, TX, USA
Status: Built

BEST INSIDE/OUTSIDE BUILDING, 1984
Location: West Brown Deer Road, Milwaukee, WI,
USA
Client: BEST Products Co., Inc.
Architect: SITE
Associate Architect: Keeva Kekst Assoc.
Structural Engineer: John Bowes and Assoc.
Consulting Engineer: V.A. Lombardi and Assoc.
Arcade Installation: M.F.I., Inc.: Mettleworks, Gene
Olson (sculpture); Creative Services International, Inc.
General Contractor: Hunzinger Construction Co.
Status: Built

BEST NOTCH SHOWROOM, 1977
Location: Arden Fair Shopping Center, 1901 Arden
Way, Sacramento, CA, USA
Client: BEST Products Co., Inc.
Concept: SITE
Associate Architect: Simpson, Stratta and Assoc.,
San Francisco, CA, USA
Consulting Engineers: Simpson, Stratta and Assoc.,
San Francisco, CA, USA
Engineer for Wandering Wall: Allied Engineering
and Production Corp., Alameda, CA, USA
General Contractor: Rudolf and Sletten, Inc.,
Mountain View, CA, USA
Status: Built

BEST PARKING LOT BUILDING, 1976
Location: Urban Shopping Center (undetermined
location)
Client: BEST Products Co., Inc.
Architect: SITE
Status: Unbuilt

BEST PEELING PROJECT, 1971
Location: 5400 Midlothian Turnpike, Richmond, VA,
USA
Client: BEST Products Co., Inc.
Concept: SITE—Cynthia Eardley
Consulting Engineer: Mario Salvadori, New York City,
NY, USA
Local Engineer: William J. Davis, Richmond, VA, USA
General Contractor: Taylor and Parrish, Richmond,
VA, USA
Status: Built

BEST REVERSIBLE PROJECT, 1978
Client: BEST Products Co., Inc.
Architect: SITE
Status: Unbuilt

BEST SCALE-REFERENCE PROJECT, 1979
Client: BEST Products Co., Inc.
Architect: SITE—Alison Sky
Status: Unbuilt

BEST TERRARIUM SHOWROOM, 1978
Location: South San Francisco, CA, USA
Client: BEST Products Co., Inc.
Architect: SITE
Status: Unbuilt

BEST TILT SHOWROOM, 1978
Location: Eudowood Mall, Goucher Boulevard,
Towson, MD, USA
Client: BEST Products Co., Inc.
Architect: SITE
Structural Engineer: Weidlinger Assoc., Inc.,
New York City, NY, USA
Mechanical Engineer: Scherr, Kopelman Assoc.,
New York City, NY, USA
Electrical Engineer: Construction Concepts,
New York City, NY, USA
General Contractor: Whiting-Turner Contracting Co.,
Baltimore, MD, USA
Status: Built

BEST TWIST SHOWROOM, 1979
Location: NJ, USA
Client: BEST Products Co., Inc.
Architect: SITE
Status: Built

BEST WORD PROJECT, 1974
Client: BEST Products Co., Inc.
Architect: SITE—Alison Sky
Status: Unbuilt

BINARY WATCH, 1998
Client: Markuse Productions, Woburn, ME, USA
Concept: SITE
Status: Manufactured

BINGHAMTON DOCK, 1972
Location: Binghamton, NY, USA
Client: Valley Development Corporation
Concept: SITE—Cynthia Eardley, Dana Draper,
Nancy Goldring, James Wines
Status: Schematic design (unbuilt)

BLACK LIGHT, 1991
Client: Foscarini Italia, Murano, Italy (commissioned
for Fiera di Mobili Exhibition, Milan, Italy)
Concept: SITE
Status: Manufactured

BRICK DESIGN CENTER, 1985
Location: 211 East 49th Street, New York City,
NY, USA
Client: Glen-Gery Corp.
Concept: SITE
Structural Engineer: Berkenfeld-Getz & Assoc.,
New York City, NY, USA
Mechanical/Electrical Engineer: Mariano D. Molina,
P.C., New York City, NY, USA
Lighting Consultant: Quentin D. Thomas, Brooklyn,
NY, USA
Status: Built

CARRARA TABLE, 1989
Client: Casigliani Italia, Carrara, Italy
Concept: SITE
Status: Manufactured

CASA FABIANI, 2000
Location: Nebbiuno, Novara Province, Piemonte,
Lago Maggiore, Italy
Client: Gianluca Fabiani
Concept: SITE—James Wines, Denise M C Lee,
Joshua Weinstein; team—Hartmut Mueller,
Patrick Head, Brian Melcher
Architect: General Planning, Milano, Italy
Consulting Engineer: General Planning, Milano, Italy
Status: Design development

CHILI'S RESTAURANT, 1999
Location: Arapahoe Crossings, Aurora, CO, USA
Client: Brinker International, Dallas, TX, USA
Concept: SITE—James Wines, Suzan Wines,
Joshua Weinstein, Denise M C Lee
Architect: The Vincent Assoc., Dallas, TX, USA
Structural Engineer: Ronald A. Roberts & Assoc.,
Dallas, TX, USA
Mechanical/Electrical Engineer: Purdy-McGuire, Inc.,

Dallas, TX, USA
Civil Engineer/Landscape Architect: CLC Assoc.,
Englewood, CO, USA
Status: Built

COLONNADE OF COLOR, 1970
Location: Richmond, VA, USA
Client: BEST Products Co., Inc.
Concept: SITE—Nancy Goldring
Structural Engineer: Mario Salvadori, New York City,
NY, USA
Status: Schematic design (unbuilt)

CORPORATE HEADQUARTERS, 2004
Location: Mumbai, India
Client: Non-disclosed upon client request
Concept: SITE—Denise M C Lee, James Wines;
team—Sara Stracey, Curtis Pittman, Jon Benner,
Brandon Coburn
Structural Engineer: Weidlinger Assoc., Inc.,
New York City, NY, USA
Mechanical/Electrical/Environmental Engineer:
Jaros Baum & Bolles, New York City, NY, USA
Status: Pre-schematic phase

COURTYARD PROJECT, 1973
Location: Intermediate School 25, New York City,
NY, USA
Client: New York Board of Education
Concept: SITE
Status: Schematic design (unbuilt)

DISNEY ANIMATION EXHIBITION, 1981
Location: New York City, NY, USA
Exhibitor: The Whitney Museum of American Art
Concept: SITE
Status: Installed

**DISNEY/MGM STUDIOS—MICKEY MOUSE
HISTORY MUSEUM AND BACK LOT REST
AREA, 1987**
Location: Disney World, Orlando, FL, USA
Client: Walt Disney and MGM Studios Collaborative
Concept: SITE
Status: Schematic design (unbuilt)

**DOOR WITHIN A DOOR WITHIN A DOOR
WITHIN A DOOR WITHIN A DOOR, 1985**
Client: Private
Concept: SITE
Status: Constructed

EDUCATION PLACE, 1970
Location: University of Northern Iowa, Cedar Falls,
IO, USA
Client: Education Department of University of
Northern Iowa
Concept: SITE—Dana Draper, Cynthia Eardley,
Nancy Goldring, James Wines
Status: Schematic design (unbuilt)

**ENVIRONMENTAL EDUCATION CENTER
AND NORTHERN TRAIL SYSTEM, 1995**
Location: Independent Hill District Park, Prince
William County, VA, USA
Client: Prince William County Park Authority
Concept: SITE
Architect: Anshen + Allen, Baltimore, MD, USA
Status: Schematic design (unbuilt)

EVERSON MUSEUM PLAZA, 1969
Location: Syracuse, New York
Client: Everson Museum of Art
Concept: SITE
Status: Schematic design (unbuilt)

FAMOLORE SHOWROOM, 1981
Location: 4 East 54th Street, New York City, NY, USA
Client: Famolore, Inc.
Concept: SITE
Status: Unbuilt

FLOATING MCDONALD'S, 1983
Location: Harem Avenue and Cermak Road,
Berwyn, IL, USA
Client: McDonald's Corp.
Concept: SITE
Structural Engineer: Weidlinger Assoc., Inc.,
New York City, NY, USA
Mechanical Engineer: Air Distribution Assoc.
Lighting Designer: Incorporation Consultants Co., Ltd.
General Contractor: Walter Daniels Contractors, Inc.
Status: Built

FLOATING ROOF SHOWROOM, 1970
Location: Richmond, VA, USA
Client: BEST Products Co., Inc.
Concept: SITE—Cynthia Eardley
Structural Engineer: Mario Salvadori
Status: Unbuilt

FORMICA COLORCORE, 1985
Location: New York City, NY, USA (traveling exhibition)
Client: Formica Corp.
Concept: SITE
Status: Constructed

FOUR CONTINENTS BRIDGE, 1988
Location: Hiroshima, Japan
Client: Sea and Island Expo Association
Concept: SITE—Joshua Weinstein, Glen Coben,
James Wines, Stomu Miyazaki
Structural Engineer: Geiger Engineers,
New York City, NY, USA
Landscape Architect: Signe Nielsen, P.C.,
New York City, NY, USA
Waterworks Consultant: Georgia Fountain Co., USA
Lighting Designer: Quentin Thomas Assoc.,
Brooklyn, NY, USA
General Contractor: Takenaka Komuten Co.,
Hiroshima, Japan
Status: Built

**FRANKFURT MUSEUM OF MODERN ART,
1983**
Location: Intersection of Domstrasse,
Berlinerstrasse, and Braubachstrasse, Frankfurt,
Germany
Client: The Municipality of Frankfurt
Concept: SITE
Structural Engineer: Weidlinger Assoc., Inc.,
New York City, NY, USA
Mechanical Engineer: Lehr Assoc., New York City,
NY, USA
Status: Competition entry (unbuilt)

GENERAL MOTORS BUILDING, 1969
Location: New York City, NY, USA
Client: General Motors Corporation
(environmental art project)
Concept: SITE—Dana Draper
Status: Schematic design (unbuilt)

GENERAL STORE—SOFT MODULES, 1980
Location: Washington, D.C., USA
Client: The General Store
Concept: SITE—Alison Sky
Status: Unbuilt

GHOST HOUSES, 1980
Location: Tract Housing Community, NJ, USA
Concept: SITE
Status: Unbuilt

GHOST PARKING LOT, 1978
Location: Hamden Plaza Shopping Center, Hamden,
CT, USA
Client: National Shopping Centers, Inc.
Concept: SITE
General Contractor: Depersia Contractors, Inc.,
Glastonbury, CT, USA
Status: Built

GLASSBRIDGE PROJECT, 1968
Location: Fallen Leaf Lake, NV, USA
Client: Non-disclosed
Concept: SITE—Cynthia Eardley
Status: Schematic design (unbuilt)

GREENING OF MANHATTEN, 1979
Location: New York City, NY, USA
Client: Commissioned for publication
Concept: SITE
Status: Published

HANDS OF THE WORLD DISPLAY, 1991
Location: Shopping centers throughout the USA
Client: Frito Lay Corp.
Concept: SITE
Status: Manufactured and installed

HIGH-RISE OF HOMES, 1981
Location: Major urban center
Concept: SITE—Patricia Philips, Alison Sky,
James Wines
Structural Engineer: Weidlinger Assoc., Inc.,
New York City, NY, USA
Status: Unbuilt

HIGHWAY 86 PROCESSIONAL, 1986
Location: 1986 World Exposition, Vancouver, BC,
Canada
Client: Expo 86
Concept: SITE—James Wines, Alison Sky,
Michelle Stone; team—Joshua Weinstein,
John de Vitry, Stomu Miyazaki, Naoto Sekiguchi
Associate Architect: Boak Alexander Architects,
Vancouver, BC, Canada
Structural Engineer: Geiger Assoc., Vancouver, BC,
Canada
Mechanical/Electrical Engineer: D.W. Thomson
Consultants, Vancouver, BC, Canada
Landscape Architect: Signe Nielsen, P.C., New York
City, NY, USA; Vaughan-Durante Ltd., Vancouver,
BC, Canada
Exhibit Contractor: EBCO Industries, Richmond, BC,
Canada
Exhibit Installer: BRITCO Installations, Vancouver,
BC, Canada
General Contractor: Halse-Martin Construction,
Vancouver, BC, Canada
Status: Built

HOROSCOPE RING—EXPO 92, 1991
Location: Toyama, Japan
Client: Toyama Expo Association
Concept: SITE—Joshua Weinstein, Amy Eggertsen;
team—James Wines, Kelley Bryant, Suzan Wines,
Hillit Meidar, Toshiyoki Ichikawa
Associated Architect: Archinocc Co., Ltd., Tokyo,
Japan
Contractor: Nomura Co., Ltd, Tokyo, Japan
Status: Built

"ICEBERG" BOTTLE, 1986
Client: Vittel Society of Mineral Water, Paris, France
Concept: SITE
Status: Limited production

**IDENTITY PEN, WATCH, CARD CASE AND
TIE, 2003**
Client: ACME Products, Inc.
Concept: SITE—Denise M C Lee, James Wines,
Patrick Head
Status: Manufactured

IGA GARDEN EXPOSITION PARK, 1996
Location: Dresden, Germany
Concept: SITE—James Wines, Hauke Stolton
Landscape Designer: Tourbier and Walmsley, NY
and Philadelphia, PA, USA; Oehme, van Sweden &
Assoc., Washington, D.C., USA
Consultant: Landmarks GMBH, Dresden, Germany
Consultant: Burkart Stelzer, Philadelphia, PA, USA
Status: Competition entry (unbuilt)

INTERSTATE 80 REST STOP PROJECT, 1974
Location: York Rest Stop, Interstate 80, NE, USA
Client: The State of Nebraska—State Bicentennial
Project
Concept: SITE—Alison Sky
Status: Schematic design (unbuilt)

ISUZU SPACE STATION, 1989
Location: Sakuragi-cho Railway Station, Naka-ku,
Yokohama, Japan
Client: Isuzu Corp., Yokohama, Japan
Architects: SITE—Joshua Weinstein, James Wines,
Glen Coben
Status: Built

**LA VILLE RADIEUSE—VENICE BIENNALE
EXHIBITION, 2000**
Location: Arsenale, Venice, Italy
Exhibitor: La Biennale de Venezia—the 7th
International Architecture Exhibition
Exhibition Title: Less Aesthetics More Ethics
Concept: SITE; I-Beam Design & Gianni Pettena
Status: Schematic design (unbuilt) and published in
Biennale catalogue

LAURIE MALLET HOUSE, 1985
Location: New York City, NY, USA
Client: Laurie Mallet
Concept: SITE—Alison Sky, James Wines,
Stomu Miyazaki
Structural Engineer: Geiger Assoc.
Lighting Consultant: Bob Davis, Inc.
Artifacts: C.S.I., Inc.; M.R.A. Assoc.
General Contractor: Gordon Construction Corp.
Status: Built

**LE PUY—CIVIC SPACE AND ADAPTIVE RE-
USE PROJECT, 1992**
Location: Le Puy-En-Velay, Haute-Loire, France
Client: Conseil General de la Haute-Loire, France
Concept: SITE
Associate Architect: George Berger Architecte
D.P.L.G., Loudes; Arch. SA., Architectes,
Saint-Etienne; Pronaos, Mirebeau-Sur-Beze
Status: Competition winner

LIVING ROOM, 2003
Location: Carate Brianza, Lombardy, Italy
Client: Matteo and Mascia Rossini
Concept: SITE—Denise M C Lee, Patrick Head,
Sara Stracey
Status: Design development

MAISON DE LA CULTURE DU JAPON, 1990
Location: 101 Quai Branly 75015, Paris, France
Client: Fondation du Japon, représentée par
l'Association pour la construction de la Maison de la
Culture du Japon à Paris
Concept: SITE
Status: Competition entry (unbuilt)

MAK BOOKSTORE ENTRANCE, 1990
Location: Vienna, Austria
Client: MAK—Museum für Angewandte Kunst
Concept: SITE
Status: Built

MELTING CANDLESTICK, 1985
Client: Swid/Powell, Inc.
Concept: SITE
Status: Produced for limited edition

**METROPOLITAN OPERA HOUSE PLAZA,
1969**
Location: Lincoln Center, New York City, NY, USA
Client: Adler Foundation
Concept: SITE
Status: Design development (unbuilt)

MIRROR PROJECT, 1970
Location: Richmond, VA, USA
Client: BEST Products Co., Inc.
Concept: SITE—James Wines
Status: Unbuilt

MOLINO STUCKY, 1978
Location: Venice, Italy
Exhibitor: La Biennale de Venezia—25th
International Art Exhibition
Exhibition Title: From Nature to Art, from Art to Nature
Concept: SITE
Status: Proposal

MONUMENTAL DESK, 1985
Location: New York City, NY, USA
Client: WilliWear Corp.
Concept: SITE
Status: Manufactured

MUSEUM OF ISLAMIC ARTS, 1997
Location: Doha, Qatar
Client: The State of Qatar
Concept: SITE—James Wines, Marcus Iglauer,
Johannes Ziegler; team—Bryan Langlands,
Denise M C Lee, Garrick Jones, Zuzana Karczenska,
Stomu Miyazaki, Jonathan Turner, Ellen Warfield
Exhibit Design: Land Design Studio, London, UK
Museum Planner: Polkinghorne Assoc., London, UK
Consulting Architect: Mimar Design, Doha, Qatar
Structural Engineer: Agassi Consulting Engineers,
NY, USA
Mechanical/Electrical Engineer: Jaros Baum &
Bolles, New York City, NY, USA
Landscape Architect: Tourbier and Walmsley, NY, USA
Environmental Consultant: The Hillier Group,
Princeton, NJ, USA
Lighting Designer: Quentin Thomas Assoc., NY, USA
Quantity Surveyor: Tillyard, NY, USA
Status: Competition entry (unbuilt)

PEEKSKILL MELT, 1972
Location: Peekskill, NY, USA
Client: Peekskill Urban Development Corp.
Concept: SITE
Status: Schematic design (unbuilt)

PERSHING SQUARE, 1986–87
Location: Los Angeles, CA, USA
Client: Pershing Square Management Assoc.
Concept: SITE
Architects: SITE with Kober Cedergreen Rippon
Structural Engineer: Geiger Assoc.
Consulting Engineer: Tsuchiayama & Kaino;
Nikolakopolus & Assoc.; Delon Hampton
Lighting Designer: George Sexton Assoc.
Landscape Architect: EDAW, Inc.; Burton & Spitz
Status: Competition winner (unbuilt)

PLATTE RIVER REST STOP, 1974
Location: Platte River Rest Stop, Interstate 80, NE,
USA
Client: The State of Nebraska—State Bicentennial
Project
Concept: SITE—James Wines
Status: Schematic design (unbuilt)

POMPIDOU GARDEN, 1989
Location: Paris, France
Exhibitor: Centre Georges Pompidou, Paris, France
Concept: SITE
Status: Design development (unbuilt)

REVENGE OF THE RIVER, 1984
Client: Dedeaux Publishing, NY, USA
Concept: SITE
Status: Printed as limited edition

ROSS'S LANDING PARK AND PLAZA, 1992
Location: Chattanooga, TN, USA
Client: The River City Company of Hamilton County
and the City of Chattanooga
Architect: SITE—James Wines; team—Glen Coben,
Joshua Weinstein, David Downs, Amy Eggertsen,
Alison Leahy, Russell Ruble
Associate Architect: Robert Seals Architects,
Chattanooga, TN, USA
Landscape Architect: EDAW, Inc., Alexandria, VA, USA
Public Artists: Jack Mackie, Seattle, WA, USA;
Stanley Townsend, Chattanooga, TN, USA
Consulting Engineers: Hensley-Schmidt, Inc.,

Chattanooga, TN, USA; Robinson Assoc., Atlanta, GA, USA
Consultants: Riverfront Downtown Planning and Design Center, Chattanooga, TN, USA
Project Management: Turner Construction Co., Nashville, TN, USA
General Contractor: Soloff Construction Co., Inc., Chattanooga, TN, USA
Status: Built

ROSSINI SCULPTURE GARDEN, VISITORS PAVILION AND MASTER PLAN, 2000–04
Location: Briosco, Italy
Client: Fondazione Rossini, Carate, Brianza, Italy
Master Planning Concept: SITE—James Wines, Denise M C Lee; team—Patrick Head, Sara Stracey, Brandon Coburn
Pavilion Concept: SITE—James Wines, Stomu Miyazaki, Denise M C Lee; team—Joshua Weinstein
Associate Architect: Corrado Sala, Paolo Fietta, Carate Brianza, Italy
Structural Engineer: Studio Losi, Carate Brianza, Italy
Mechanical Engineer: Colciago Roberto, Carate Brianza, Italy
Interior Designer: D Studio, Milano, Italy
General Contractor: Impresa di costruzioni F.lli Boffi – S.r.l.
Status: Under construction

SANTA FE RAILYARD PARK, 2002
Location: Santa Fe, NM, USA
Client: Trust for Public Land
Concept: SITE—James Wines, Denise M C Lee, Patrick Head, Stomu Miyazaki, Sara Stracey
Associate Architect: Marie Wilkinson, Santa Fe, NM, USA; Van Amburgh+Pares Studio, Santa Fe, NM, USA
Landscape Designer: Design with Nature, Santa Fe, NM, USA
Landscape Architect: David Carlson, Santa Fe, NM, USA
Public Artist: Chrissie Orr, Santa Fe, NM, USA
Advisor: Regenesis, Santa Fe, NM, USA; Earth & Water, Santa Fe, NM, USA; Anthony Dorame and Assoc., Tesuque Pueblo, NM, USA
Status: Competition entry (unbuilt)

SAUDI ARABIAN NATIONAL MUSEUM AND DARAT AL MALIK ABD AL-AZIZ, 1996
Location: Riyadh, Al Muraba, Saudi Arabia
Client: Ar-Riyadh Development Authority
Concept: SITE—James Wines, Denise M C Lee, John de Vitry, Michelle Stone
Associate Architect: Benoy Architects, London, UK; Omrania, Riyadh, Saudi Arabia
Landscape Architect: EDAW, Inc., London, UK
Exhibit Designer: LAND Design Studio, London, UK
Consulting Engineer: Buro Happold, Bath, UK
Museum Planner: LORD, Toronto, Canada
Status: Competition entry (unbuilt)

SAUDI ARABIAN PAVILION, 1992
Location: Seville, Spain
Client: H.H. The Commissioner, Prince Abdullah Bin Faisal Bin Turki Al Saud, Kingdom of Saudi Arabia
Concept: SITE—James Wines, Michelle Stone, Joshua Weinstein; team—John de Vitry, Glen Coben, Alison Leahy, Amy Eggertsen, Jacqueline Tatom, Jim Petroulas, Katsu Takemata
Project Management: Al-Shathry Consulting Engineers, Riyadh, Saudi Arabia; Buro Happold, Bath, UK
Associate Architect: Fitch-Benoy, London, UK
Exhibit Designer: Fitch-Benoy, London, UK
Consulting Engineer: Interstudio, Seville, Spain
Landscape Architect: Signe Nielsen, P.C., NY, USA
Lighting Designer: Quentin Thomas Lighting, Brooklyn, NY, USA
Quantity Surveyor: Symonds Chartered Quantity Surveyors, London, UK
General Contractor: Dumez-Copisa, Seville, Spain
Status: Built

SHAKE SHACK, 2004
Location: Southeast corner of Madison Square Park, East 23rd–East 26th Streets between Fifth and Madison Avenues, Manhattan, NY, USA
Client: Madison Square Park Conservancy; The Union Square Hospitality Group
Concept: SITE—Denise M C Lee, James Wines; team—Cheryl Woo, Sara Stracey, Brandon Coburn
City Agency: City of New York Parks & Recreation
Structural Engineer: Concept— Weidlinger Assoc., Inc., New York City, NY, USA
Consulting Engineer: Marino Gerazounis & Jaffe Assoc.
Kitchen Designer: Clevenger Frable LaVallee
Lighting Designer: Thompson + Sears Lighting
Signage Designer: Pentagram
Associate Architect: Kullman Industries
General Contractor: Kullman Industries
Sitework Contractor: Qwest Contracting
Status: Built

SHINWA RESORT, 1991
Location: Kisokoma-Kogen, Japan
Client: Yutaka Tanaka, Shinwa Resort Corp.
Concept: SITE
Landscape Architect: EDAW, Inc.
Consultant: Hashimoto/Platz Design, Inc.
Status: Schematic design (unbuilt)

SITE BUILDINGS AND SPACES, 1980–81
Client: BEST Products, Co., Inc.
Exhibitor: Virginia Museum, Richmond (traveling exhibition)
Concept: SITE
Films: Howard Silver Films, NY, USA
Graffiti: The Dirty Ones, Brooklyn, NY, USA
Carpentry: Tana Construction, NY, USA
General Contractor: Blitman Construction Co., NY, USA
Status: Installed

SPLIT HOUSE, 2003
(Villa Claudia)
Location: Ogiata, Roma, Italy
Client: Giandomenico Fabiani
Concept: SITE—James Wines, Denise M C Lee, Patrick Head, Sara Stracey
Status: Schematic design (unbuilt)

STATEN ISLAND 9/11 MEMORIAL SATELLITE CONNECTION, 2002
Location: New York City, Borough of Staten Island, NY, USA
Client: NYC Economic Development Corporation
Designer: SITE—Denise M C Lee, Patrick Head, Sara Stracey
Status: Competition entry (unbuilt)

TENNESSEE AQUA CENTER AKA AQUATORIUM, 1993
Location: Kirkman Hill, Chattanooga, TN, USA
Client: City of Chattanooga
Concept: SITE—James Wines, Joshua Weinstein; team—Jonathan Rothstein, Denise M C Lee, Toshiyoki Ichikawa
Status: Schematic design (unbuilt)

TERRA TAVOLA, 1999
Client: Saporiti Italia, Milan, Italy
Concept: SITE—James Wines, Denise M C Lee
Status: Manufactured

THE PAZ BUILDING, 1985
Location: 179 Marcy Avenue, Williamsburg, Brooklyn, NY, USA
Client: Paz Holding Corp. and 185 Marcy Corp.
Concept: SITE
Structural Engineer: Weidlinger Assoc., Inc., New York City, NY, USA
Electrical/Mechanical Engineer: Lehr Assoc., New York City, NY, USA
Status: Unbuilt

THE WORLD ECOLOGY PAVILION, 1992
Location: Seville, Spain
Client: EXPO 92 – 1992 Universal Exposition
Concept: SITE
Status: Schematic design (unbuilt)

TÖÖLÖNLAHTI PARK, 1997
Location: Helsinki, Finland
Client: Municipality of Helsinki
Concept: SITE—James Wines; team—Bryan Langlands, Denise M C Lee, Christian Klimaschka, Zuzana Karczenska, Johannes Ziegler
Landscape Architect: Tourbier and Walmsley, NY, USA
Status: Competition entry (unbuilt)

TRAWSFYNYDD INTERNATIONAL ENERGY COMMUNICATIONS CENTER, 1994–95
Location: Trawsfynydd, North Wales, UK
Client: British Broadcasting Corp. and the City of Trawsfynydd, Nuclear Electric, The Development Board for Rural Wales, The Training and Enterprise Council for North West Wales, UK
Concept: SITE—James Wines, Kriz Kizak-Wines
Status: Schematic design (unbuilt)

USA PAVILION—2000 HANNOVER WORLD EXPO, 1998
Location: Hannover, Germany
Client: US Commissioner General and USA at Hannover 2000, Inc.
Concept: SITE—James Wines, Denise M C Lee, Stomu Miyazaki; team—Suzan Wines, Joshua Weinstein, Marcus Iglauer
Landscape Consultant: Michael Van Valkenburgh Assoc., Boston, MA, USA
Structural Engineer: Weidlinger Assoc., Inc., New York City, NY, USA
Cost Consultant: Tillyard, New York City, NY, USA
Status: Schematic design (unbuilt)

VIRGIN RECORDS, 1987
Location: New York City, NY, USA
Client: Virgin Records, Inc.
Concept: SITE
Status: Unbuilt

WILLIWEAR HARRODS SHOP, 1983
Location: Harrods, London, UK
Client: WilliWear, Ltd.
Concept: SITE
General Contractor: Bernard Exhibition Design
Status: Built

WILLIWEAR RETAIL STORE, 1988
Location: Lower Fifth Avenue, New York City, NY, USA
Client: WilliWear, Ltd.
Concept: SITE
Consulting Engineer: Jetmatrix; Kaback Enterprises
Lighting Designer: Kruger Assoc.
Landscape Design: Madelyn Simon & Assoc.
General Contractor: Gordon Construction Corp.
Status: Built

WILLIWEAR SHOWROOM, 1982
Location: 209 West 38th Street, New York City, NY, USA
Client: WilliWear, Ltd.
Concept: SITE
Showroom Installation: Architectural Assoc.
General Contractor: Gordon Construction Corp.
Status: Built

XERION CAPITAL PARTNERS OFFICES, 2004
Location: 450 Park Avenue, New York City, NY, USA
Client: Xerion Capital Partners
Concept: SITE—Denise M C Lee, Sara Stracey
Audio Visual Consultant: Excel Media Systems, Inc.
Holographic Film Manufacturer: DNP
Art Installation Assistant: Alan Ho
General Contractor: R C Dolner LLC
Status: Built

SITE BIBLIOGRAPHY

MONOGRAPHS AND EXHIBITION CATALOGUES

Beret, Chantal & Revoire, Michel. *James Wines Dessins d'Architecture*. (Catalogue for a Wines drawing exhibition at Galerie Cour de Mai in Paris and Museum of Contemporary Art in Lyon, France.) Paris, France: Les Editions du Demi-Cercle, 1989.

Bossiere, Oliver. *Gehry, Site, Tigerman: Trois Portraits de l'Artiste en Architecte*. (Book on three American architects featuring SITE work until 1981.) Paris, France: Editions du Moniteur, 1981.

Byeon, Wooil. *James Wines and Site*. (Monograph. Interview with James Wines.) Seoul, Korea: Korea International Publisher, 1996.

Dietsch, Deborah. *American Visions Series, "Site"*. (Monograph catalogue.) USA: Champion International Paper Company, 1989.

Graaf, Vera. *Du Magazine "Site"*. (Special monograph issue on work of SITE up to 1988.) Zurich, Switzerland: Du Verlag, January 1988.

Intervista—James Wines. (Monograph based on a dialogue with J.W. concerning his views of environmental design. Interview by Francesco Cirillo.) Napoli, Italy: CLEAN Edizioni, 1999.

James Wines & Site—Architecture in Context. (Catalogue and Monograph based on the Architecture in Context Exhibition on 35 years of James Wines and SITE's built and unbuilt projects, showing James Wines' early Landsite sculptures, watercolor renderings, and SITE's architectural models.) Orléans, France: Musée des Beaux-Arts d'Orléans, France—Collection FRAC Centre—HYX, 2002.

Muschamp, Herbert (with notes by James Wines). *Folio VII: The Frankfurt Museum of Modern Art*. (Monograph folio on SITE's competition entry for the Museum of Modern Art, Frankfurt, West Germany.) London, England: The Architectural Association, 1986.

Muschamp, Herbert; Nakamura, Toshio & Sakane, Itsuo. *SITE*. (Book on the work of SITE from 1970 to 1986.) Tokyo, Japan: A+U Publishing Company, 1986.

Phillips, Patricia & Wines, James. *The High-rise of Homes*. (Catalogue for traveling exhibition of high-rise architecture by SITE.) New York City, New York, USA: Rizzoli International Publications, 1982.

Restany, Pierre & Zevi, Bruno. *Site: Architecture as Art*. (Monograph on the work of SITE from 1970 to 1980.) London and New York, UK and USA: Academy Editions and St. Martins Press, 1980.

SITE & Zevi, Bruno. *Site—Projects and Theories*. (Monograph on the complete work of SITE from 1970 to 1978.) Bari, Italy: Dedalo Libri, 1978.

Site Agenda 1995. (Monograph. Diary/appointment book featuring 25 years of drawings by James Wines for SITE projects.) Milano, Italy: Edizioni L'Archivolto, 1995.

SITE. (Monograph on the complete work of SITE through 1987. Interview and text by Herbert Muschamp.) New York City, New York, USA: Rizzoli International Publications, 1987.

Smith, C. Ray. *Site: Buildings and Spaces*. (Catalogue for 10 year retrospective exhibition of SITE's projects and proposals at the Virginia Museum, Richmond, Virginia.) Richmond, Virginia, USA: The Virginia Museum, 1980.

Sokolowski, Thomas. *SITE on McDonald's: the American Landscape*. (Catalogue for an exhibition at the Chrysler Museum at Seaboard Center featuring a McDonald's building by SITE.) Norfolk, Virginia, USA: The Chrysler Museum, 1984.

Toraldo di Francia, Cristiano. *Site: Architetture 1971–1988*. (Monograph to accompany the SITE retrospective in Florence, Italy.) Milano, Italy: Officina Edizioni, 1988.

BOOKS AND CATALOGUES FEATURING SITE

1000 Architects. (Publication as an international pictorial directory of leading architectural firms.) Melbourne, Australia: Images Publishing Group, 2004.

7th International Architecture Exhibition: Citta: Less Aesthetics More Ethics (3 volumes). (Catalogue featuring participating architects and designers at la Biennale di Venezia.) Venezia, Italy: Marsilio, 2000.

8th International Architecture Exhibition: Next (2 volumes). (Catalogues featuring participating architects and designers at la Biennale di Venezia.) Venezia, Italy: Marsilio, 2002.

Architectural References. (Catalogue for exhibition at Vancouver Art Gallery featuring three projects by SITE.) Vancouver, Canada: Vancouver Art Gallery, 1979.

Barrie, David (Editor). *Power to Change: Architecture for a New Age of Nuclear Waste and Decommissioning*. (Documentation of four design teams commissioned to examine the decommissioning of a nuclear power station in Wales. SITE project commentary and illustrations by James Wines, including interviews.) London, England: British Broadcasting Corporation, 1995.

Brayer, Marie-Ange & Simonot, Beatrice (Editors). *Archilab's Earth Buildings—Radical Experiments in Land Architecture*. (Catalogue for the 3rd annual architectural exhibition featuring young architects and designers.) New York City, New York, USA: Thames & Hudson, 2003.

Brayer, Marie-Ange (Introduction and text). *Architectures Experimentales 1950–2000—collection du FRAC Centre*. (Catalogue featuring FRAC Center's collection, including SITE's BEST Indeterminate Façade, BEST Forest Showroom, High-rise of Homes.) Orléans, France: HYX, 2003.

Cantico 2000. (Museum catalogue on exhibition Ethics and Environment at Museo della Permanente, featuring Habitable Sculpture Garden Pavilion for the Rossini Family. Curated by Ivan Rizzi.) Milano, Italy: Stampa Inedita, 2000.

Crosby, Michael & Wines, James. *Green Architecture—A guide to sustainable design featuring five projects by SITE*. Rockport, Massachusetts, USA: Rockport Publishers, Inc., 1994.

DaimlerChrysler Design Awards 1993–1999. (Publication featuring award recipients and related works.) Detroit, Michigan, USA: DaimlerChrysler Design Awards, 1999.

Des-Res Architecture. Vol. 69 No.1/2. (Book on residential architecture featuring the Mallet House. Mixed authors.) London, UK: Architectural Design Publishers, 1999.

Dixon, John. *Urban Spaces*. (Book on public spaces featuring 25 architects and landscape architects.) New York City, New York, USA: Retail Reporting Publishers, 1999.

Documenta 8. (Catalogue for Documenta International Art Exhibition featuring five projects by SITE.) Kassel, West Germany: Fridericianum Veranstaltungs GmbH, 1987.

Drexler, Arthur. *Buildings For Best Products*. (Catalogue for exhibition at Museum of Modern Art featuring five projects by SITE.) New York City, New York, USA: Museum of Modern Art, 1979.

Eaton, Ruth. *Ideal Cities*. (Book on historical urban architecture.) Antwerp, Belgium: Mercatorfonds N.V., 2001.

Envisioning Architecture. (Drawings from the Museum of Modern Art.) New York, USA: Museum of Modern Art, 2002.

Gossel, Peter & Leuthauser, Gabriele. *Architecture in the Twentieth Century*. Cologne, Germany: Reprint by Taschen Verlag, 2002.

Goulet, Patrice. *Temps Sauvage et Incertain* (Catalogue for traveling exhibition featuring four projects by SITE.) Paris, France: Les Editions du Demi-Cercle, 1989.

Guenzi, Carlo. *La Affinita Elettive*. (Catalogue for the Triennale di Milano featuring a special exhibit by SITE.) Milano, Italy: Electa Editrice, 1985.

Jodidio, Philip (Editor). *New Forms—Architecture in the 1990s—Taschen's World Architecture series*. Cologne, Germany: Taschen Verlag, 1997.

Jodidio, Philip. *Building a New Millennium*. (Book on contemporary architecture.) Cologne, Germany: Taschen Verlag, 1999.

Jodidio, Philip. *Contemporary American Architects—Vol. II*. (Pictorial book featuring work of 16 architects and/or firms.) Cologne, Germany: Benedikt Taschen, 1996.

Jodidio, Philip. *Contemporary American Architects*. (Pictorial book featuring the work of 15 firms.) Cologne, Germany: Benedikt Taschen, 1993.

Kelley, James. *The Sculptural Idea* (4th Ed.) "Humanity and Technology; Environment and Action/Reaction." (Including SITE's BEST Indeterminate Façade, BEST Notch Showroom, Ghost Parking Lot and Ranger Pavilion.) Long Grove, Illinois, USA: Waveland Press, 2003.

Kostelanetz, Richard. *Dictionary of the Avant-Gardes*. (Book on music, film, visual arts, dance and theater.) New York City, New York, USA: Schirmer Books, 2000.

Landscape and the Zero Degree of Architectural Language. (Documents the Conference led by Bruno Zevi in Modena, Italy, September 1997.) Venezia, Italy: Canal E Stamperia Editrice. 1999.

Lear, Edward. *Non-Sense*. Children's book. Illustrated by James Wines. New York City, New York, USA: Rizzoli International Publications, 1994.

Miller, R. Craig (Introduction). *US Design 1975–2000*. "Points of View in American Architecture" by David DeLong. Germany: Prestel, 2002.

Nakamura, Toshio & Wines, James. *Architecture and Urbanism*. "SITE, Green Architecture." (Special issue featuring environmental work by SITE.) Tokyo, Japan: A+U Publishing Company, December 1990.

Porter, Tom. *Architectural Drawing Masterclass*. (Pictorial book of different architects' graphic techniques featuring three projects by SITE.) New York City, New York, USA: Charles Scribner's Sons, 1993.

Project on the City. "High Architecture" by Daniel Herman. Cologne, Germany: Taschen Verlag, 2002.

Protetch, Max with Krimko, Stuart (Introduction). *A New World Trade Center—Design Proposals from Leading Architects Worldwide*. New York, USA: Regan Books, Harper Collins Publishing House, 2002.

Raggi, Franco (Editor). *A Proposal of Molino Stucky*. (Catalogue for the 1975 Venice Biennale featuring a special project by SITE.) Milano, Italy: Alfieri Publishers, 1975.

Rohrer, Judith. *Matrix: A Changing Exhibition of Contemporary Art*. (Catalogue of one-man show at the Wadsworth Atheneum featuring the work of SITE from 1970 to 1975.) Hartford, Connecticut, USA: Wadsworth Atheneum Publications, 1975.

Ruano, Miguel. *Eco Urbanismo*. (Book on ecological urbanism featuring SITE's master plans for IGA Park in Dresden, Germany and Hôtel du Departement in Le Puy-en-Velay, France.) Barcelona, Spain: Gustavo Gili Publishers, 1999.

Slessor, Catherine (Introduction). *100 of the World's Best Houses*. Melbourne, Australia: Images Publishing Group, 2002.

Ten Years—Chrysler Design Awards—A Decade of Design. (Publication of award winners 1992 to 2002, including James Wines and SITE as the 1995 winner.) Wilton, Connecticut, USA: The Magazine Works, November 2002.

Unbuilt America. (Historical reference book by Alison Sky and Michelle Stone.) New York City, New York, USA: McGraw Hill Publishers, 1976.

Wines, James (Editor). *The Architecture of Ecology*. London, UK: Architectural Design Publishers, May 1997.

Wines, James (Foreword, texts by multiple authors). *On Energy—Analytical compilation of essays on the energy issue in architecture*. New York City, New York, USA: ON SITE Publications, 1974.

Wines, James (Introduction). *James Culter—Contemporary World Architects series*. (Monograph on James Culter's architectural works.) Rockport, Massachusetts, USA: Rockport Publishers, 1997.

Wines, James (Introduction). *Massimiliano Fuksas—Contemporary World Architects Series*. (Monograph on Massimiliano Fuksas' architectural works.) Rockport, Massachusetts, USA: Rockport Publishers, 1998.

Wines, James. *De-Architecture*. (Book of critical essays on architecture and environmental art.) New York City, New York, USA: Rizzoli International Publishers, 1987.

Wines, James. *Green Architecture*. (Historical and philosophical book on architecture and the natural environment, with an emphasis on recent green architects.) Cologne, Germany: Taschen Verlag, 2000.

Wiseman, Carter. *Twentieth-Century American Architecture—the Buildings and their Makers*. (Book on American architecture.) New York City, New York, USA: W.W. Norton & Company, 2000.

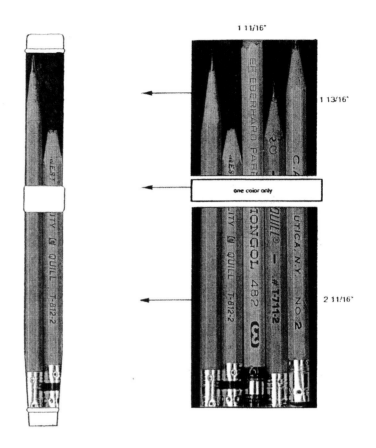

1 11/16"

1 13/16"

one color only

2 11/16"

^ **Pencil—Pen concept for ACME Products**
2001

v **Illustration for Edward Lear's** *Non-Sense*
Rizzoli
1994

PHOTOGRAPHY CREDITS

SITE EXCEPT FOR:

PETER AARON OF ESTO—Best Forest Showroom, SITE 65 Bleecker Street Studio

PHILIPPE RAGNON—Landsite Model V, James Wines & SITE—Architecture in Context

PETER MAUSS OF ESTO—Madison Square Park Kiosk, aka Shake Shack—p 210–211

ANDREAS STERZING—WilliWear Men's Harrods Shop, Fifth Avenue, Glen Gery Brick Design Center, Laurie Mallet House, Avenue Five, Highway 86, ALLSTEEL Showroom & Archaeology, 65 Bleecker Street, SITE 25 Maiden Lane Studio

PAUL WARCHOL—Laurie Mallet House

ROBERT SMITHSON
Spiral Jetty
Great Salt Lake, Utah, USA
1970

ALICE AYCOCK
Low Building with Dirt Roof
New Kingston, Pennsylvania, USA
1973

GORDON MATTA-CLARK
Splitting
Englewood, New Jersey, USA
1974

MERET OPPENHEIM
Fur-lined Tea Cup
1936

MICHAEL MCDONOUGH
Grid House
Boston, Massachusetts, USA
1978

LE CORBUSIER
Proposal for Algiers Viaduct Block
1934

MAN RAY
Marcel Duchamp, photographed by Man Ray,
Elevage de Poussiere from the Green Box
1934

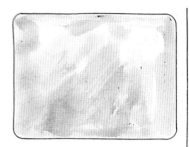

starts with fogged screen.

Screen explodes

Image of smoke and dwindling fire inside the broken screen area.

Image of the V.J. appears after smoke settles — sitting inside of the TV set, surrounded by the actual electronics, still on fire.

V.J. disappears leaving black interior and last flickering electrical fire glow — with logo.

ACKNOWLEDGMENTS

The past and present members of SITE extend a special thanks to the following people who, from 1970 to the present, gave us a variety of support in the form of patronage, advocacy, guidance, inspirational dialogue, and the benefits of their infinitely valuable friendship.

Clients:
Daniel Arbess (Xerion)
Enrico Baleri (Baleri Italia)
Duane Beckhorn (Private Koenig Foundation)
Roger Enrico (Pepsico)
Jackie Fowler
Carey Hanlin (Rivercity Company)
Masatake Kitamoto (Country Communications)
Malcolm Knapp
Debbie Landau (Madison Square Park Conservancy)
Susan Lewin (Formica)
Sydney and Frances Lewis (BEST Products)
Laurie Mallet (WilliWear)
Danny Meyer (Union Square Hospitality Group)
Barbara Pine
Alberto Rossini (Fondazione Rossini)
Rafaele Saporiti (Saporiti Italia)
Jun Shinzawa (Dentzu)
Willli Smith (WilliWear)
Abby Terkuhle (MTV)
Roger Thomson (Brinker International)
Tom Trybus (ALLSTEEL)
Georgy Venn (ALLSTEEL)

Art Galleries and Museums:
Centre Pompidou (Jean Dethier)
Centre Pompidou, Paris (Frédéric Migayrou)
Cooper Hewitt Museum, New York (Marilyn Symmes)
Corcoran Gallery of Art (David Levy)
Fonds Régional d'Art Contemporain du Centre, Orléans, FRAC (Marie-Ange Brayer)
Marlborough Gallery, New York (Frank Lloyd)
Max Protetch Gallery, New York (Max Protetch)
Museum of Modern Art, New York (Arthur Drexler and Stuart Wrede)
Osterreichisches Museum für Angewandte Kunst (Peter Noever)
Ronald Feldman Gallery, New York (Ronald Feldman)
Senior and Shopmaker Gallery, New York (Betsy Senior and Lawrence Shopmaker)
Virginia Museum (R. Peter Mooz)
Whitney Museum of American Art (Tom Armstrong)

Architects, Artists, and Engineers:
Peter Aaron
Hazem Abu Naba
Vito Acconci
Emilio Ambasz
Alice Aycock
Donna Brueger
Peter Cook
Tarik & Nayana Currimbhoy
Dawn Dedeaux
David Gissen
Alvin Gordon
Paul Gossen
Karan Grover
Nancy Holt
Nam June Paik
Frederick Kiesler
Donald Kunze
Matthys Levy
Max Limsgrüth
Darla Lindberg
Federica Marangoni
Gordon Matta-Clark
Miralda
Mariano Mollina
Donald Mongitore
Evaristo Nicolao
Alain Peskine
Bret Peters
Gianni Pettena
Franco Raggi
László Rajk
Mario Salvadori
Denise Scott Brown
Robert Smithson
Alan Sonfist
Michael Sorkin

Andreas Sterzing
Alan Swanson
Robert Venturi
Anthony Walmsley
Straud Watson
Aaron West
Suzan Wines

Foundations:
Graham Foundation (Carter Manny and Richard Solomon)
Kaplan Foundation (Joan Davidson)
Kress Foundation (Marilyn Perry and Mary Davis)
National Endowment for Arts—Design (Bill Lacy and Michael Pittas)
New York State Council for the Arts (Trudi Grace)
Rockefeller Foundation (Harold Snedcof)

Authors:
Fulvia Angrisano
Chantel Béret
Oliver Boissiére
Cesare Casati
Douglas Davis
Andrea Dean
Ruth Eaton
Marc Emery
Odile Fillion
Charles Gandee
Ada Louise Huxtable
Charles Jencks
Elaine Louie
Michael McDonough
Herbert Muschamp
Pierre Restany
Leslie Scherr
Vincent Scully
C. Ray Smith
Karen Stein
Pilar Vilades
Tom Wolfe
Bruno Zevi

Publishers and Editors:
A + U Japan (Toshio Nakamura)
Academy Editions (Andreas Papadakis)
Architecture (Donald Canty, Deborah Dietsch, and Reed Kroloff)
Architectural Record (Mildred Schmertz)
Artforum (Ingrid Sischy)
Connaissance des Arts (Philip Jodidio)
Images Publishing Group (Paul Latham and Alessina Brooks)
Interiors (Beverly Russell)
Interior Design (Stanley Abercrombie)
Landscape Architecture (Bill Thompson)
L'arca (Cesare Casati)
L'architecture d'ajourd'hui (Marc Emery)
McGraw Hill (Jeremy Robinson and Virginia Fechtmann)
Projetto (Luigi Prestinenza-Puglisi)
Rizzoli International (Gianfranco Monacelli)
Terrazzo (Ettore Sottsass)

Professional Advisors:
Emin Balcioglu
John Brockman
Alvin Boyarsky (Architecture Association)
George Collins (Columbia University)
Doris Freedman (Public Art Fund)
Leonard Garment
Anthony and Roseanna Lee
Sharyn Lewis
Kate Norment
Suha Özkan
Adolph Placzek (Columbia University)
Neil Porterfield (Penn State University)
Silas Rhoades (School of Visual Art)
George Sadek (Cooper Union)
Corrine Trang
Richard Wookey

BIOGRAPHIES

JAMES WINES

President and Creative Director

James Wines was educated at Syracuse University, where he studied art history, sculpture and literature, graduating with a Bachelor of Arts in 1956. He is the founder and President of SITE, the former Chair of Environmental Design at Parsons School of Design, and currently a Professor of Architecture at Penn State University. At both Parsons and Penn State he has worked on the development of graduate and professional programs in architecture.

He has given lectures at more than 1000 colleges, universities and conferences in 24 countries, and written many essays for books and magazines in the USA, Europe, and Asia. His book *DE-ARCHITECTURE* was published in 1987 by Rizzoli International and, in 2000, Taschen Verlag in Germany released his book *GREEN ARCHITECTURE*. During the past decade, there have been 22 monographs and museum catalogues produced on Mr. Wines' projects for SITE and their related models and drawings. He has designed more than 150 architecture, landscape, interior and exhibition projects for both private and municipal clients. Winner of 25 art and design awards, including the 1995 Chrysler Award for Design Innovation, he is also the recipient of fellowships and grants from the National Endowment for the Arts, The Kress Foundation, The American Academy in Rome, The Guggenheim Foundation, The Rockefeller Foundation, The Graham Foundation, The Ford Foundation, and the Pulitzer Prize for Graphics.

James Wines lives and works in New York City, exhibits with the Max Protetch Gallery and frequently travels abroad for projects, research, lectures, and writing assignments.

DENISE M C LEE

Senior Associate

Denise Lee graduated with a Bachelor of Planning and Design and Bachelor of Building from the University of Melbourne, Australia. She has worked extensively over the past 14 years in New York, Hong Kong, and Australia. Denise Lee has been with SITE on various levels of project responsibility since 1992, recently working as Project Designer and Coordinator on a variety of architecture, public space, urban and master planning projects.

In addition to her responsibilities at SITE, Denise Lee has been a guest critic at the Chinese University in Hong Kong, the Fashion Institute of Technology, Penn State University and Tulane University. Also, she has lectured and participated in symposia at various professional conferences in the USA, Europe, and Asia. Most recently she was the keynote speaker at the "Sensazioni e Bennessere" at the Bioarchitettura conference in Como, Italy.

Denise Lee lives and works in New York City and frequently travels abroad for projects and lectures.

SARA STRACEY

Artist

Sara Stracey was educated at Sweet Briar College, where she studied philosophy, literature, and biology prior to graduating with a B.F.A. in Painting with European Honors from the Rhode Island School of Design.

Ms. Stracey has been with SITE since 2001 and has contributed to projects including A New World Trade Center, New York, USA for Venice Architettura Biennale, Venice, Italy; Xerion Capital Partners—Listening to Architecture, New York, USA; SITE Architecture in Context— A Retrospective Exhibition, Musée des Beaux Arts, Orléans, France; Santa Fe Railyard Park, Santa Fe, New Mexico, USA; Rossini Foundation—Fires; Briosco, Italy; and India Projects.

STOMU MIYAZAKI

Associate, Senior Designer

Stomu Miyazaki graduated from the California College of Arts and Crafts (B.F.A. in Sculpture) and the Nippon University in Tokyo, Japan (B.S. in Physics). With his diversified academic background in art and science and his training in design, his creative work has been exhibited in numerous galleries in Tokyo, Oakland, and Manhattan. His furniture and lighting designs have both been awarded in international design competitions. Throughout his years at SITE since 1984, he has been in the design team associated with projects like Highway 86 for Expo '86, Vancouver; Theater for the New City, New York; SITE studios at the Bayard Building, New York; USA Pavilion for EXPO 2000, Hannover, Germany; and the Garden Pavilion, Briosco, Italy. By affiliation, he is an architectural design consultant for commercial and residential real estate developments in New York, Los Angeles, Philadelphia, and Miami.

JOSHUA WEINSTEIN

Architect
(Director of SITE II, Minneapolis, Minnesota)

Joshua Weinstein brings his 30 years of professional experience to SITE. Mr. Weinstein has given the firm its capacity to create fusions of art and architecture and to see the projects through to realization. He is involved in every stage of development, from conceptual ideas and design development to final on-site supervision. His unique role includes an involvement in the complex philosophical issues, their translation into architectural terminology, and a "hands-on" approach to building.

Mr. Weinstein graduated in architecture from Pratt Institute in Brooklyn, New York, with further studies in Paris, London, and Stockholm. Before joining SITE in 1982 as Director of Design Development, Joshua Weinstein worked with several large design offices where he specialized in adaptive/reuse projects and was responsible for an Award of Merit presented by the Regional Conference of Historical Agencies. Mr. Weinstein is a registered architect in Minnesota, and is certified by the National Council of Architectural Registration Boards.

In addition to his responsibilities at SITE, Joshua Weinstein has taught in the Environmental Design Department at Parsons School of Design, and currently teaches graduate design studio at the University of Minnesota. Also, he has lectured, judged competitions and participated in symposia at various colleges and professional conferences in North America, Europe, and Asia.

DEDICATION

This book is dedicated to the memory of David Bermant, whose patronage, friendship, and faith in the work of SITE spanned 22 unforgettable years.

With profound gratitude from SITE

^ **David Bermant**
Photo by David's loving wife,
Susan Hopmans Bermant

Annmarie Garden — Amphitheater area